AUTO-BIOGRAPH

GW01066349

This page enables you to compile a list of useful data on your Cavalier, so that whether you're ordering spares or just checking the tyre pressures, all the key information - the information that is 'personal' to your car - is easily within reach.

Registration number: ....

Model: ....

Body colour: ....

Paint code number: ....

Date of first registration:..

Date of manufacture (if different): ....

VIN (or 'chassis') number: ....

Engine number:...

Ignition key number: ....

Door lock key/s number/s: ....

Fuel locking cap key number (if fitted): ....

Alarm remote code (if fitted):...

Alarm remote battery type:...

Radio/cassette security code (if fitted): ....

Tyre size

    Front:............................Rear: ....

Tyre pressure (normally laden)

    Front:............................Rear: ....

Tyre pressure (fully laden)

    Front:............................Rear: ....

Insurance

    Name and address of insurer:..

    ....

Policy number:

    ....

Modifications

    Information that might be useful when you need to purchase parts:...

    ....

Suppliers

    Address and telephone number of your garage and parts suppliers:...

    ....

First published in 1995 by Porter Publishing Ltd.

Porter Publishing Ltd.
The Storehouse
Little Hereford Street
Bromyard
Hereford HR7 4DE
England

British Library Cataloguing in Publication Data.

A catalogue record for this book is available from the British Library.

ISBN 1-899238-11-5

Series Editor: Lindsay Porter
Design: Martin Driscoll, Lindsay Porter and Lyndsay Berryman.
Layout and Typesetting: Pineapple Publishing, Worcester.
Printed in England by The Trinity Press, Worcester.

Every care has been taken to ensure that the material contained in this Service Guide is correct. However, no liability can be accepted by the authors or publishers for damage, loss, accidents, or injury resulting from any omissions or errors in the information given.

Titles in this Series:

Absolute Beginners' Service Guide
Caravan Owner's Manual & Service Guide
Classic 'Bike Service Guide
Diesel Car Engines Service Guide
Ford Escort (Front Wheel Drive) & Orion Service Guide
Ford Fiesta (All models to 1995) Service Guide
Ford Sierra (All models) Service Guide
Land Rover Series I, II, III Service Guide

Land Rover Defender, 90 & 110 Service Guide
Metro (1980 - 1990) Service Guide
Mini (all models 1959-1994) Service Guide
MGB (including MGC, MGB GT V8 and MG RV8) Service Guide
Vauxhall Astra & Belmont (All models - 1995) Service Guide
VW Beetle Service Guide

- With more titles in production -

Vauxhall Cavalier
Service Guide & Owner's Manual
by
Andrew MacQuillan & Lindsay Porter

K350 RNP

OIL AND WATER DON'T MIX

It is important to remember that even a small quantity of oil is harmful to water and wildlife. And tipping oil down the drain is as good as tipping it into a river. Many drains are connected directly to a river or stream and pollution will occur.

Each year the National Rivers Authority deals with over 6,000 oil related water pollution incidents. Many of these are caused by the careless disposal of used oil.

The used oil from the sump of just one car can cover an area of water the size of two football pitches, cutting off the oxygen supply and harming swans, ducks, fish and other river life.

OIL POLLUTES WATER USE YOUR BRAIN- NOT THE DRAIN!

Follow the Oil Care Code

◆ *When you drain your engine oil - don't oil the drain!* Pouring oil down the drain will cause pollution. It is also an offence.

◆ Don't mix used oil with other materials, such as paint or solvents, because this makes recycling very difficult.

◆ Take used oil to an oil recycling bank. Telephone FREE on 0800 663366 to find the location of your nearest oil bank, or contact your local authority recycling officer.

OIL CARE
FOLLOW THE CODE

This book is produced in association with Castrol (U.K.) Ltd.

"Cars have become more and more sophistated. But changing the oil and brake fluid, and similar jobs are as simple as they ever were. Castrol are pleased to be associated with this book because it gives us the opportunity to make life simpler for those who wish to service their own cars. Castrol have succeeded in making oil friendlier and kinder to the environment by removing harmful chlorine from our range of engine lubricants which in turn prolong the life of the catalytic convertor (when fitted), by noticeably maintaining the engine at peak efficiency. In return, we ask you to be kinder to the environment too... by taking your used oil to your Local Authority Amenity Oil Bank. It can then be used as a heating fuel. Please do not poison it with thinners, paint, creosote or brake fluid because these render it useless and costly to dispose of."

Castrol (U.K.) Ltd

CONTENTS

Introduction

Over the years, I have run any number of cars, from superb classic cars and modern cars, to those with one foot in the breakers yard. And I know only too well that any car is only enjoyable to own if it's safe, reliable and basically sound - and the only way of ensuring that it stays that way is to service it regularly. That's why we have set about creating this book, which aims to show the owner interested in DIY car servicing that there's nothing to fear; you really can do it yourself!

Making It Easy! Porter Publishing Service Guides are the first books to give you all the service information you might need, with step-by-step instructions, along with a complete Service History section for you to complete and fill in as you carry out regular maintenance on your car over the months ahead. Using the information contained in this book, you will be able to:

◆ see for yourself how to carry out every Service Job, from weekly and monthly checks, right up to longer-term maintenance items.
◆ carry out regular body maintenance and rustproofing, saving a fortune in body repairs over the years to come.
◆ enhance the value of your car by completing a full Service History of every maintenance job you carry out on your car.

I hope you enjoy keeping your car in trim while saving lots of money by servicing your car yourself, with the help of this book. Happy motoring!

Lindsay Porter
Porter Publishing Ltd

Lindsay Porter

Andrew MacQuillan

Acknowledgements

There's been help from many people and companies in preparing 'my' part of this book, ranging from the huge multinational concern that we know as Vauxhall, through to the lady who made my tea.

Especially helpful were two Vauxhall dealers - Cowies (Leicester) Ltd and Erringtons of Evington (Leicester), whose service personnel were helpful to beyond the call of duty, so a big "thank you" to Richard Mawdsley and Jeremy Page. From my experience around the country, the service and help given by these two dealerships is typical of that available anywhere and is a credit to the Vauxhall organisation.

I owe a great deal to the efforts of our publisher, Lindsay Porter, and his staff for "holding my hand" through each stage of preparation of this book - their guidance (and patience!) are much appreciated.

Finally, the most important person behind this book has so far received scant mention, other than for her efforts at tea-making: my wife Adele, whose encouragement, support and forbearance made it all possible, and not forgetting Megan and Lizzie for making it worthwhile.

Andrew MacQuillan

SPECIAL THANKS

The Publisher would like to thank: Vauxhall Motors for their advice and use of illustrative material - Diedre Davis, for allowing her car to be photographed for the cover, and Simon Bowley for his assistance - Gunsons for equipment, line drawings and advice - Dinitrol for their kind assistance with Chapter 5 - and our good friends at Castrol for their continuing support, assistance and advice.

CHAPTER 1 - SAFETY FIRST!

You must always ensure that safety is the first consideration in any job you carry out. A slight lack of concentration, or a rush to finish the job quickly can easily result in an accident, as can failure to follow the precautions outlined in this Chapter. Whereas skilled motor mechanics are trained in safe working practices you, the home mechanic, must find them out for yourself and act upon them.

Remember, accidents don't just happen, they are caused, and some of those causes are contained in the following list. Above all, ensure that whenever you work on your car you adopt a safety-minded approach at all times, and remain aware of the dangers that might be encountered.

Be sure to consult the suppliers of any materials and equipment you may use, and to obtain and read carefully any operating and health and safety instructions that may be available on packaging or from manufacturers and suppliers.

PART I: IMPORTANT POINTS

Vehicle Off Ground

ALWAYS ensure that the vehicle is properly supported when raised off the ground. Don't work on, around, or underneath a raised vehicle unless axle stands are positioned under secure, load bearing underbody areas, or the vehicle is driven onto ramps, with the wheels remaining on the ground securely chocked to prevent movement.

ALWAYS ensure that the safe working load rating of any jacks, hoists or lifting gear used is sufficient for the job, and that lifting gear is used only as recommended by the manufacturer.

NEVER attempt to loosen or tighten nuts that require a lot of force to turn (e.g. a tight oil drain plug) with the vehicle raised, unless it is safely supported. Take care not to pull the vehicle off its supports when applying force to a spanner. Wherever possible, initially slacken tight fastenings before raising the car off the ground.

ALWAYS wear eye protection when working under the vehicle and when using power tools.

Working On The Vehicle

ALWAYS seek specialist advice unless you are justifiably confident about carrying out each job. The safety of your vehicle affects you, your passengers and other road users.

DON'T lean over, or work on, a running engine unless it is strictly necessary, and keep long hair and loose clothing well out of the way of moving mechanical parts. Note that it is theoretically possible for fluorescent striplighting to make an engine fan appear to be stationary - double check whether it is spinning or not! This is the sort of error that happens when you're really tired and not thinking straight. So...

...DON'T work on your car when you're over tired.

ALWAYS work in a well ventilated area and don't inhale dust - it may contain asbestos or other harmful substances.

REMOVE your wrist watch, rings and all other jewellery before doing any work on the vehicle - and especially when working on the electrical system.

DON'T remove the radiator or expansion tank filler cap when the cooling system is hot, or you may get scalded by escaping coolant or steam. Let the system cool down first and even then, if the engine is not completely cold, cover the cap with a cloth and gradually release the pressure.

NEVER drain oil, coolant or automatic transmission fluid when the engine is hot. Allow time for it to cool sufficiently to avoid scalding you.

ALWAYS keep antifreeze, brake and clutch fluid away from vehicle paintwork. Wash off any spills immediately.

TAKE CARE to avoid touching any engine or exhaust system component unless it is cool enough not to burn you.

Running The Vehicle

NEVER start the engine unless the gearbox is in neutral (or 'Park' in the case of automatic transmission) and the hand brake is fully applied.

NEVER run catalytic converter equipped vehicles without the exhaust system heat shields in place.

TAKE CARE when parking vehicles fitted with catalytic

converters. The 'cat' reaches extremely high temperatures and any combustible materials under the car, such as long dry grass, could be ignited.

Personal Safety

NEVER siphon fuel, antifreeze, brake fluid or other such toxic liquids by mouth, or allow contact with your skin. There is an increasing awareness that they can damage your health. Best of all, use a suitable hand pump and wear gloves.

BEFORE undertaking dirty jobs, use a barrier cream on your hands as a protection against infection. Preferably, wear thin gloves, available from DIY outlets.

WEAR GLOVES for sure when there is a risk of used engine oil coming into contact with your skin. It can cause cancer.

WIPE UP any spilt oil, grease or water off the floor immediately, before there is an accident.

MAKE SURE that spanners and all other tools are the right size for the job and are not likely to slip. Never try to 'double-up' spanners to gain more leverage.

SEEK HELP if you need to lift something heavy which may be beyond your capability. Don't forget that when lifting a heavy weight, you should keep your back straight and bend your knees to avoid injuring your back.

NEVER take risky short-cuts or rush to finish a job. Plan ahead and allow plenty of time.

BE METICULOUS and keep the work area tidy - you'll avoid frustration, work better and lose less.

KEEP children and animals right-away from the work area and from unattended vehicles.

ALWAYS tell someone what you're doing and have them regularly check that all is well, especially when working alone on, or under, the vehicle.

PART II: HAZARDS

Fire!

Petrol (gasoline) is a dangerous and highly flammable liquid requiring special precautions. When working on the fuel system, disconnect the vehicle battery earth (ground) terminal whenever possible and always work outside, or in a very well ventilated area. Any form of spark, such as that caused by an electrical fault, by two metal surfaces striking against each other, by a central heating boiler in the garage 'firing up', or even by static electricity built up in your clothing can, in a confined space, ignite petrol vapour causing an explosion. Take great care not to spill petrol on to the engine or exhaust system, never allow any naked flame anywhere near the work area and, above all, don't smoke.

Invest in a workshop-sized fire extinguisher. Choose the carbon dioxide type or preferably, dry powder but never a water type extinguisher for workshop use. Water conducts electricity and can make worse an oil or petrol-based fire, in certain circumstances.

DON'T disconnect any fuel pipes on a fuel injected engine while the ignition is switched on. The fuel in the line is under very high pressure - sufficient to cause serious injury. Remember that many injection systems have residual pressure in the pipes for days after switching off. Consult the workshop manual or seek specialist advice before carrying out any work.

Fumes

In addition to the fire dangers described previously, petrol (gasoline) vapour and the types of vapour given off by many solvents, thinners, and adhesives are highly toxic and under certain conditions can lead to unconsciousness or even death, if inhaled. The

risks are increased if such fluids are used in a confined space so always ensure adequate ventilation when handling materials of this nature. Treat all such substances with care, always read the instructions and follow them with care.

Always ensure that the car is out of doors and not in an enclosed space when the engine is running. Exhaust fumes contain poisonous carbon monoxide, even when the car is fitted with a catalytic converter, since 'cats' sometimes fail and don't function when the engine is cold.

Never drain petrol (gasoline) or use solvents, thinners adhesives or other toxic substances in an inspection pit as the extremely confined space allows the highly toxic fumes to concentrate. Running the engine with the vehicle over the pit can have the same results. It is also dangerous to park a vehicle for any length of time over an inspection pit. The fumes from even a slight fuel leak can cause an explosion when the engine is started. Petrol fumes are heavier than air and will accumulate in the pit.

Mains Electricity

Best of all, avoid the use of mains electricity when working on the vehicle, whenever possible. For instance, you could use rechargeable

tools and a DC inspection lamp, powered from a remote 12V battery - both are much safer. However, if you do use mains-powered equipment, ensure that the appliance is wired correctly to its plug, that where necessary it is properly earthed (grounded), and that the fuse is of the correct rating for the appliance is fitted. For instance, a 13 amp fuse in lead lamp's plug will not provide adequate protection. Do not use any mains powered equipment in damp conditions or in the vicinity of fuel, fuel vapour or the vehicle battery.

Also, before using any mains powered electrical equipment, take one more simple precaution - use an RCD (Residual Current Device) circuit breaker. Then, if there is a short, the RCD circuit breaker minimises the risk of electrocution by instantly cutting the power supply. Buy one from any electrical store or DIY centre. RCDs fit simply into your electrical socket before plugging in your electrical equipment.

The Ignition System
You should never work on the ignition system with the ignition switched on, or with the engine being turned over on the starter, or running.

Touching certain parts of the ignition system, such as the HT leads, distributor cap, ignition coil etc, can result in a severe electric shock. This is especially likely where the insulation on any of these components is weak, or if the components are dirty or damp. Note also that voltages produced by electronic ignition systems are much higher than those produced by conventional systems and could prove fatal, particularly to people with cardiac pacemaker implants. Consult your handbook or main dealer if in any doubt.

An additional risk of injury can arise while working on running engines, if the operator touches a high voltage lead and pulls his or her hand away on to a sharp, conductive or revolving part.

The Battery
Never cause a spark, smoke, or allow a naked light near the vehicle's battery, even in a well ventilated area. Highly explosive hydrogen gas will be given off as part of the charging process.

Battery terminals on the car should be shielded, since a battery contains energy and a spark can be caused by any metal object which touches the battery's terminals or connecting straps.

Before working on the fuel or electrical systems, always disconnect the battery earth (ground) terminal. (But before doing so, read the relevant **FACT FILE** in *Chapter 3* regarding saving computer and radio settings.)

When using a battery charger, care should be taken to avoid causing a spark by switching off the power supply before the battery charger leads are connected or disconnected. Before charging the battery from an external source, disconnect both battery leads before connecting the charger. If the battery is not of the 'sealed-for-life' type, loosen the filler plugs or remove the cover before charging. For best results the battery should be given a low rate trickle charge overnight. Do not charge at an excessive rate or the battery may burst.

Always wear gloves and goggles when carrying or when topping up the battery. Even in diluted form (as it is in the battery) the acid electrolyte is extremely corrosive and must not be allowed to contact the eyes, skin or clothes.

Brakes and Asbestos
Obviously, a car's brakes are among its most important safety related items. ONLY work on your vehicle's braking system if you are trained and competent to do so. If you have not been trained in this work, but wish to carry out the jobs described in this book, we strongly recommend that you have a garage or qualified mechanic check your work before using the car.

Whenever you work on the braking system's mechanical components, or remove front or rear brake pads or shoes: i) wear an efficient particle mask; ii) wipe off all brake dust from the brakes after spraying on a proprietary brand of brake cleaner (never blow dust off with compressed air); iii) dispose of brake dust and discarded shoes or pads in a sealed plastic bag; iv) wash your hands thoroughly after you have finished working on the brakes and certainly before you eat or smoke; v) replace shoes and pads only with asbestos-free shoes or pads. Note that asbestos brake dust can cause cancer if inhaled.

Brake Fluid
Brake fluid absorbs moisture rapidly from the air and can become dangerous resulting in brake failure. Castrol (U.K.) Ltd. recommend that you should have your brake fluid tested at least once a year by a properly equipped garage with test equipment and you should change the fluid in accordance with your vehicle manufacturer's recommendations or as advised in this book if we recommend a shorter interval than the manufacturer. You should buy no more brake fluid than you need, in smaller rather than larger containers. Never store an opened container of brake fluid. Dispose of the remainder at your Local Authority Waste Disposal Site, in the designated disposal unit, not with general waste or with waste oil.

Engine Oils
Take care to observe the following precautions when working with used engine oil. Apart from the obvious risk of scalding when draining the oil from a hot engine, there is the danger from contamination contained in all used oil.

Always wear disposable plastic or rubber gloves when draining the oil from your engine. i) Note that the drain plug and the oil are often hotter than you expect. Wear gloves if the plug is too hot to touch and keep your hand to one side so that you are not scalded by the spurt of oil as the plug comes away; ii) There are very real health hazards associated with used engine oil. In the words of one manufacturer's handbook "Prolonged and repeated contact may cause serious skin disorders, including dermatitis and cancer." Use a barrier cream on your hands and try not to get oil on them. Always wear gloves and wash your hands with hand cleaner soon after carrying out the work. Keep oil out of the reach of children; iii) NEVER, EVER dispose of old engine oil into the ground or down a drain. In the UK, and in most EC countries, every local authority must provide a safe means of oil disposal. In the UK, try your local Environmental Health Department for advice on waste disposal facilities.

Plastic Materials
Work with plastic materials brings additional hazards into workshops. Many of the materials used (polymers, resins, adhesives and materials acting as catalysts and accelerators) contain dangers in the form of poisonous fumes, skin irritants, and the risk of fire and explosions. Do not allow resin or 2-pack adhesive hardener, or that supplied with filler or 2-pack stopper, to come into contact with skin or eyes. Read carefully the safety notes supplied on the can, tube or packaging and always wear impervious gloves and goggles when working with them.

Jacks and Axle Stands
Throughout this book you will see many references to the correct use of jacks, axle stands and similar equipment - and we make

SAFETY FIRST!

no apologies for being repetitive. This is one area where safety cannot be overstressed - your life could be at stake!

Special care must be taken when any type of lifting equipment is used. Jacks are made for lifting the vehicle only, not for supporting it while it is being worked on. Never work under the car using only a jack to support the weight. Jacks must be supplemented by adequate additional means of support, positioned under secure load-bearing parts of the frame or underbody. Axle stands are available from most auto. parts stores. Drive-on ramps are limiting because of their design and size but they are simple to use, reliable and offer the most stable type of support. We strongly recommend their use.

Full details on jacking and supporting the vehicle will be found near the beginning of *Chapter 3.*

Fluoroelastomers

MOST IMPORTANT! PLEASE READ THIS SECTION!

If you service your car in the normal way, none of the following may be relevant to you. Unless, for example, you encounter a car which has been on fire (even in a localised area), subject to heat in, say, a crash-damage repairer's workshop or a vehicle breaker's yard, or if any second-hand parts have been heated in any way.

Many synthetic, rubber-like materials used in motor cars contain a substance called fluorine. These materials are known as fluoroelastomers and are commonly used for oil seals, wiring and cabling, bearing surfaces, gaskets, diaphragms, hoses and 'O' rings. If they are subjected to temperatures greater than 315 degrees C, they will decompose and can be potentially hazardous. Fluoroelastomer materials will show physical signs of decomposition under such conditions in the form of charring of black sticky masses. Some decomposition may occur at temperatures above 200 degrees C, and it is obvious that when a car has been in a fire or has been dismantled with the assistance of a cutting torch or blow torch, the fluoroelastomers can decompose in the manner indicated above.

In the presence of any water or humidity, including atmospheric moisture, the by-products caused by the fluoroelastomers being heated can be extremely dangerous. According to the Health and Safety Executive, "Skin contact with this liquid or decomposition residues can cause painful and penetrating burns. Permanent irreversible skin and tissue damage can occur". Damage can also be caused to eyes or by the inhalation of fumes created as fluoroelastomers are burned or heated.

After a vehicle has been exposed to fire or high temperatures:

1. Do not touch blackened or charred seals or equipment.

2. Allow all burnt or decomposed fluoroelastomer materials to cool before inspection, investigations, tear-down or removal.

3. Preferably, don't handle parts containing decomposed fluoroelastomers, but if you must, wear goggles and PVC (polyvinyl chloride) or neoprene protective gloves whilst doing so. Never handle such parts unless they are completely cool.

4. Contaminated parts, residues, materials and clothing, including protective clothing and gloves, should be disposed of by an approved contractor to landfill or by incineration according to national or local regulations. Oil seals, gaskets and 'O' rings, along with contaminated material, must not be burned.

PART III: GENERAL WORKSHOP SAFETY

1. Always have a fire extinguisher of the correct type at arm's length when working on the fuel system.

If you do have a fire, DON'T PANIC. Use the extinguisher effectively by directing it at the base of the fire.

2. NEVER use a naked flame anywhere in the workplace.

3. KEEP your inspection lamp well away from any source of petrol (gasoline) such as when disconnecting a carburettor float bowl or fuel line.

4. NEVER use petrol (gasoline) to clean parts. Use paraffin (kerosene), white spirits, or a proprietary degreaser.

5. NO SMOKING. There's a risk of fire or of transferring dangerous substances to your mouth and, in any case, ash falling into mechanical components is to be avoided.

6. BE METHODICAL in everything you do, use common sense, and think of safety at all times.

CHAPTER 2 - BUYING GUIDE

In this Chapter, we show you how to go about buying a second hand car. We also look at which parts wear out, and we explain when they are likely to need replacement, so that whether you are giving your own car the once-over, or you're looking at a prospective purchase, you'll know what to expect; and we examine the best ways of buying parts for your pride and joy.

PART I: BUYING A SECOND-HAND CAR

In general, the safest - but also the most expensive - way of buying second hand is through a main dealer: NOT the same as a general second-hand dealer, whose standards are almost certain to be lower! We *strongly* recommend the use of HPI Autodata checks mentioned on page 110, because even main dealers can make 'mistakes', but once you've done that, and selected the main-dealer car you want, it's better to have an AA or RAC inspection carried out rather than carry out your own checks. But for many people, it's a question of saving money and buying privately, and that's what this Chapter is mainly about. But don't find yourself with the *worst* of both worlds...

Spot The Rogue Trader

One of the biggest dangers with buying privately is that you might encounter a real cheat: a trader masquerading as a private seller. Cars offered by such people are likely to be among the worst on offer, they may have had their mileometers tampered with and deep seated faults may have been cleverly concealed. Here's how to spot them:

• take note of the way traders often word their advertisements. Key phrases include: "a very clean car", "very straight", "a beautiful motorcar" and other glib phrases.

• when you telephone in response to an ad., *always* say, "I'm calling about the car..." If the person on the other end asks, "Which car?", put the 'phone down before the spiel starts.

• if you get past the telephone stage, take careful note of the attitude of the seller. Part-time, 'black economy' dealers often seem blase, even bored by the whole thing, and slicker than most private sellers.

• insist on looking at the Registration Document. If the seller isn't the registered keeper, why not?

How To Inspect A Used Vehicle

STAGE ONE: Even if you know very little about cars, you can root out the obvious no-hopers before arranging for a local main agent, AA or RAC inspection. The text in italics explains the problems.

• catch the light along all sides of the car. Can you see any ripples? Check for overspray inside wheel arches, inside engine bay and on tyres and trim. Does all the paint match? *All indicate poorly carried out crash repairs.*

• Look at the gaps between panels. Also, look very carefully inside the engine bay and inside the boot for evidence of rippling in the metal. Look low down, mainly in the vicinity of structural members. *Tell-tale signs of crash damage.*

STAGE TWO: If your car passes Stage One, look more closely at the bodywork - the most expensive part to repair.

• check the sills by lifting the carpets just inside the doors and also check the footwells, especially around the edges. *Rust!*

• look inside the engine bay especially at the tops of struts. *Check for corrosion.*

• check the bottoms of wings, the 'skirts' beneath front and rear bumpers and the tops of wing panels for corrosion. *Rust covered with filler will quickly burst through again.*

SPECIALIST SERVICE: It's hardly worth trying to check beneath a car without the use of a hoist. Leave it to the pro. inspection mentioned earlier, or see if you can persuade a local garage to lend or hire their hoist:

• check around spring mountings, the joints between floors and sills, all box-section 'chassis' members and anywhere that suspension components are fixed to the car's body structure.

• check all brake pipes and hoses. *Look for rubbing or corrosion.*

• look at the shock absorbers. *Fluid leakage means failure.*

• check the exhaust. *Look for rust, holes or patches.*

• examine each tyre carefully for bulges or splits. *Tyres worn more on one side than the other might mean that the car's tracking needs checking - easily adjustable - or it might indicate suspension damage, maybe from an accident.*

 *If you are buying an older car which needs work doing to it, try making the owner an offer 'subject to MoT test'. Then, you can have the car tested as an inexpensive (though not necessarily complete) condition check.*

Mechanical Components

• before starting up, remove the oil filler cap. *Grey sludge around the cap is a certain indicator that the engine is on its last legs.*

• pull out the dipstick. Is the oil level very low? Is the oil a dirty black and does it feel gritty between finger and thumb? *Not a well maintained car! Does it have droplets of water on it? Big problems! Probably a blown head gasket.*

• check inside the radiator cap (ONLY if the engine is cold!). Do you see anti-freeze colour? *Good!* Do you see rust? *Bad!* Do you see droplets of oil? *Disastrous! See previous paragraph.*

• start the car and note whether the starter motor sounds lively or whether it is struggling to keep up. *Could be duff battery; or tired starter motor.*

• undo and remove the oil filler cap again. (N.B. Most engines spray oil around in *copious* quantities. Ensure that you don't get covered!) *If oil mist chugs out, the engine bores are badly worn. Also...*

• ...look at the exhaust. Steam (especially in colder weather) and even water dripping out is no problem, although it should go away after the car has been driven. 'Rev' the engine, hard and several times. *If you see puffs or even clouds of black smoke (not grey steam), the engine is probably on the slippery slope.*

• does the oil pressure warning light flicker with engine cold? *Low oil pressure equals an engine rebuild?*

• bonnet open. Does the 'top' of the engine rattle on start up? *Mechanical tappets: adjustment needed.* If the rattle continues after 30 seconds, *the engine may need an expensive replacement camshaft.* Hydraulic tappets: *noise is always expensive!*

• rev the engine. Does it rattle in a deep, growly way, low down in the engine? *The big end and/or main bearings are gone - replacement engine time!*

Static Checks

• are the carpets wet? *water is leaking in. Windscreen seal leaks can often be cured easily. But if the car is old the screen surround may have corroded, requiring expensive welding. Alternatively, water coming in from beneath suggests that the car's lower structure has as much future as an old car park ticket. If water is leaking from the heater, remember that it can be expensive and tricky to replace.*

• seat rips can be a pain and devalue the car. *It can be difficult to find the right colour match on second hand seats.* Do your knees come up as your backside goes down. *The seat springing has gone.*

• can you live with headlining rips or severe discolouration? *It's difficult to clean easily and replacement is usually expensive.*

• take a *close* look at seat belts and mountings. *Life saver - and quite expensive to replace.*

• check that the heater works properly. *Or you'll end up hating the car!*

• take time to check every switch, accessory and electrical fitting on the car. *Replacements can be expensive.* Check that the stereo works - *and check that it's included with the car!*

• don't accept lame excuses when things don't work! *If things are so easy to fix, why haven't they been done already?*

• check the spare wheel and the condition (existence?) of the jack and toolkit. *More expense!*

• open and close windows and sunroof. *(Also look for stains around sunroof aperture - they can leak!)*

Finally, but perhaps most important of all, make sure that the person who is selling the car actually owns it!

• ask to see the Registration Document. *If it's not available it could be: the 'owner' has a) lost it; b) has it but it doesn't show the 'owner's' name because he is a trader; c) the car doesn't belong to the seller. If you can't see the Registration Document, walk away!*

• ask to see the owner's original purchase receipt and check that the car is owned by the 'owner' and is not subject to a finance agreement. See below. *IMPORTANT NOTE: You may be amazed to learn that, if you pay for a car that is subsequently found to belong to someone else, you will lose the car and the money!*

• check that the VIN (Vehicle Identification Number) shown on the Registration document is the same as those on the VIN plate riveted to the car. See "Fact File" later in this chapter for the precise location of these numbers. *If any of the numbers in these three locations are different, missing, or have obviously been tampered with, then under no circumstances consider buying the car unless the seller can provide an explanation, in writing, satisfactory to a third party, such as an AA or RAC inspector, or the Police!*

Spot The Rogue Car

Before buying *any* used car, check it out with HPI Autodata. (See Page 110.) A postal or telephone enquiry (cheques or credit card payments accepted) will (i) confirm that the vehicle details shown (make, model, colour, engine size, fuel type) are all correct, (ii) tell you if the vehicle is reported as stolen, or subject to an outstanding finance agreement, (iii) tell you if the vehicle has been logged as having a major insurance claim (not foolproof; many don't show up), (iv) identify vehicles which have had a registration plate change.

PART II: WHAT WEARS, AND WHEN

The following list provides a great way of checking what is *likely* to be worn on your Cavalier, and at what stage it is likely to need replacement - useful when checking your own car, or when buying another. Please bear in mind that the mileages shown are only intended as an approximation of the lifespan of each component. In real life, some will wear out faster and some slower, of course but the chart below provides a useful rough guide.

> **SAFETY FIRST!**
> **Read and take note of Chapter1, Safety First! and the Safety information in Chapter 3 before carrying out any of these checks.**

COMPONENT:	COULD NEED REPLACEMENT AT:	CHECKS OR SYMPTOMS:
Alternator	70,000 miles	Fails without warning.
Battery	4 to 7 years (original); 1 to who-knows (non-original)	Goes flat, even though disconnected.
Brake Pads - Front	15 to 20,000 miles	See Job 71.
Brake Pads/Shoes - Rear	35 to 40,000 miles	See Jobs 73 and 74.
Cambelt	36,000 miles	Should be renewed - see Job 100.
Clutch	Up to 75,000 normally	Check for slipping when pulling away, or hill climbing.
Diesel Glowplugs	60,000 miles	Engine reluctant to start from cold and smokes (when battery in good condition).
Diesel Injectors	75,000 miles	Excessive smoke; engine misfires.
Exhaust Mounting Rubbers	Rears go every year or two.	Examine visually; twist manually.
Exhaust pipe	(Vauxhall parts) Up to 4 years (non-original parts) 1 to 3 years	Examine visually - see Job 35; listen for blowing.
Shock absorbers	(front) 40,000 miles	Clean off and look for oil leaks. Grasp and twist,
Shock absorbers	(rear) 60,000 miles	looking for wear in bushes top and bottom.
Starter motor	150,000 miles	Turns engine slowly or fails to engage when battery and connections in good condition.
Turbocharger	(diesel) 140,000 miles	Seal failure leads to engine oil being consumed
Turbocharger	(petrol) 100,000 miles	- engine smokes through exhaust when turbo operates.
Tyres	(most models) 15 - 20,000 miles	Check visually, especially inside
Tyres	(4x4 models) 7 - 10,000 miles	tyre walls and spare.

PART III - BUYING SPARES

One of the great advantages of DIY servicing is that you can choose which parts you buy, where you buy your parts, and how much you pay for them, whereas if the dealer services your car you buy their parts at their prices!

Of course, you must take care not to buy poor quality parts, but it's worth bearing in mind that many of the car makers' parts are the same as those available from 'independents'.

Buying The Right Parts

All manufacturers change the parts they use on the production line, often with startling frequency. The only way of ensuring that the parts you buy are the right ones for your car is to take your car's Vehicle Identification Number (VIN) and engine number with you when buying spares.

Main Dealers

Main dealers more than anyone else should be able to match your car's VIN number to the precise part you need, so have it to hand. This can also be the key to a more helpful approach by some Parts Department staff! Also, try to avoid calling on the parts department in the early mornings and other busy periods, and you may find that staff have more time to help you. Consumable items are almost certain to be too expensive from your main dealer. Try high street auto accessory stores or out-of-town Superstores for best prices.

Auto Accessory Stores

Local parts factors and big-name motor accessory shops can be extremely useful for obtaining servicing parts at short notice - many 'accessory' outlets open late in the evening, and on both days at weekends. You'll find that the high-street shops and Superstores will usually be open when you need them, their prices are usually the keenest of all, because they can buy-in in great quantities, and the quality of the parts is excellent from the best-known shops, since they use the same big-name manufacturers as many of the original car makers.

Buying Second-Hand

Purchasing any safety-related items second-hand - braking, steering or suspension parts - is something to avoid. That's not to decry buying second-hand altogether. Replacing a worn out distributor or carburettor, for instance, with a second-hand component that you know to be 'low mileage' can make a lot of sense. Equally, non-performance related items, such as wheel trims, interior trim and other interior parts can often be obtained at a fraction of the 'new' cost.

Reconditioned Parts

These are best obtained from reputable retail suppliers. When buying, always enquire about the terms of the guarantee. Don't buy if there isn't a good one! 'Exchange' alternators and starter motors are good value - but only buy from a reputable source.

Steering racks are invariably available as exchange items. Ensure that you rotate the operating shaft fully from lock to lock, feeling for any undue free play, roughness, stiffness, or 'notchiness' as you do so. Reject any units showing signs of any of these problems.

Tyres

We recommend buying only good quality radial ply tyres. Cheaper tyres rarely perform as well as top brands, even when they are the cheaper brand of a top manufacturer. Your car may steer more erratically, have less grip on cornering and braking and be noisier than if you pay the small extra amount required for top brand tyres - and they usually last longer, too. Remould tyres are available at lower initial cost, but life expectancy is not as long as with new tyres and we don't recommend them.

Shopping Around

If you want to buy good quality parts *and* save money, you must be prepared to shop around. Ring each of your chosen suppliers with a shopping list to hand, and your car's personal data, from the Auto-Biography at the front of this book, in front of you. Keep a written note of prices - including VAT, delivery etc - whether the parts are proper 'brand name' parts or not and - most importantly! - whether or not the parts you want are in stock. Parts expected 'soon' have been known never to materialise. A swivel pin in the hand is worth two in the bush. (Bad pun!)

FACT FILE: IDENTIFICATION NUMBERS

All manufacturers change the parts they use on the production line, often with startling frequency. The only way of ensuring that the parts you buy are the right ones for your car is to take your car's Vehicle Identification Number (VIN) and engine number with you when buying spares.

There are three main numbers you will need to know in order to buy parts and touch-up paint for your car. The VIN is your car's internationally unique number and tells your parts supplier exactly which model and year the car is. Quote the VIN whenever you buy spares for your car.

1. The Cavalier's VIN plate is positioned on the front or "slam"-panel of the engine and the number should be the same as that shown on your vehicle documents.

2. The VIN number is also stamped onto the floorpan at manufacture and is found beneath a small flap in the carpet between the drivers' seat and the door sill. Make sure it is the same as that shown on the VIN plate!

3. The engine number will usually be found on the engine block, on

a small flat area beneath the righthand-most spark plug, but may be embossed into a small aluminium plate.

INSIDE INFORMATION: On V6 models, Vauxhall mechanics use a torch and a dentist's mirror, the number being badly concealed by the shape of the cylinder head!

4. INSIDE INFORMATION: If you need an exact paint colour match, you'll need the car's paint code number. Although the VIN plate will carry the basic colour code, the paint/trim code plate will contain precise details of the shade and the type of trim fitted. It is situated also on the front "slam" panel, to the right of the VIN plate and is usually painted in the body colour.

Most aerosol paints won't relate to this number, although at least one brand claims to be able to produce cans matched to your car's code colour, to special order. Alternatively, have your local paint factor mix a small quantity of matching paint for you.

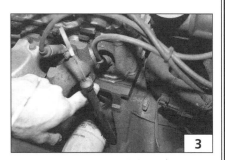

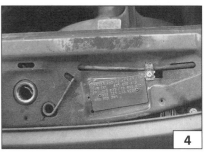

CHAPTER 3 - SERVICING YOUR CAR

Every Cavalier owner wants their car to start first time, run reliably and last longer than the average. And there's no magic about how to put yours into that category; it's all a question of thorough maintenance! If you follow the Service Jobs listed here or have a garage or mechanic do it for you, you can almost *guarantee* that your car will still be going strong when others have fallen by the wayside... or the hard shoulder. Mind you, we would be among the first to acknowledge that this Service Schedule is just about as thorough as you can get; it's an amalgam of all the maker's recommended service items plus all the 'Inside Information' from the experts that we could find. If you want your Cavalier to be as well looked after as possible, you'll follow the Jobs shown here, but if you don't want to go all the way, you can pick and choose from the most essential items in the list. But do bear in mind that the Jobs we recommend are there for some very good reasons:

◆ *body maintenance* is rarely included in most service schedules. We believe it to be essential.

◆ *preventative maintenance* figures very high on our list of priorities. And that's why so many of our service jobs have the word "Check..." near the start!

◆ *older vehicles* need more jobs doing on them than new cars - it's as simple as that - so we list the jobs you will need to carry out in order to keep any Cavalier in fine fettle.

USING THE SERVICE SCHEDULES

At the start of each Service Job, you'll see a heading in bold type, looking a bit like this:

☐ **Job 48. Check/adjust spark plugs.**

Following the heading will be all the information you will need to enable you to carry out that particular Job. Please note that different models of car might have different settings. Please check *Chapter 8, Facts and Figures.* Exactly the same Job number and heading will be found in the Service History chapter, where you will want to keep a full record of all the work you have carried out. After you have finished servicing your car, you will be able to tick off all of the jobs that you have completed and so, service by service, build up a complete Service History of work carried out on your car.

You will also find other key information immediately after each Job title and in most cases, there will be reference to an illustration - a photograph or line drawing, whichever is easier for you to follow - usually on the same page.

If the Job shown only applies to certain vehicles, the Job title will be followed by a description of the type of vehicle to

which the Job title applies. For instance, Job 25 applies to DIESEL ENGINES ONLY - and the text in capitals tells you so.

Other special headings are also used. One reads **OPTIONAL,** which means that you may wish to use your own discretion as to whether to carry out this particular Job or whether to leave it until it crops up again in a later service. Another is **INSIDE INFORMATION.** This tells you that here is a Job or a special tip that you wouldn't normally get to hear about, other than through the experience and 'inside' knowledge of the experts who have helped in compiling this Service Guide, while MAKING IT EASY! are hints and tips designed to do just that. Another heading is **SPECIALIST SERVICE,** which means that we recommend you to have this work carried out by a specialist. Some jobs, such as setting the tracking or suspension are best done with the right measuring equipment while other jobs may demand the use of equipment such as an exhaust gas analyser. Where we think you are better off having the work done for you, we say so!

Throughout the Service Schedule, each 'shorter' Service Interval is meant to be an important part of each of the next 'longer' Service Interval, too. For instance, under *Every 1,500 Miles,* in Job 15 you are instructed to check the tyres for wear or damage. This Job also has to be carried out at 1,500 miles,

3,000 miles, 6,000 miles, 9,000 miles, and so on. It is therefore shown in *Appendix 3* to be carried out in each of these 'longer' Service Intervals but only as a Job number, without the detailed instructions that were given the first time around!

> *SAFETY FIRST!*
> *The other special heading is the one that could be the most important one of all! SAFETY FIRST! information must always be read with care and always taken seriously. In addition, please read the whole of Chapter 1, Safety First! before carrying out any work on your car. There are many hazards associated with working on a car but all of them can be avoided by sticking to the safety rules. Don't skimp on safety!*

The 'Catch-up' Service

When you first buy a used Cavalier, you never know for sure just how well it's been looked after. So, if you want to catch-up on all the servicing that may have been neglected on your car, just work through the entire list of Service Jobs listed for the **36,000 miles - or Every Three Years** service, add on the 'Longer Term' servicing Jobs, and your car will be bang up to date and serviced as well as you could hope for. Do allow

several days for all of this work, not least because it will almost certainly throw up a number of extra jobs - potential faults that have been lurking beneath the surface - all of which will need putting right before you can 'sign off' your Cavalier as being in tip-top condition.

The Service History

Those people fortunate enough to have owned a Cavalier from new, or one that has been well maintained from new, will have the opportunity to keep a service record, or 'Service History' of their car, usually filled in by a main dealer. Until now, it hasn't been possible for the owner of an older car to keep a formal record of servicing but now you can, using the complete tick list in *Appendix 3, Service History*. In fact, you can go one better than the owners of new cars, because your car's Service History will be more complete and more detailed than any manufacturer's service record, with the extra bonus that there is space for you to keep a record of all of those extra items that crop up from time to time. New tyres; replacement exhaust; extra accessories; where can you show those on a regular service schedule? Now you can, so if your battery goes down only 11 months after buying it, you'll be able to look up where and when you bought it. All you'll have to do is remember to fill in your Service Schedule in the first place!

RAISING THE CAR BEFORE WORKING ON IT

> *Raising a Car - Safely!*
> *You will often need to raise your car off the ground in order to carry out the Service Jobs shown here. To start off with, here's what you must never do - never work beneath a car held on a jack, not even a trolley jack. Quite a number of deaths have been caused by a car slipping off a jack while someone has been working beneath. On the other hand, the safest way is by raising a car on a proprietary brand of ramps. Sometimes, there is no alternative but to use axle stands. Please read all of the following information and act upon it!*

When using car ramps:

(I) Make absolutely certain that the ramps are parallel to the wheels of the car and that the wheels are exactly central on each ramp.

Always have an assistant watch both sides of the car as you drive up. Drive up to the end 'stops' on the ramps but never over them!

Apply the hand brake firmly, put the car in first or reverse gear, or 'Park', in the case of an automatic.

I

(II) Chock both wheels remaining on the ground, both in front and behind so that the car can't move in either direction.

INSIDE INFORMATION: wrap a strip of carpet into a loop around the first 'rung' of the ramps and drive over the doubled-up piece of carpet on the approach to the ramps. This prevents the ramps from skidding away, as they are inclined to do, as the car is driven on to them.

II

On other occasions, you might need to work on the car while it is supported on an axle stand or a pair of axle stands. These are inherently less stable than ramps and so you must take much greater care when working beneath them. In particular:

• ensure that the axle stand is on flat, stable ground, never on a surface where one side can sink in to the ground.

• ensure that the car is on level ground and that the hand brake is off and the transmission in neutral.

• raise the car with a trolley jack - invest in one if you don't already own one; the car's wheel changing jack is often too unstable. Place a piece of cloth over the head of the jack if your car is nicely finished on the underside. Ensure that the floor is sufficiently clear and smooth for the trolley jack wheels to roll as the car is raised and lowered, otherwise it could slip off the jack.

(III) Place the jack beneath the front subframe or another load-bearing area, such as immediately behind the wheel-change jacking point, when raising the front of the car...

(IV) ...and place the axle stands beneath body-mounts or suspension mounts, but NEVER under the engine or gearbox.

(V) At the rear of the car, place the jack head, beneath the rear body jacking points or rear suspension mounting points, or beneath the rear 'axle'/torsion beam.

(VI) Take care to locate the top of the axle stands on a strong, level, stable part of the car's underside: you should never use a movable suspension part (because the part can move and allow the axle stand to slip) or the floor of the car (which is just too weak).

Just as when using ramps - only even more importantly! - apply the hand brake firmly once the car is supported on the axle stands, put the car in first or reverse gear (or 'Park', in the case of an automatic) and chock both wheels remaining on the ground, both in front and behind.

Be especially careful when applying force to a spanner or when pulling hard on anything, when the car is supported off the ground. It is all too easy to move the car so far that it topples off the axle stands. And remember that if a car falls on you, *YOU COULD BE KILLED!*

Whenever working beneath a car, have someone primed to keep an eye on you! If someone pops out to see how you are getting on every quarter of an hour or so, it could be enough to save your life!

Do remember that, in general, a car will be more stable when only one wheel is removed and one axle stand used than if two wheels are removed in conjunction with two axle stands. You are strongly advised never to work on the car with all four wheels off the ground, on four axle stands. The car would then be very unstable and dangerous to work beneath.

Before lowering the car to the ground, remember to remove the chocks, release the hand brake and place the transmission in neutral.

Raising The Car In An Emergency

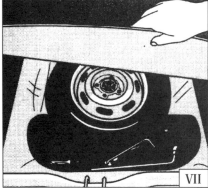

It happens too often - a roadside puncture, probably in the dark, probably in the rain, the spare is flat, you don't know where the car jack is, or the wheelbrace, and even if you did you don't know where the jack should go, and the wheel bolts are far too tight to be shifted by that bit of bent rod they call a wheelbrace! If you've never done it before, changing a wheel is a daunting prospect, so practise the wheel-change routine at home, before the worst happens to you.

(VII) START by finding where the jack and the wheelbrace are normally stowed - lift the spare wheel cover, as shown, on the Cavalier. CHECK that the spare hasn't gone flat, because you check it every week, along with the other wheels/tyres. PREPARE by ensuring that in the boot and/or glovebox you have an old waterproof, something to kneel on, rag to clean your hands if necessary, but also protective gloves, and a torch. (Illustration, courtesy Vauxhall Motors Ltd.)

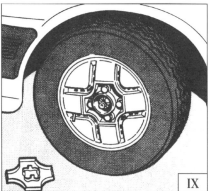

(VIII) Wheel bolts should be done up to a specified degree of tightness, but all too often they're done up by a chap behaving like a gorilla with a toothache! Give yourself a better chance by buying one of these extendible wrenches, complete with the right-sized socket to fit your wheel nuts or bolts. Its superior strength and leverage will shift wheel bolts that the car-kit brace wouldn't even look at - it's an absolute 'must', not just for those who haven't got the strength of a raging gorilla but to replace that feeble wheel brace in the boot, for everyone!

(IX) In many instances, you will first have to lever off a wheeltrim - or plastic caps over the bolts that look like the real thing but are not! The car-kit wheelbrace might have a flattened end made for the job, otherwise find yourself perhaps a suitable screwdriver (keep it in the car) and lever carefully around the circumference of the trim: note where the tyre valve protrudes through, making a pencil mark if necessary. Once the wheeltrim is partly unclipped - it often needs vigorous levering, so watch that bodywork! - you may be better off doning your gloves and pulling. (Illustration, courtesy Vauxhall Motors Ltd.)

(X) With the wheel still on the ground, loosen the wheel bolts. For your physical wellbeing you should always bear down on the wheelbrace, rather than pull it upwards - if you're stuck with that bent-rod car-kit brace, you'll probably need a length of pipe to slip over it to extend its leverage but it will probably be a struggle to keep it on the nut... If you try slackening the wheel bolts *after* you've raised the wheel, all you'll do it rotate the wheel, not the bolt!

(XI) Make sure now that you know exactly where and how the car jack locates, and how it is operated. If you are unsure, seek the advice of your car dealer. Do it NOW, so that you'll know when you need it!

(XII) On all Cavaliers, the wheel-changing jack locates at one of these positions.

(XIII) In the case of CD and SRi models before 1988, a plastic cover has to be removed.

(XIV) The jack winding handle has to be unfolded from the jack.

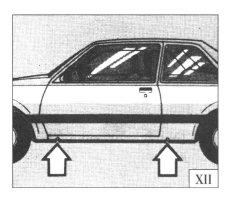

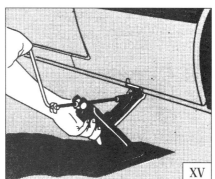

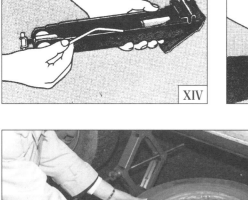

(XV) Jacking takes place as shown here.

Remember to carry a piece of timber in the boot that can be placed beneath the jack to spread the load and prevent it from sinking into soft ground. Once the car is raised, have the handbrake on, and there are purpose-made chocks you can buy that you can wedge each side of the wheel opposite to the one you are changing, to guard against the car rolling. In an emergency, use any old pieces of wood or bricks that you can find. Wind the jack handle until the wheel is clear of the ground, remembering that if the tyre is flat, you need enough clearance for a wheel with a fully pumped up tyre. Do not put any part of your body beneath a car which is supported only on a jack.

(XVI) SAFETY FIRST! and INSIDE INFORMATION
Always place the spare wheel, or the wheel you've just removed, under the car: partly for safety to help guard against being crushed; partly so that if the car topples off the wheel-change jack (and they DO, especially on soft ground) you'll be able to reposition the jack and start again.

(XVII) Once the required wheel is clear of the ground, fully undo the bolts, leaving the one 'at the top' until last so you can get your balance and a secure grip before lifting away the wheel. Because bolts are used, it can be a bit of a struggle to try to locate the wheel on something (maybe some sort of projection on the hub/drum face) while you attempt to align the bolt holes and insert at least one bolt with one hand while steadying the wheel with the other! Nip the bolts up finger-tight, then lower the wheel to the ground for final tightening, working diagonally, a little at a time, on each bolt: do them up as tight as you can, using all your strength if it's the car-kit wheelbrace, slightly less than full strength if it's the extended wrench.

making it easy! Since your Cavalier's wheels are held on with bolts, have your local garage supply you with two pieces of threaded rod - bolts with heads cut off would be ideal. You can screw them into two of the holes in the hub, 'hang' the wheel on them while you put in the 'proper' wheel bolts to the other holes, then unscrew them with your fingers and fit the two remaining wheel retaining bolts. Remember to carry them with you! ii) You can also try levering the wheel up into place with a shovel, a length of wood or anything else you can lay your hands on, by the roadside.

Every 500 Miles, Weekly, or Before a Long Journey

These are the regular checks that you need to carry out to help keep your car safe and reliable. They don't include the major Service jobs but they should be carried out as an integral part of every 'proper' service.

Every 500 Miles - The Engine Bay

☐ **Job 1. Engine oil level.**

Although some engines barely need their sump oil topping-up between major services, even healthy ones sometimes have an unusual appetite for it (especially early Cavaliers), while worn ones will certainly burn it. New or old can develop an oil leak. An engine low on oil runs the risk of internal damage, over-heating and eventual seizure - all of them ruining the engine.

Before you check the oil level, the engine should be switched off and left standing for a while to ensure that all oil has returned to the sump - obviously first thing in the morning after garaging overnight is the ideal time.

INSIDE INFORMATION: Never overfill the engine, as any excess could find its way past an overloaded oil seal, or lead to overheating and other problems.

1A. Obviously, too, the car should be on level ground when you check the dipstick. The dipstick on all 4-cylinder Cavaliers is situated at the front of the engine. Lift it out, wipe clean with a piece of cloth or tissue, put it back in and lift out again. The oil level should be clearly visible on the lower part of the 'stick' but if not, wipe clean and try again, turning the stick so that it goes into the tube at a different angle.

1B. On some models, the dipstick goes right into a hole in the block, rather than a tube. (Illustration, courtesy Vauxhall Motors Limited)

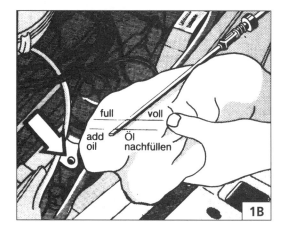

1C. On the V6 engine the dipstick is just in front of the oil filler cap.

1D. The oil level should be somewhere between the MIN and MAX markings on the stick - the difference between the two is also marked on the stick, in this case 1 litre, to give some idea of how much to add. Ideally, the oil level seen on the dipstick should be on or pretty close to the maximum (or 'max') mark, not close to the minimum (or 'min') mark. The lower mark is, of course, the danger level. But it could also be unwise to exceed the maximum mark - a shade over won't matter, but substantial over-filling can also lead to over-heating and other problems.

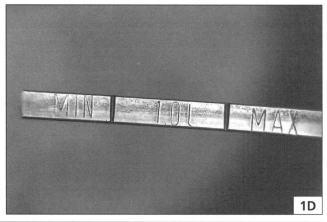

Many thanks are due to Cowies of Leicester for their help in preparing this section of the book.

1E. If you do need to top-up, the oil filler cap is situated on top of the engine and is removed by turning a 1/4 turn to the left (anti-clockwise) and lifting off. Add the oil a little at a time and allow a minute or so for the fresh oil to drain down into the sump before you recheck the level, not forgetting to start with a clean dipstick again.

1F. For topping-up when only small quantities of oil are required, a small measuring jug, plastic bottle or funnel-measure like that shown here, is useful to pour the oil in; spills are less likely and you can also keep a check on oil consumption between service intervals.

☐ Job 2. Check coolant level.

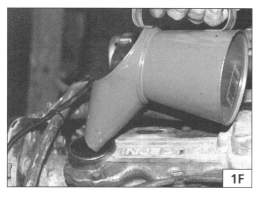

SAFETY FIRST!
i) The coolant level should only ever be checked WHEN THE SYSTEM IS COLD. If you remove the pressure cap when the engine is hot, the release of pressure can cause the liquid in the system to quickly boil and spurt several feet in to the air, with the risk of severe scalding. ii) Take precautions to prevent antifreeze coming into contact with the skin or eyes. If this should happen, rinse immediately with plenty of clean water.

Again, this is a check that should be made first thing in the morning, before the engine has been run. There are two reasons for this: (i) Hot coolant expands, so you'll only get a true level reading when it's cold; (ii) Hot coolant (like a boiling kettle) can be extremely dangerous, and removal of the filler cap can release a scalding blast of steam and liquid. See *Safety First!* above.

Generally speaking, an engine is at its most efficient when running at a temperature close to that of boiling water - and generally speaking it is water, with an anti-freeze content, that is used for the coolant. And water under pressure can reach a higher temperature than normal without boiling, thus avoiding all the attendant dangers of its dissipating away in steam, or even 'exploding' the system!

It is important that all engines have the correct proportion of anti-freeze in the coolant. This not only helps prevent freezing in the winter, but also overheating in summer temperatures. In addition, it also helps to prevent internal engine corrosion. NEVER use salt water or water which may have a salt content, regardless of the presence of an anti-freeze content. Doing so will certainly result in engine corrosion.

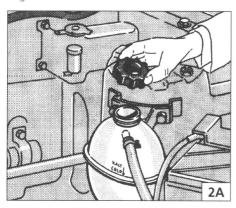

Having located the position of the coolant header tank for your model from the photographs below, check the coolant level against the mark on the outside of the tank.

If topping-up is required, turn the cap a quarter-turn anti-clockwise to release any slight pressure in the system, then turn fully and remove. NEVER ATTEMPT TO REMOVE THE FILLER CAP WHEN THE ENGINE IS HOT. If, in emergency, the cap needs to be removed before the engine has completely cooled, wrap rag around both the cap and your hands and open the cap in two stages, the first quarter turn to release any remaining internal pressure. Keep face and body well clear.

Add a mixture of 50% anti-freeze and water, even in summer (see note below). It is important that the tank is not overfilled.

2A. On 1981 to '88 petrol engined models the header tank is situated on the right-hand side of the engine bay (as you look towards the rear of the car) just behind the battery. (Illustration, courtesy Vauxhall Motors Limited)

2B. On 1982 to '88 diesel engines, the tank is on the opposite side. (Illustration, courtesy Vauxhall Motors Limited)

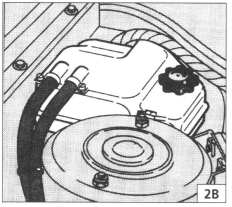

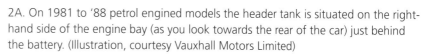

making it easy! The coolant header tank on all models is made from a semi-transparent material in order for the coolant level to be readily seen without needing to remove the cap. However, the inner surface of the tank often becomes discoloured making this impossible, but is easily cured by cleaning the inner surface with a long-handled brush, such as those used in the kitchen for washing dishes.

2C. From 1988-on all models (including diesels up to 1992, but excluding the V6) have the tank situated on the left-hand-rear corner of the engine bay (viewed from the front of the car) to the left of the brake fluid reservoir. Note the position of the 'FULL' mark on the tank.

2D. Diesel engined models from 1992 - position of coolant header tank at rear of engine bay, towards the right-hand side.

2E. V6 engined models - position of coolant header tank on righthand side of engine bay behind battery.

2F. With the cap removed, add coolant from a measuring jug or bottle. If only a small quantity is required it is quite permissible to use neat antifreeze straight from the bottle as here. There is no danger in increasing the concentration provided that you don't go over about 60% antifreeze to water.

When the level is correct, replace the cap, making sure it is not cross-threaded and that it is fully tightened down, otherwise coolant leakage could lead to overheating and serious engine damage.

INSIDE INFORMATION: Although the word 'Antifreeze' is used throughout this book as a generic term, it is more strictly correct to refer to it as 'Antifreeze/Summer Coolant' due to the corrosion-inhibiting qualities of most good-quality modern products. All Cavalier cylinder heads are made of alloy which needs such inhibitors on an all-year-round basis, even in temperate countries where frost isn't present. Vauxhall recommend a mixture of 45% antifreeze to water, although a 50/50 ratio is easier to remember and mix!

DIESEL ENGINES ONLY

INSIDE INFORMATION: Because of the high rate of heat transfer around the injector nozzles, diesel engines should NEVER be run without coolant, even for short periods of time. Serious injector damage could result.

☐ Job 3. Brake fluid level.

Check/top-up brake fluid level as required.

> **SAFETY FIRST!**
> **i) If brake fluid should come into contact with the skin or eyes, rinse immediately with plenty of clean water. ii) The brake fluid level will fall slightly during normal use as the brake-pad friction material wears down, but if it falls significantly below the MIN mark on the reservoir, stop using the car and seek specialist advice. iii) Use only new brake fluid from an airtight container, as brake fluid is able to absorb moisture from the atmosphere, which could cause the brakes to fail when carrying out an emergency stop or other heavy use of the brakes.**

Even though all models are fitted with a device to monitor the brake fluid level in the reservoir and operate a warning lamp on the instrument panel when the level drops below the MIN mark, it is wise to check the level physically while carrying out these other checks, as failure of the warning-light system (i.e. the bulb!) could go unnoticed. There's no need to remove the cap on the reservoir which is translucent, making the fluid level easily seen.

2C

2D

2E

2F

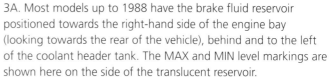

3A.

3A. Most models up to 1988 have the brake fluid reservoir positioned towards the right-hand side of the engine bay (looking towards the rear of the vehicle), behind and to the left of the coolant header tank. The MAX and MIN level markings are shown here on the side of the translucent reservoir.

3B. This is the location on post-1988 cars; on all types it is necessary to keep the reservoir clean, not only so that the level can be seen but to prevent any grit or dirt entering if and when the cap is removed for topping-up.

3C. If the cap is to be removed (after cleaning!), hold the centre section of the cap and the sensor wires steady while the outer part is unscrewed anti-clockwise.

3D. Before lifting the cap clear of the reservoir, allow the fluid contained in the sensor 'tube' on the underside of the cap to drain away - remember, brake fluid is damaging to paintwork, even that in the engine bay! When drained, place the cap on a piece of rag or tissue to catch any remaining drips.

3E. Before adding fresh fluid position a piece of rag around the filler neck to catch any spillages. Don't overfill the reservoir, and remember to leave some space to allow for the displacement of fluid by the sensor tube when the cap is replaced afterwards.

INSIDE INFORMATION: i) Check the ground on which the car has been parked, especially beneath the engine bay and inside each road wheel, for evidence of oil, clutch or brake fluid leaks. If any are found, investigate further before driving the car.

3B.

Note that on all disc-braked cars a gradual drop in the fluid level over a lengthy period is natural. This is because, as the disc pads' friction material wears, the pad backing plates move nearer to the disc, the brake caliper pistons (in contact with the backing plates) move further out of their bores, the fluid follows the pistons, and more fluid from the reservoir flows into the system to fill the extra space thus created.

SAFETY FIRST!
Should the fluid level drop quite markedly over a short period, the cause must be investigated immediately - it could be dangerous to drive the car until the fault is found and rectified. Although modern dual-circuit hydraulic brake systems should retain some braking ability provided any leakage is confined to just one of the circuits, leakage in an earlier single-circuit system could threaten sudden and total brake failure.

3C.

3D.

3E.

☐ Job 4. Battery electrolyte

SAFETY FIRST!
i) The gas given off by a battery is highly explosive. Never smoke, use a naked flame or allow a spark to occur in the vicinity of the battery. Never disconnect a battery (which can cause sparking) while the filler cap or caps are removed. ii) Batteries contain sulphuric acid; if spillage occurs and the acid comes into contact with the skin or eyes, wash immediately with plenty of clean water and seek medical advice.iii) Do not check the battery levels within half an hour of the battery being charged with a separate battery charger because the addition of fresh water could then cause the highly acid and corrosive electrolyte to flood out of the battery.

FACT FILE: COMPUTER PROTECTION

Many vehicles depend on a constant power supply from the battery and you can find yourself in all sorts of trouble if you simply disconnect the battery on those vehicles. You might find that the car alarm will go off, you could find that the engine management forgets all it has ever "learned" and the car will feel very strange to drive until it has re-programmed itself, and you could find that your radio refuses to operate again unless you key in the correct code. And if you've bought the car second-hand and don't know the code, you would have to send the set back to the manufacturer for re-programming. So, you must ensure that the vehicle has a constant power supply even though the battery is removed. To do so, you will need a separate 12 volt battery supply. You could put a self tapping screw into the positive lead near the battery terminal before disconnecting it, and put a positive connection to your other battery via this screw. But you would have to be EXTREMELY CAREFUL to wrap insulation tape around the connection so that no short is caused. The negative terminal on the other battery would also have to be connected to the car's bodywork.

A better way is to use something like the Sykes-Pickavant Computer Saver shown here.

Clip the cables to your spare battery and plug it into your cigarette lighter. (You may have to turn the ignition switch to the "Auxiliary" setting to allow the cigarette lighter to function.)

You have to hold in the red button on the Computer Saver while inserting it into the cigarette lighter, and if two green lights still show after the button is released, you have a good connection and your battery can now be disconnected and removed.

Be sure not to turn on any of the car's equipment while the auxiliary battery is connected.

Where the battery is provided with screw caps to the individual cells, or obviously removable strips which plug into or over a number of cells at a time, it is obviously intended that its electrolyte content should be topped up as and when required. But note that a so-called 'maintenance-free' battery may have flush-fitting strips over its cells which can be prised up for the addition of electrolyte, perhaps prolonging its life beyond general expectation!

INSIDE INFORMATION: Do not confuse this latter type of maintenance-free battery with those supplied as original equipment on new Cavaliers - these are marked 'AC-DELCO Freedom Battery' and cannot be opened up.

4A. All Cavaliers are fitted with a 'maintenance-free' battery when new and as the name suggests, these are sealed-for-life units that do not require topping-up and no provision is made for doing so. These batteries are provided with a 'condition indicator' on the top surface, as shown here.

If the indicator is darkened and shows a green dot, it is charged and in good condition. No green dot indicates the battery is part-charged, although this may not be noticeable in normal use. If the indicator shows yellow then the battery is in poor condition and may need replacement: DO NOT ATTEMPT to re-charge or jump-start (using jump-leads) the car if the battery is in this state.

4B. 'Ordinary' batteries: If the battery case is translucent, look for a level mark scribed or moulded on the side, otherwise a general recommendation is that the electrolyte level should be just above the tops of the plates which you can see with the cell caps or strips removed.

INSIDE INFORMATION: Note that here is an instance where it is preferable that the battery should be warm, such as after a run, before checking the level, since the electrolyte expands with heat. If it were topped up while cold there is a danger that later the fluid would overflow, leading to corrosion of the terminals and accumulated dirt.

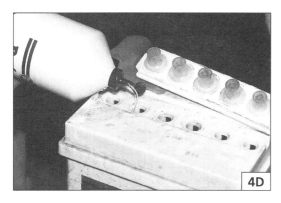

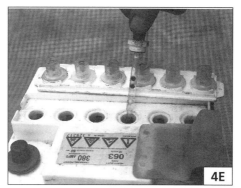

4D. Top up only with distilled ('de-ionised') water, never ordinary tap water, which may contain impurities which would damage the plates and shorten the battery's life. Mop up any accidental spillage immediately, and make sure the entire battery exterior is clean and dry.

4E. Here's how to check the strength, or specific gravity, of the battery electrolyte. You place the end of a hydrometer into the electrolyte liquid, squeeze and release the rubber bulb so that a little of the electrolyte is drawn up into the transparent tube and the float or floats inside the tube (small coloured beads are sometimes used) give the specific gravity. Check each cell and if one (or more) is significantly lower than the others, with battery topped up, the battery is probably on its way out.

making it easy! Use the hydrometer bulb for drawing up a small quantity of distilled water, as a spill-free way of topping up the battery.

INSIDE INFORMATION: Since only water evaporates out of a battery, not acid, topping up with distilled water is sufficient. If a battery is run flat, use a small battery charger, following the instructions and disconnecting the battery on your car first. A battery that goes flat in normal use can be checked by a garage. Otherwise, you could try disconnecting the battery and seeing if it still goes flat - if it does, it probably has an internal problem and requires replacement.

4F. Check the tightness of the battery clamp. A loose, rattling battery will have a shorter life than one that is held down securely.

If checking now reveals corroded terminals (typically, a white, powdery growth) refer to *Job 86. Battery terminals*.

Job 5. Screenwash level.

Check the screenwash fluid level reservoir and top-up if necessary.

It can be positively dangerous to run out of screenwash fluid in mid-journey, so check the washer bottle level regularly!

On all models the screen wash reservoir is positioned on the right-hand side of the engine bay as you look to the rear of the car, but changes to its position and appearance have occurred over the years - and note that, while yours may not look *identical* to these, the principles remain the same:

5A. On models up to 1988 the reservoir is positioned between the suspension turret and the bulkhead. If a headlamp wash/wipe system is fitted the tank will appear slightly larger than that shown, due to its increased capacity. (Illustration, courtesy Vauxhall Motors Limited)

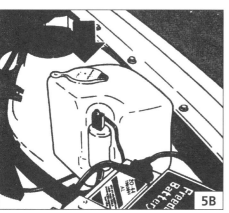

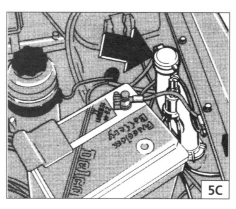

5B. On models from 1988 onwards the reservoir is positioned in front of the turret and serves both front and rear washers, but not the headlamp wash/wipe system if fitted - see below. (Illustration, courtesy Vauxhall Motors Limited)

5C. Post-1988 cars fitted with headlamp wash/wipe have the reservoir situated beneath the front wing, with the filler neck and cap positioned just to the rear of the battery. (Illustration, courtesy Vauxhall Motors Limited)

5D. Don't forget to check the rear washer bottle on pre-1988 models; it is found on the right-hand side of the boot (behind a trim panel) on saloons, or just in front of the tailgate opening on the back panel of hatchback models. (Illustration, courtesy Vauxhall Motors Limited)

5E. Make sure the reservoir is kept fully topped up, using a good brand of screen-wash additive that promises not to freeze up in winter and helps clean the screen in summer. Stick to the recommended concentration - never add cooling system anti-freeze, since, like brake fluid, this is also an effective paint stripper!

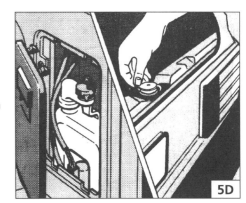

5D

Every 500 Miles - Around the Car

☐ Job 6. Check tyre pressures.

This is another job that is best done 'cold', for certainly after any appreciable run the tyres will have warmed up and the air inside will have expanded, giving you a higher pressure reading.

Correct tyre pressures will not only prolong tyre life, they will also make for safer driving. The tyre pressures for the various tyre sizes are shown in *Chapter 8, Facts and Figures.*

6A. Garage airline readings can be unreliable, so use a good quality gauge of your own to check that the tyre pressures accord with your handbook recommendations. Provided the garage is little more than 'just down the road', you can drive there to use the airline, checking afterwards with your own gauge that you have got the pressures right. Of course, having your own footpump, of a good make, is also a good idea! Observe the utmost cleanliness, and don't forget to replace the valve caps afterwards.

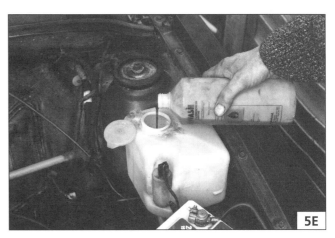

5E

6B. Don't forget to check the spare wheel in the boot, otherwise it may not be usable when you need it! The 'pencil' type gauge shown here is available quite cheaply from most accessory shops and is sufficiently accurate if not mistreated.

☐ Job 7. Check headlights, sidelights and front indicators.

SPECIALIST SERVICE It is not possible to set headlamp alignment accurately at home. They will need to be checked by a garage with proper headlamp beam setting equipment.

6A

SAFETY FIRST!
i) It is important, for reasons both of safety and legality, that your car's lights work correctly and that the reflectors and lenses are in good condition. Replace faulty bulbs as soon as possible and get any damaged lens renewed. ii) If removing a headlamp bulb be aware that these items get extremely hot in use and are capable of burning fingers for some minutes after switching off; allow at least five minutes for the bulbs, and their holders, to cool before attempting to remove them. NEVER hold a headlamp bulb while it is switched on - it will burn you before you can let it go!

6B

Check ALL lights operate correctly and with equal brightness on each side of the car; in other words, that both left and right-hand sidelights are equally bright.

making it easy! When checking the rear lights it helps to have an assistant stand at the rear of the car to confirm each light is working, but the job can be done alone if the car is reversed close to a garage door or wall so that the reflections of the lights can be seen from the driver's seat. Also, test the stoplights with the sidelights already switched on, then the indicators with the stoplights held on; this test causes maximum current to flow through the earth circuit of each rear-light cluster, which sometimes suffer from poor earth connections.

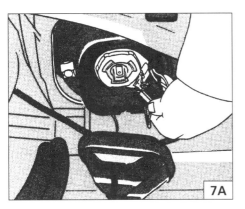

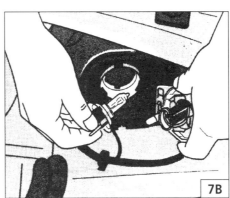

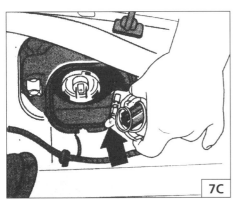

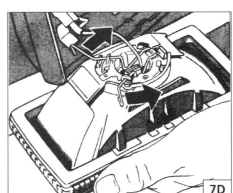

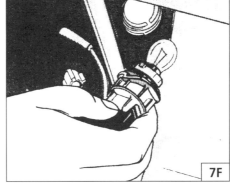

CARS FROM 1981 TO '88 ONLY

7A. HEADLAMP BULB REPLACEMENT. On these earlier models, the headlamp bulb is reached by first removing the dust cover and the plug socket from the back of the lamp unit. (Illustration, courtesy Vauxhall Motors Limited)

7B. The retaining ring is pressed in and turned anti-clockwise and this allows you to remove the bulb from the lamp unit. When you fit a replacement bulb, ensure that the fixing lugs on the bulb holder engage the recesses in the lamp unit. UNDER NO CIRCUMSTANCES SHOULD YOU TOUCH THE BARE GLASS OF A NEW BULB. (Illustration, courtesy Vauxhall Motors Limited)

7C. FRONT SIDELAMP REPLACEMENT. With the headlamp dust cover and retaining ring removed as before, the sidelamp bulb (arrowed) can be removed from the bulb holder and replaced. (Illustration, courtesy Vauxhall Motors Limited)

7D. FOG LAMPS. Remove the cross-headed screw from the bottom of the lamp and remove the reflector housing. You can now disengage the bulb retainer by pinching the spring clips (arrowed) and swivel the retainer. (Illustration, courtesy Vauxhall Motors Limited)

7E. You can now remove the bulb from the holder and detach the wire. When you install the new bulb, make sure that the recesses on the bulb socket coincide with the reflector lugs. ON NO ACCOUNT SHOULD YOU TOUCH THE BULBS WITH YOUR BARE HANDS. If you accidentally do so, clean the glass with methylated spirit or white spirit. (Illustration, courtesy Vauxhall Motors Limited)

7F. **FRONT INDICATOR LAMP.** Disengage the bulb holder from the lamp with a twisting motion and remove the bulb from the holder. The new bulb can now be fitted. (Illustration, courtesy Vauxhall Motors Limited)

500 MILE/WEEKLY SERVICE

CARS FROM 1988 TO '95 ONLY

7G. **HEADLAMP BULBS.** Headlamp bulbs are changed by removing the black plastic cover inside the engine bay and pressing down on the tab at the top of the cover. This exposes the headlamp bulb connector - gently pull this off and you will then see a two-legged spring clip which secures the bulb's flange to the reflector.

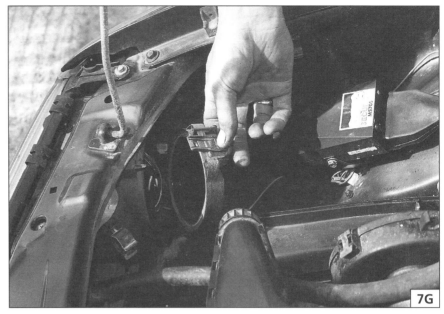

7G

7H. Squeeze the clip at the two loops and it will easily come away, allowing the bulb to be lifted out and replaced.

7I. Take care not to touch the glass envelope of the bulb as even minute traces of oil from the fingers can cause it to 'blow'; handle the bulb by its metal base only. New bulbs sometimes come with a paper or card sleeve over the glass envelope for safer handling, but remember to remove the sleeve before fitting!

7H

7J. Front sidelamps are situated in the headlamp reflectors with the bulb and holder positioned adjacent to the headlamp bulb, so access to it follows that described above for the headlamp.

7I

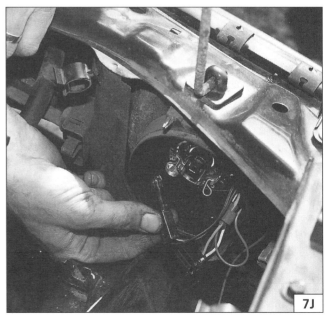

7J

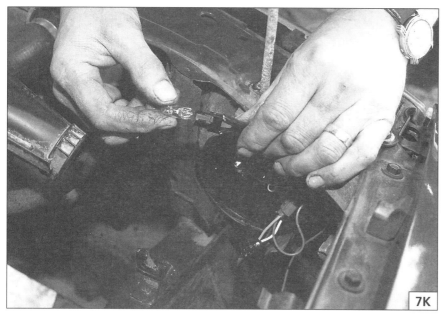

7K. The bulb and holder is simply a push-fit in the reflector and is easily withdrawn rearwards. The bulb too is a push-fit in its holder and can be fitted either way round.

7L. **INDICATOR BULBS.** The front indicator bulb is changed by first loosening the screw that secures the lens assembly to the headlights shell. A long Phillips-type screwdriver is used to undo the screw one or two turns - there is no need to remove it completely.

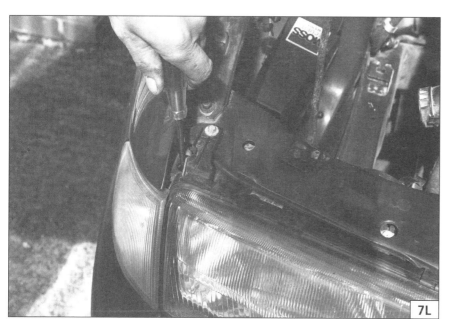

7M. The indicator lens can now be drawn out a few inches. The bulb holder is undone by turning it through 90 degrees anti-clockwise when the lens can be lifted away.

7N. The bulb can be removed from the holder by pushing down slightly against the sprung contact and turning anti-clockwise.

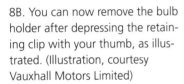

Job 8. Rear lights and indicators.

CARS FROM 1981 TO '88 ONLY

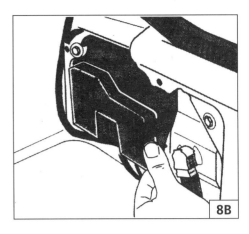

8A. **REAR INDICATORS, SIDE, BRAKE AND REVERSE LAMP BULBS.** On saloon models, remove the retaining plugs (arrowed) from the cover and on hatchback models, release the carpet fasteners. On saloons, the cover is now tilted downwards, while on hatchbacks, it is tilted to one side. (Illustration, courtesy Vauxhall Motors Limited)

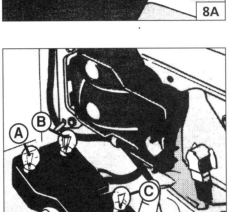

8B. You can now remove the bulb holder after depressing the retaining clip with your thumb, as illustrated. (Illustration, courtesy Vauxhall Motors Limited)

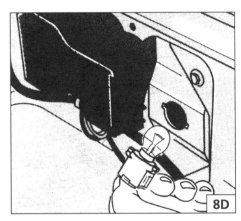

8C. The three bulbs found in the bulb holder block can be identified as follows: bulb A is the indicator bulb; bulb B is the side/brake lamp bulb, with twin filaments, and bulb C is for the reverse lamp. When fitting a new side and brake lamp bulb, you have to be sure that the offset pegs on the bulb are the right way round, otherwise the bulb will not clip into place. (Illustration, courtesy Vauxhall Motors Limited)

8D. **REAR FOG LAMP BULB.** You have to remove the lamp cover in the boot as described in 8A and the bulb holder can be found next to the main bulb holder block. This smaller bulb holder can be removed by twisting until the pegs on the bulb holder line up with the slots. A new bulb is fitted in the normal way before re-inserting the bulb holder to the bodywork. (Illustration, courtesy Vauxhall Motors Limited)

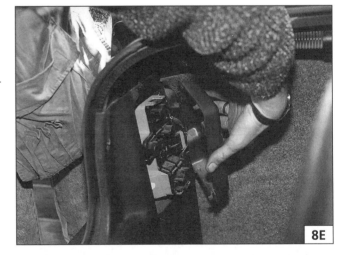

CARS FROM 1988 TO '95 ONLY

8E. The rear lamp cluster on all models can be found by removing a small trim panel on the interior of the car immediately behind the lamps and lifting off the plastic cover.

8F. The one-piece lamp cluster is held by lugs top and bottom; squeezing them and pulling the cluster rearwards releases it.

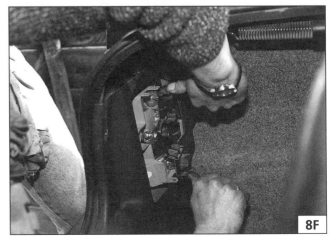

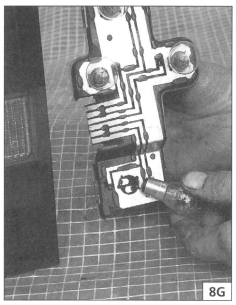

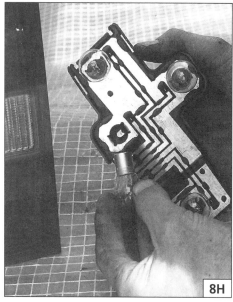

8G. This is the sidelight bulb which is rated at 5 watts. It is removed by pushing down slightly against the sprung contact and turning anti-clockwise.

8H. The indicator bulb shown here is rated at 21 watts and is removed as for the sidelight bulb above.

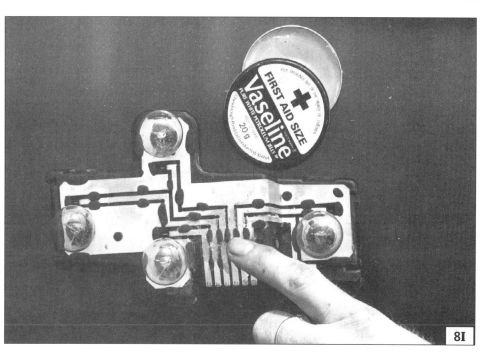

8I. INSIDE INFORMATION: As mentioned above, earthing problems can arise on the rear lamp multi-bulb holder, mainly due to damp which causes corrosion of the metal 'tracks', or conductors, that connect each bulb to the wiring harness. To prevent this problem, smear petroleum jelly over the tracks and the edge connector terminals to protect them from the effects of moisture and air.

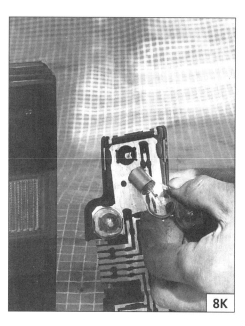

CARS FROM 1988 TO '95 ONLY

REVERSING AND REAR FOG LAMPS

8J. This shows removal of the reversing light bulb, rated at 21 watts...

8K. ...while here is the rear foglamp bulb, also 21 watts.

☐ Job 9. Interior lights.

9A. Prise the lamp cover away with a screwdriver but take care to damage neither headlining nor bulb holder. (Illustration, courtesy Vauxhall Motors Limited)

9B. Push the bulb against the spring clip and remove. (Illustration, courtesy Vauxhall Motors Limited)

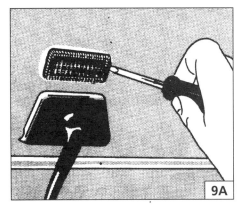
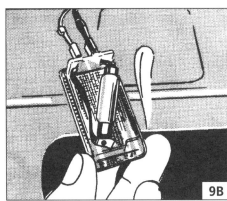

☐ Job 10. Number plate lights.

10A. The rear number plate lamp is situated in the rear bumper (except estates - see below) and is removed by springing-up the bumper-coloured surround...

10B. ...then squeezing on a tab to remove the lens and bulb holder.

10C. The lens and bulb holder are separated by means of another tab and the bulb can then be simply pulled out. Clean the inner surface of the lens before refitting.

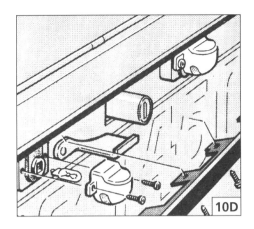

10D. The number plate lamp on the estate version contains two bulbs and is accessed by removing four screws that secure the tailgate handle. Two further screws secure each lens to the respective bulb holder - remove these and the bulb can be pulled straight from its holder and a new one pushed in. Clean the lens inner surface before refitting. (Illustration, courtesy Vauxhall Motors Limited)

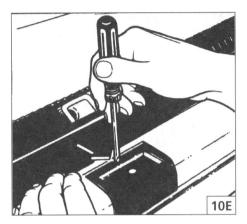

10E. On this later type (saloons and hatchbacks, again!), the complete lamp is disengaged with a screwdriver. (Illustration, courtesy Vauxhall Motors Limited)

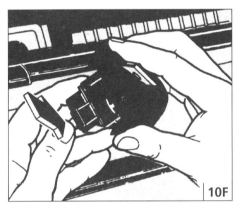

10F. The base is removed by pressing in the lug (arrowed)... (Illustration, courtesy Vauxhall Motors Limited)

10G. ...and the bulb can now be removed. (Illustration, courtesy Vauxhall Motors Limited)

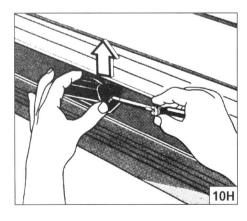

10H. On earliest cars, the lamp is eased out from this angle - check to see where Vauxhall put the screwdriver slot on your car. (Illustration, courtesy Vauxhall Motors Limited)

☐ Job 11. Side repeater light bulbs.

11A. Side repeater bulbs are removed by first turning the orange lens a quarter turn to the left and lifting it away.

11B. The bulb is a push-fit in its holder and is recessed quite deeply, which makes removal difficult. To remove the bulb more easily wrap a short piece of masking tape around the protruding glass and squeeze the excess into a small 'handle' as shown.

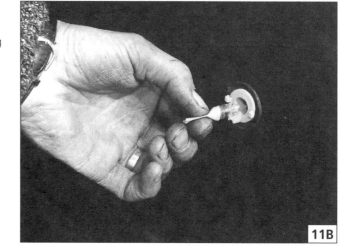

FACT FILE: HORN LOCATION

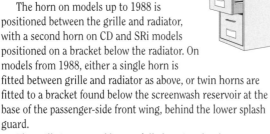

The horn on models up to 1988 is positioned between the grille and radiator, with a second horn on CD and SRi models positioned on a bracket below the radiator. On models from 1988, either a single horn is fitted between grille and radiator as above, or twin horns are fitted to a bracket found below the screenwash reservoir at the base of the passenger-side front wing, behind the lower splash guard.

The grille is removed by carefully levering the three top clips from the bonnet slam-panel and lifting the grille away. Access to the later "below-wing" type is gained by removing three screws from the forward part of the splash guard and gently bending it down.

☐ Job 12. Check horn.

12. Try the horn button. If the horns fail to work, examine the wiring to the horns themselves if the horn is accessible, otherwise seek professional advice.

SPECIALIST SERVICE: Horn wiring and connections are more complex than they appear at first. For instance, both terminals at the horn should be 'live'! If there is no obvious problem with the wiring connections, have the horn circuitry and switches checked over by a specialist.

☐ **Job 13. Check windscreen wipers.**

13A. Check the wiper blades for splitting (as here), hardening of the rubber blade, and that no metal part of the blade carrier is contacting the screen, which will quickly score and ruin the glass - which is also a possible MoT failure. Wipe each blade with methylated spirit to remove traces of oil and dirt that would otherwise be smeared across the screen. Don't forget the rear tailgate wiper and/or headlamp wipers if fitted to your model.

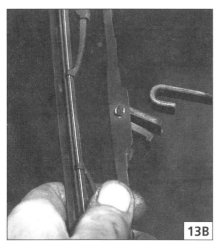

13B. Worn or damaged blades are easily replaced by squeezing this clip and pushing the blade towards the bottom of the arm, then lifting clear. Refit by placing the blade over the 'hook' of the arm and engaging the plastic clip. If new blades are being fitted, new clips also will be included.

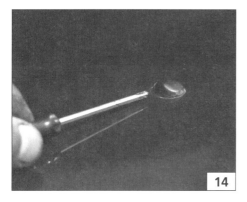

☐ **Job 14. Windscreen washers.**

14. The windscreen washer jets are situated on the bonnet and although they're non-adjustable, make sure there is no build-up of dried polish or other debris which might obstruct them. If the spray from one of the jets seems uncertain or is non-existent, and you're sure the feed tube to the jet is secure, try poking the jet with a pin to clear possible blockage. Don't forget to check the rear screen washer, if fitted.

Every 1,500 Miles - or Every Month, whichever comes first

1,500 Miles - Around the Car

☐ **Job 15. Check tyres.**

SAFETY FIRST!
Tyres that show uneven wear tell their own story, if only you know how to speak the language! If any tyre is worn more on one side than another, consult your specialist Vauxhall dealer or tyre specialist. It probably means that your suspension or steering is out of adjustment - probably a simple tracking job but conceivably symptomatic of suspension damage, so have it checked. If a tyre is worn more in the centre or on the edges, it could mean that your tyre pressures are wrong, but once again, have the car checked. Incorrectly inflated tyres wear rapidly, can cause the car's handling to become dangerous and can even cause the car to consume noticeably more fuel. When checking your tyres, don't forget to include the spare.

See also *Chapter 8, Getting Through the Mot* for a more detailed explanation of tyre wear and problems likely to be encountered.

15A. Check the tyres for sufficient depth using a tread depth gauge and note that in the UK, the minimum legal tread depth is 1.6mm. However, tyres are not at their safest at that level, particularly in the wet, and you might want to replace them earlier. Measure the tread across the width of the tyre, at three or four places around the circumference. This will give early warning of any uneven wear pattern, perhaps caused by a steering or suspension fault, or a defect in the tyre itself.

15A

15B. Check the inner and outer sidewalls for bulges and splits, also the wheel rims if kerbstones etc. have been driven over (accidentally, of course!). Raise each wheel off the ground, supporting the axle on an axle stand, otherwise you won't be able to see the inside of each tyre properly, nor will you be able to check that part of the tyre in contact with the ground. If you find any splits or other damage, the tyre(s) should be inspected immediately by a tyre specialist who will advise whether repair is possible or replacement is the only answer.

☐ Job 16. Check spare tyre.

Don't forget the spare wheel - on all models it will be found beneath the boot floor covering. Check it as for the road wheels, but additionally check all over the sidewalls for signs of scuffing or other damage which can occur if the tyre isn't fixed firmly in the wheel well, or by loose stone chips or odd screws which work their way under the tyre. Check the pressure of the spare wheel, too.

15B

INSIDE INFORMATION: You should inflate the spare to the maximum recommended for high speed or high load running. Then, if you have a puncture while on a journey, you'll be okay. It's always easier to carry a tyre pressure gauge with you and let some air out than put some in!

☐ Job 17. Wash bodywork.

INSIDE INFORMATION: Many people choose to wash their cars weekly, which is commendable, while others seem never to wash them at all! But there's no denying that regularly washed-and-waxed bodywork lasts longer and helps maintain a car's value. Getting into a regular car-washing routine has the advantage that minor damage to the bodywork does not go unnoticed and can be quickly treated before corrosion gets a hold.

Wash paintwork, chrome and glass with water and a suitable car wash detergent, taking care not to get 'wax-wash' on the glass. Finish by washing the wheels and tyre walls. Leather the paintwork dry. Use a separate leather on the glass to avoid transfer of polish from paintwork.

CONVERTIBLE CARS ONLY

Don't wash the roof covering with soap and water or shampoo; a soft brush worked in the direction of the pile is all that is recommended by the manufacturer. The plastic rear screen should be cleaned with a soft damp cloth or chamois leather. Finally, DO NOT use petrol, thinners, tar remover or similar chemicals on the roof material or rear screen.

☐ Job 18. Touch-up paintwork.

18. Treat small areas of damage, like the stonechip shown here, as soon as possible, otherwise corrosion of the exposed metal will soon get a hold and prove difficult (and expensive!) to eradicate. 'Touch-Up' type products are available from accessory shops and garages in the form of paint 'pens' and even colour-matched film that is simply 'stuck' over the damaged area. These products may not give an invisible repair, but they do offer protection from road-salt and water.

☐ Job 19. Aerial/antenna

19. Clean each section of an extending aerial with a maintenance spray and work the aerial up and down a few times. With electrically operated antennae it is especially important to keep the sections clean, otherwise the operating motor and/or gears will be over-stressed and quickly fail. Do not leave lubricating oil on the aerial sections as this will simply encourage the adherence of grit and dirt.

☐ Job 20. Valet interior.

20. Regularly vacuuming the seats and carpets will not only make the car more pleasant to drive, but will remove a surprising amount of abrasive grit and dust, the main cause of 'baldness' in these items. For stains and grease-marks use one of the many domestic upholstery cleaning materials, although some severe stains can only be effectively removed by the use of white or methylated spirit - test these on an unseen area first though, to check for colour-fastness of the upholstery.

☐ Job 21. Improve visibility.

21. Use a proprietary glass cleaner on the windscreen (and other windows) both inside and out. Tar-spots and dead flies can be removed with special cleaners available from accessory shops. 'Traffic-film' can build up unnoticed and is a mixture of oil and grime thrown from the wheels of other vehicles, resulting in dangerous smearing of the windscreen in the wet, and which ordinary washer additives can't shift. Proprietary traffic film removers are instantly effective however, and last quite well.

1,500 Miles - Under the Car

☐ **Job 22. Clean mud traps.**

22. Use a strong water jet to clean underneath the wheelarches front and rear. If available, a high-pressure washer is the most effective method but take care: on a powerful spray, they'll blast away underseal!

INSIDE INFORMATION: Even where the car is fitted with plastic 'inner' linings, mud can build-up around the edges and will act like a sponge to salt-laden water thrown from the tyres. The result is bubbling and flaking of paint from around the edges of the wheelarches.

22

Every 3,000 Miles - or Every Three Months, whichever comes first

3,000 Miles - The Engine Bay

☐ **Job 23. Generator drive belt.**

23A. Check the tension of the alternator drivebelt by deflecting with a finger or thumb, halfway along the top 'run' with firm pressure. The amount of movement should be no more than 12mm (0.5in). Check also the general condition of the belt, looking for signs of cracking and frayed edges.

23B. Tension the drivebelt (if necessary) by slackening the nut and bolt shown - loosen it just sufficiently to allow movement of the alternator but maintaining a degree of 'grip'.

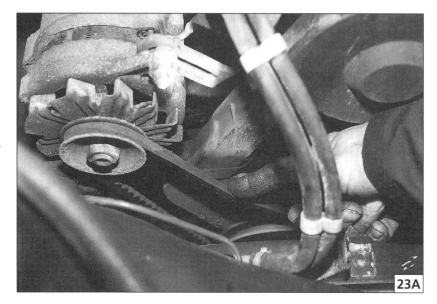

23A

making it easy! 23C. Use a length of wood to apply sideways pressure to the alternator body (as near to the bracket end as possible) moving it away from the engine against belt tension. Provided the alternator bracket bolt hasn't been loosened too much, the alternator should 'stay-put' while the nut and bolt are tightened. However, if you find this procedure difficult (it takes practice!) ask an assistant to hold the wood while you tighten the bolt.

23B

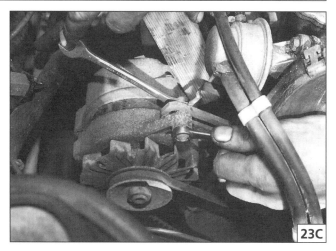

23C

☐ **Job 24. Check brake/fuel lines.**

SAFETY FIRST! AND SPECIALIST SERVICE.
Fuel injection systems remain pressurised even when the engine is switched off and require special procedures to make them safe - UNDER NO CIRCUMSTANCES loosen or remove fuel pipes on a fuel injection system. If pipework requires repair, take the car immediately to a fuel injection specialist or your Vauxhall dealer.

Make a physical check of all the pipework and connections in the engine bay. Bend the flexible fuel lines in order to expose hairline cracks or deterioration which may not be immediately obvious. Look for signs of rust or weeping on the brake lines and unions. Start the engine and (taking the usual precautions) check that there are no fuel leaks.

SAFETY FIRST!
As everyone is aware, petrol is highly flammable and only a small spark is necessary to ignite it, with potentially disastrous consequences. If a fuel leak (however slight) is suspected or detected; don't smoke, switch off all car accessories (but don't disconnect the battery which often creates sparks as the terminal is removed) and mop-up any spilt or dripping fuel with rags which should be taken out of doors. Don't drive the car until professional advice is sought and the problem rectified.

☐ **Job 25. Drain fuel filter.**

DIESEL ENGINES ONLY

SAFETY FIRST!
Whenever you are dealing with diesel fuel, it's essential to protect your hands by wearing plastic gloves.

Drain the diesel-fuel filter of any water residue.

INSIDE INFORMATION: The fuel filter is designed so that any water which passes through it will collect at the bottom of the filter, immediately above the drain plug. This means that any water present will be drained first, and the drain plug can be closed as soon as fuel begins to flow. Under normal conditions the amount of water likely to be present is usually very small, although under extreme conditions of high humidity or widely varying day-to-night temperatures, more will be present, so the wise owner will want to check this at shorter intervals, such as 3,000 miles.

25. The filter is located at the back of the engine bay. Drain it by partly unscrewing the plastic drain-plug fitted to the base of the filter unit (arrowed), after placing a number of rags beneath the filter to catch any water and fuel that may escape.

☐ **Job 26. Renew engine oil.**

DIESEL ENGINES UP TO 1987 ONLY

OPTIONAL: This job is specified by Vauxhall at 3,000 miles but with no time limit specified. We include it here regardless, but if your car only covers a small mileage, say 1,000 miles or less in three months, you may wish to include the job in the 6 monthly checks described later in this chapter.

Refer to *Job 45* later in this chapter for precise instructions: The diesel engine is identical to the petrol version as far as oil changing is concerned and follows the same procedure.

☐ **Job 27. Replace oil filter.**

DIESEL ENGINES UP TO 1987 ONLY

OPTIONAL: This job is specified by Vauxhall at 3,000 miles but with no time limit specified; we include it here regardless, but if your car only covers a small mileage, say 1,000 miles or less in three months, you may wish to include the job in the 6 monthly checks described later in this chapter.

Refer to *Job 45* later in this chapter for precise instructions: The diesel engine is identical to the petrol version as far as oil filter changing is concerned and follows the same procedure.

CHAPTER THREE

3,000 Miles - Around the Car

☐ Job 28. Check wheel bolts.

28. Check the tightness of all wheel bolts. The wheel brace supplied with the car is merely intended for use in an emergency and we strongly recommend the use of a torque wrench for this job. This will avoid over-tightening the bolts and the inherent danger of stripped threads or over-stressed bolts causing the bolts to loosen or shear.

To 'torque' the wheel bolts correctly, first slacken each bolt and check that the threads aren't stiff or corroded, then tighten with the wrench to the specified torque figure - 9kg.m. (65 ft.lb.).

☐ Job 29. Check brake/fuel lines.

From under the car, check the remainder of the pipe-work for signs of rust or weeping unions - severe rust or even the tiniest of leaks render the car dangerous to drive, and it must not be driven until the problem has been put right.

29. Bend flexible brake hoses to show up signs of cracking - if any are found, the hose must be renewed immediately. They must also be free from bulges or oil contamination.

INSIDE INFORMATION: Bend double, especially near the pipe ends and check visually. Also, have an assistant press hard on the brake pedal and check the pipes for bulging, which means they need replacement.

☐ Job 30. Check handbrake adjustment.

This is another job that might these days be considered as non-essential at this mileage/period and, for low mileage cars this may be true, but we recommend it at this point on grounds of safety.

Raise the rear of the car sufficiently to enable the rear wheels to turn, and support it on axle stands - see *Raising the Car Safely* at the beginning of this chapter.

30A. Apply the handbrake by three clicks of the ratchet, when it should just be possible to turn each wheel by heavy hand pressure. If one or other of the wheels is too stiff to turn, or turns freely, then adjustment may be necessary. However, the cause could be the result of wear or sticking of the mechanism, so check these before proceeding - see Job 73. In the case of cars with rear disc brakes, separate handbrake drums are fitted. Dismantling involves removal of the brake calipers, which is a **SPECIALIST SERVICE** job. Note that the wheels should most certainly be locked at five clicks of the ratchet.

30B. While the rear of the car is raised, make a visual check of the handbrake cables across the rear 'axle' (correctly called the torsion beam) and the quadrant tubes shown here, through which the cables pass just inboard of the rear wheels, applying a spot of grease to these points. Look for signs of chafing or fraying of the multi-strand cable. NOTE: This component has been removed as a unit from the car, to make photography and identification easier.

SPECIALIST SERVICE: Due to the design of the handbrake cables and the method of adjustment, a 'rolling-road' brake tester is required so that application of the handbrake results in an equal 'pull' on both sides of the car. Although an 'adjuster' is present on the rear torsion beam, mis-adjustment will produce unequal braking and instability, so we recommend the actual adjustment be carried out by a reputable garage or Vauxhall agent.

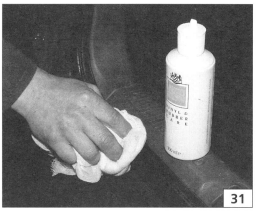

Job 31. Door and tailgate seals.

31. To preserve the weather-protection efficiency of door and tailgate (or bootlid) seals, they should be regularly cleaned and occasionally treated with a proprietary 'conditioning' product. Treat sunroof seals similarly.

Job 32. Check windscreen.

32. Check the windscreen for chips and scratches, a potential MoT Test failure depending on size and position - see *Chapter 7, Getting Through the MoT* for what is and is not acceptable according to UK regulations. Most chips can be repaired by specialists, while light scratches and scuff-marks can often be polished-out by the same people.

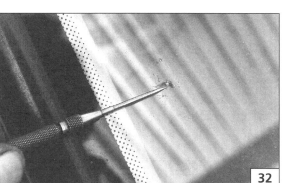

Job 33. Rear view mirrors.

33. Check your rear view mirrors, both inside and outside the car, for cracks and crazing. Also ensure that the interior rear view mirror is soundly fixed in place since they can come loose and when they do, the vibration can get so bad that you can't tell whether you're being followed by a long distance truck or one of the boys in blue!

3,000 Miles - Under the Car

Job 34. Check exhaust system.

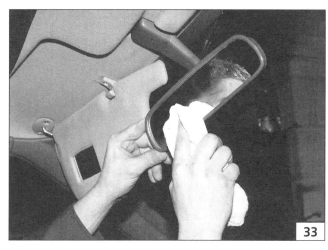

SAFETY FIRST!
Never run your car's engine in an enclosed space, only ever out of doors. Exhaust gases can be toxic and an exhaust leak can allow gases into the car as you drive along. Check the condition and security of the entire exhaust system, looking carefully for any signs of corrosion on the pipes and silencers, or leakage at the joints. Replace gaskets if necessary.

34A. Examine the silencers (as far as safe access will allow) for signs of corrosion, especially along seams and around welded joints.

34B. Check joints where parts of the exhaust system are fitted together, for signs of 'sooty' deposits indicating a leak, as seen here.

INSIDE INFORMATION: If you suspect a leak but its location isn't obvious, start the engine and try pressurising the system by holding a piece of board or similar so that it blocks off the tailpipe - under pressure, the leak should become more noisy, enabling you to track it down. Get an assistant to help if you can, but remember an exhaust system gets extremely hot - neither of you should actually touch the pipe-work anywhere, or you risk a severe burn ESPECIALLY when a catalytic converter is fitted.

Job 35. Check exhaust mountings.

If exhaust mountings break or come loose, the extra stresses on your exhaust system will soon cause fracturing. Replace split rubber mountings *before* they break - a case of a stitch in time saving nine!

---

making it easy! Jobs 36, 37, 38 and 39 all require the front of the car to be raised and the wheels clear of the ground; you may prefer to carry them out together, possibly after completing Job 64 (front brakes) and Job 29 (brake hoses).

Job 36. Check steering rack gaiters.

SAFETY FIRST!
*This operation requires the steering to be swung from lock-to-lock so the use of axle stands is necessary. Refer to **Raising the Car Safely** at the beginning of this chapter for details of how this can be done safely.*

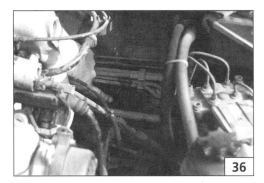
36

The steering rack gaiters - also sometimes called 'boots'- are made of convoluted rubber, their purpose being to exclude dust and grit from the steering rack mechanism while keeping lubricant inside it, and at the same time allowing the 'push-pull' effect of the steering arms as the steering wheel is turned.

Obviously, this continual movement; plus attack from flying grit and stones from the road surface, can lead to splits in the gaiter; lubricant gets out, abrasive dirt gets in and very soon the rack mechanism is prematurely worn out.

37A

36. With the steering turned on full lock (that is, turned fully left or right) check the gaiter that is extended for splits, chafing, perishing etc., feeling with the hand for damage on those parts of the gaiter not visible. Turn the steering to the other direction and check the second gaiter. Also make sure the clips securing the gaiter are firm and doing their job. Replacement of gaiters involves removal of the steering arms and for most, this will be a **SPECIALIST SERVICE** job. But running with a split gaiter will *very* quickly ruin an expensive steering rack!

Job 37. Check drive-shaft gaiters.

Drive-shaft gaiters perform a similar function to the steering gaiters i.e. keeping lubricant in and dirt out, while allowing movement of the driveshaft and universal joint within it. There are two gaiters to each driveshaft - inner and outer, the latter being more prone to wear and failure due to the larger range of movement necessary for the steering, and also because of the harsher conditions present at the exposed roadwheel end.

37B

37A. Turn the steering on to full lock so that the outer driveshaft gaiter is put under tension, then slowly turn the road wheel and examine the gaiter around its circumference, checking for damage and signs of escaping grease. Also ensure the clips at each end of the gaiter are secure.

37B. Check the inner gaiters (where the driveshaft enters the gearbox) in a similar fashion, but note there is no need to turn the steering to full lock.

INSIDE INFORMATION: Driveshaft gaiters play a vitally important part in keeping the universal joints they enclose free of dirt and grit, which would otherwise severely limit their lifespan. If damage or signs of leakage are apparent, have the gaiter replaced as soon as possible and the joint checked for wear - both SPECIALIST SERVICE jobs.

38

Job 38. Steering joints.

Steering joints, or 'track rod ends', provide the link between the steering arms and the roadwheel/hub. A small rubber bellows forms part of the assembly and is vital to the life of the joint. Splits or cracks will allow abrasive dirt to enter the joint and ruin it.

38. Put the steering on full lock so that each steering joint can be seen at the rear and to the inside of, the wheel. Check the rubber boot on each track rod end (TRE). If torn, renew the complete track rod end. In theory, you can replace the boot but it's a

false economy for the following reasons. i) Chances are that the old TRE will be worn because the boot has split and because of the resulting absence of lubricant, and ii) the TRE has to be removed from the steering arm in any case. This can be such a devil of a job to carry out that you might as well get it over with and fit a relatively inexpensive, new TRE whilst you're at it.

SPECIALIST SERVICE: This is a tricky job for the inexperienced mechanic to carry out! A ball-joint separator is required and the 'tracking' of the front wheels will need re-setting afterwards.

Job 39. Check suspension ball-joints.

Suspension ball-joints provide the link between the hub/roadwheel assembly and the lower track control arm and allow the hub to rise and fall with changes in the road surface, while also allowing the hub to swivel under the influence of the steering. The ball-joint itself is protected by a small rubber bellows, similar to the steering joint, whose condition is vital to the joint it protects.

39. This check requires the wheel to be removed ideally, so that the joint can be thoroughly examined for splits and/or cracking. If grease is evident on the outer surface of the rubber then it is a good bet there is a leak somewhere, but as the bellows is in a somewhat 'squashed' and restricted position such a leak may not be readily obvious.

INSIDE INFORMATION: Test for wear in the ball-joint by grasping the road wheel at the six o'clock position and 'rocking' it, feeling for any play or slackness from the joint. If play is felt, have an assistant apply the footbrake and repeat the test - if play is still evident then the joint is worn, but if the play disappears then the wheel bearing could be faulty.

Job 40. Inspect for leaks.

While under the car, look out for fluid leaks, such as hydraulic fluid spotted on a tyre wall, or oil dripping from beneath the engine or transmission. It is better to spot such leaks early, before danger threatens or major expense is incurred.

3,000 Miles - Road Test

Job 41. Clean controls.

41. Clean the door handles, controls and steering wheel: they may well have become greasy from your hands while you were carrying out the rest of the service work on your car. Start up the engine while you are sitting in the driver's seat.

Job 42. Check instruments.

Before pulling away, and with the engine running, check the correct function of all instruments and switches.

Job 43. Throttle pedal.

Check the throttle pedal for smooth operation. If the throttle does not operate smoothly, turn off the engine and check the cable itself for: a cracked or broken casing, kinks in the casing, or fraying at the cable ends, especially where the ends of the cable 'disappear' into the cable 'outer'. If you find any of these faults, replace the throttle cable.

Job 44. Brakes and steering road test.

SAFETY FIRST!
Only carry out the following tests in daylight, inclear dry conditions when ther are no other road users about and no pedestrians. Use your mirrors and make sure that there is no traffic following you when carrying out the following brake tests.

Only a proper brake tester at an MoT testing station will be able to check the operation of the brakes accurately enough for the MoT test, but you can rule out one of the worst braking problems in the following way: drive along a clear stretch of road and, gripping the steering wheel fairly lightly between the thumb and fingers of each hand, brake gently from a speed of about 40 mph. Ideally, the car should pull up in a dead straight line without pulling to one side or the other. If the car pulls to the left (when being driven on the left-hand side of the road) or to the right (when being driven on the right-hand side of the road, such as in many countries outside the UK), it might be that there is no problem with your brakes but that the camber on the road is causing the car to pull over. If you can find a stretch of road with no camber whatsoever, you may be able to try the brake test again or failing that, find a one-way-street where you can drive on the 'wrong' side of the road and see if pulling to one side happens in the opposite direction. If it does not, then you've got a problem with your brakes. Before assuming the worst, check your tyre pressures; try switching the front wheels and tyres from one side of the car to the other. If after carrying out these modifications in turn, the problem doesn't go away, seek SPECIALIST SERVICE.

The second test is to ensure that the self-centring effect on the steering works correctly. If the steering stiffens up over a period of time, you can easily get used to it so that you don't notice that it doesn't operate as it should. After going round a sharp bend, the steering should tend to move back to the straight-ahead position all by itself without having to be positively steered back to the straight-ahead position again by the driver. This is because the swivel pins are set slightly ahead of the centre line of the wheels so that the front wheels behave rather like those on a supermarket trolley - or at least those that work properly! If the steering swivels have rusted, or the steering rack is damaged, the steering will be stiff and no self centring will be evident. Drive round a sharp bend and, as you come out of the bend, you should feel the steering wheel tend to turn itself back to the straight-ahead position. If it doesn't and you have to pull the wheel back to the straight-ahead, you've got a problem with the steering and should seek a little more of that SPECIALIST SERVICE.

4,500 Miles Service

☐ **Job 45. Change engine oil and filter.**

SAFETY FIRST!
If the car has just been used and the engine is hot, allow thirty minutes at least for it cool down, or you could be scalded by hot oil when the plug is removed. Also, used engine oil may contain chemicals and by-products of combustion that can irritate and inflame the skin and in some cases have found to be carcinogenic (cancer inducing), so it is essential to wear latex or plastic gloves to prevent oil coming into contact with the hands. Oil drain plugs are often overtightened. i) Take care that the spanner does not slip causing injury to hand or head. (Use a socket or ring spanner - never an open-ended spanner - with as little offset as possible, so that the spanner is near to the line of the bolt.) ii) Take great care that the effort needed to undo the drain plug does not cause the vehicle to fall on you or to slide off ramps - remember those wheel chocks.

DIESEL ENGINES FROM 1987 - 1992 ONLY

OPTIONAL: This job is specified by Vauxhall at 4,500 miles but with no time limit specified. We include it here at six months as this mileage is 'average', but if your car only covers a small mileage, say 3000 miles or less in three months, you may wish to include the job in the 9-monthly checks described later in this chapter. Refer to Job 46 for details of the procedure.

Every 6,000 Miles or Every Six Months, whichever comes first

6,000 Miles - The Engine Bay

Carry out the 3000-mile/3-month service operations, plus the following:

☐ **Job 46. Change engine oil/oil filter.**

SAFETY FIRST!
See above, under Job 45.

OIL CARE FOLLOW THE CODE

PETROL ENGINES ONLY

See pages 4 and 46.

46A

OPTIONAL: Vauxhall recommend 9,000 mile intervals for all cars. Pre-1987 the recommendation is 'six months or 9,000 miles; post-1987, it is 12 months or 9,000 miles'. We recommend playing safe and going for this shorter interval if you want to maximise engine life.

DIESEL ENGINES 1992-ON ONLY

As above, except that Vauxhall now recommend 7,500 mile oil change interval for 1992-on vehicles. Even on these vehicles, we recommend playing safe and changing at 6,000.

46A. This is the location of the oil drain plug on the great majority of Cavalier engines, viewed from the back of the car looking forwards. As stated elsewhere, the plug will often be tight and require some force to move initially, when it may suddenly 'give' and offer little or no resistance - be careful not to rap your knuckles! Rubber or plastic gloves can compromise your grip on the spanner, so it may be wise to leave them off for the initial 'tug', but remember to don them immediately the plug has been slackened.

---

making it easy! *Apart from small differences in location of the oil filter and the sump drain plug, the procedure is the same for all models. Before draining the sump, run the engine (if cold) for around five minutes to warm the oil slightly, so that it will drain more freely - but not so hot that it will scald. Use an oil drainage container to catch the oil as it drains from the sump - note that the oil will fall in an arc away from the drain hole, so position the container to allow for this. Spread newspaper on the floor beneath the engine bay to protect it from oil spills and drips. Before undoing the drain plug, take off the oil filler cap: this relieves any partial vacuum in the system - the faster the oil can drain from the sump the more debris it will drag out with it.*

Probably the one service operation on which most DIY motorists will 'cut their teeth' is an engine oil change - that is emptying the old oil out through the sump drain plug situated beneath the engine and, later pouring in a specified quantity of new oil through the oil filler, found on the valve cover at the top of the engine. And no matter how technically complex the engine, an oil change still remains basically a simple operation.

46B. Once the plug has started to move in its thread it can be undone with the (gloved) fingers; remember to hold onto the plug when fully unscrewed.

46C. INSIDE INFORMATION: Be ready to reposition your bowl - the angle of 'spurt' changes as the oil flows out of the sump! We're now looking backwards from the front of the car.

46D. The drain plug has a copper or nylon sealing washer - examine the latter for signs of distortion or splitting, renewing it if in doubt. New ones are obtainable from most accessory shops and it is a good idea to buy a new copper one with the oil and filter. They are designed to crush when the plug is tightened and are not meant to be reused.

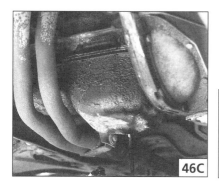

☐ Job 47. Replace oil filter.

The oil filter is positioned either on the front or to the rear left-hand side of the engine, depending on model and year.

---

making it easy! *47A. Oil filter removal tool types are numerous, to cope with various engine types, but this 'chain-wrench' type is suitable for all Cavaliers and is cheaply available from most good accessory shops. You'll almost never get it undone by hand!*

47B. One full turn of the filter using the wrench is usually enough to get it started, when it can then be undone by hand.

Note that some oil loss will occur, so position the oil tray or container under the engine to catch it. (With the front-mounted filter shown here, it is also a good idea to place a rag beneath the filter to prevent oil dribbling down the engine side).

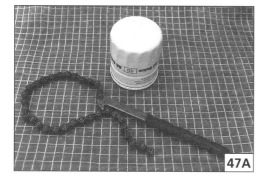

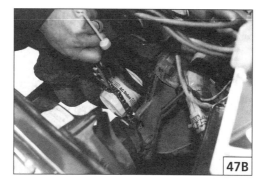

47C. Make sure the new rubber sealing ring is in place on the new filter (there is a 'channel' into which the ring will snugly fit) and apply a little clean oil to the seal, to prevent it buckling as the filter is screwed home.

47D. Screw the filter onto the threaded stub, taking care it is centrally placed and the thread isn't 'crossed'. Most filters have tightening instructions printed on the casing, but essentially all filters are fitted by screwing on by hand only. When the sealing ring contacts its seat make a further three-quarters of a turn and leave it - there's no need to tighten it any further as to do so will only make removal more difficult next time.

Before refitting the sump drain plug, wipe around the drain hole with a piece of clean rag to remove any grime or grit that might be picked-up on the plug and transferred to the engine internals. Check the sealing washer is fitted to the plug and refit it to the sump.

47C

making it easy! Although it has a large bolt-type head, the plug certainly doesn't need to be tightened to the degree such a size would suggest. Simply grip the spanner so that the thumb rests upon the spanner head, thereby limiting the amount of leverage applied to it, applying 'firm' pressure only.

47E. Pour the recommended amount of fresh oil into the engine (figures are given in *Chapter 8, Facts and Figures)* at a steady rate - too much too soon will cause it to overflow as the air displaced from inside the engine tries to escape. It's a good idea to place a piece of rag around the filler anyway, as drips and spills from the oil can will inevitably occur.

Check the level on the dipstick when the approximately measured amount has been poured in, but note that the level shown at this stage is likely to be above the MAX mark - this is normal and will go down once the engine has been started and the new filter becomes 'charged' with oil.

47F. Clean the filler cap of any sludge and traces of old oil before refitting it.

INSIDE INFORMATION: Also make sure the sealing ring on its inner side is in good condition, as some engines require the cap to provide an airtight seal for the emission control system.

47G. On models after 1987, check the rubber hose that connects to the valve cover. This carries fumes from the engine to the air filter housing and can sometimes perish or crack. Replace it if necessary.

47D

47E

47F

47G

48A

Finally after the vehicle has been lowered to the ground, run the engine for a minute or so then re-check the oil level on the dipstick, topping-up if necessary. Take a look beneath the car to check for any leaks around the sump plug or filter, tightening if required.

☐ Job 48. Check/adjust spark plugs.

PETROL ENGINES ONLY

48A. Look to see if the spark plug leads are numbered; if not, mark the plug caps with a spot of paint - typists' correction fluid is used by many mechanics as it is easy to apply and dries very quickly. Number them from the drive-belt end of the engine in the sequence one, two, three, four. (Identification of the plug leads is important as if incorrectly replaced, the engine will not run!).

48B. When this is done the plug caps can be pulled off. Be careful not to tug on the lead itself as you may pull it from the cap, which will remain on the plug!

48C. Some engines will have the plug caps protected from the hot exhaust manifold by a steel tube as here; treat them the same as those above.

48D. Unscrew the spark plugs. They may be 'tight' to begin with so take care to keep the plug spanner or socket in line with the plug body, otherwise the porcelain insulator of the plug can break.

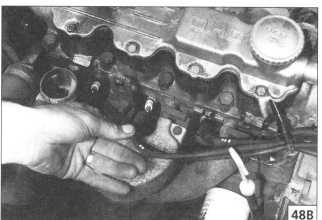
48B

INSIDE INFORMATION: If you are trying to remove a plug which gets ever tighter as you turn it, there's every possibility that it is cross threaded. Once out, it probably won't go back in again. Tighten it up again and take the car to a Vauxhall dealer or specialist who may be able to chase out the threads with a purpose-made tool. If this can't be done, he will have to add a thread insert to your cylinder head. It pays to take great care when removing and fitting spark plugs, especially when dealing with aluminium cylinder heads!

48E. Clean the plug electrodes by vigorous use of a wire brush to remove any carbon deposits. If the electrodes of the plug look 'rounded' and worn (compare them to a new plug) they should be renewed.

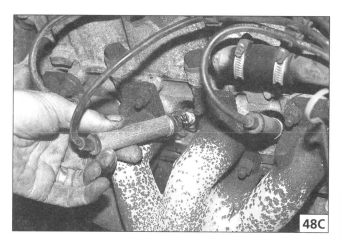
48C

making it easy! Leave the spark plug in the socket spanner while using the wire brush - this is kinder on the fingers and lessens the risk of dropping the plug and breaking it.

48D

48E

48F. If using a flat feeler gauge select the 'blade' of the correct thickness *(see Chapter 8, Facts and Figures)* and slide it between the electrodes as shown. The gap between the two electrodes should provide a sliding fit, with no 'slack'. If necessary, adjust the gap as shown below.

The gap is adjusted by slightly bending the side electrode either closer or further-away from the centre electrode. With the gapping tool as shown, this is easy and carries little risk of damaging the plug, which can occur if the electrode is moved by use of a screwdriver or pliers. Replace the plugs once the gaps are correct, adding just a slight smear of grease to the threads to make future removal easier. There is no need to screw the plugs down with great force - just tighten them firmly.

IMPORTANT NOTE: Some owners renew spark plugs every 12 months; others do so when they look eroded or the insulation is damaged - essential in both cases. We prefer to renew at 12,000 miles, irrespective of appearance - but the choice is yours!

☐ Job 49. Distributor.

Certain models up to 1986 are fitted with a vacuum-operated advance/retard mechanism - check with 49B to see if your car has one, marked with arrow 'C': if so, test the mechanism by disconnecting the plastic pipe from the capsule and attaching a short length of rubber tube; sucking on the tube should cause the advance/retard operating arm - marked with arrow 'D' - to retract and rotate the distributor base plate by several degrees. If the arm fails to move and/or there is no resistance felt when the tube is sucked, have the distributor checked over by a competent garage. You'll probably need an exchange replacement.

1300cc MODELS UP TO 1986 ONLY

While the dwell meter can give an accurate measurement of the points gap, it gives little indication of the actual condition of the points themselves, so a physical examination is necessary. The most common problem affecting CB points is the eroding of one contact and the build-up of metal (in the form of a 'pip') on the other. In its early stages this condition may well have little detrimental effect on the production of a spark and a dwell reading will take it into account, but as the pip increases in size the spark is liable to become unstable and/or unreliable. While removing the points and smoothing-away the pip with emery is feasible, it is far more sensible, and cost-effective in the long-run, to simply renew the inexpensive points assembly as a whole.

49A. Remove the two spring clips securing the distributor cap and place it to one side - there is no need to disconnect any of the High Tension leads at this point. NOTE: some distributor caps may be secured by two small screws in place of the spring clips. Lift the cap away and the rotor arm can be pulled from the shaft - it is a push-fit. The points will be found, either beneath a metal outer-bearing plate (Bosch distributors) or beneath a plastic protective shield (Delco Remy). Prise the points gently open using a small screwdriver and examine the faces of the contacts, looking for signs of metal transfer between the contacts (i.e a 'pip' and a 'pit') and general wear.

INSIDE INFORMATION: A blue-ish colour on the contacts indicates overheating caused by a faulty condenser. Replacement is both easy (see below) and cheap.

making it easy! *While it is obviously possible to measure and adjust the contact breaker gap physically, as when new points are fitted for instance, such a method does not guarantee accuracy and the stated gap is regarded only as a starting-point so that the engine may be started and a more accurate 'dwell' measurement taken. Dwell meters are used with the engine running and therefore automatically take into account small (but significant) deviations and wear patterns in the distributor components and points, and they also require no dismantling of the engine to make a measurement. The type of multi-meter described in* **Chapter 9, Tools and Equipment** *will allow the dwell to be measured simply by attaching three wires, to the battery and coil, enabling an accurate reading to be taken without disturbing the distributor, and in a fraction of the time a physical measurement would take.*

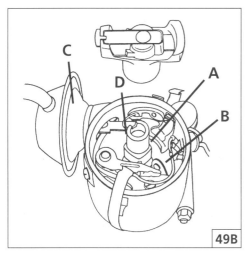

49B

49B. Both types of distributor feature a small felt pad in the centre of the cam rotor (A) - apply a little oil to it, just enough to soak in without depositing oil on the points, which could prevent them working. Also, apply a smear of grease to the sides of the cam rotor (B) but again, be economical so that none can transfer to the points themselves.

49C. On reassembly, clean the rotor arm of any dust or grime, also the inside of the distributor cap, with a soft cloth. In winter, spray the outside of the cap with a very small amount of water repellant, such as Castrol DWF maintenance spray which helps prevent condensation forming and possibly 'shorting' the spark to earth - what mechanics call 'tracking'.

Job 50. Ignition timing.

NOT DIESEL OR V6, OR 1.6, 1.8 AND 2.0 LITRE MODELS AFTER 1987

OPTIONAL: This job requires a stroboscopic timing light to make any worthwhile check on the timing; however, some owners may prefer to have this check carried out professionally by a garage or tuning specialist.

49C

> *SAFETY FIRST!*
> *THE ELECTRONIC IGNITION SYSTEM INVOLVES VERY HIGH VOLTAGES!*
> *Vauxhall recommend that only trained personnel should go near the high-tension circuit (coil, distributor and HT wiring) while the engine is running and it is ESSENTIAL that anyone wearing a medical pacemaker device does not go near the ignition system. Also, stroboscopic timing requires the engine to be running - take great care that parts of the timing light or parts of you don't get caught up in the moving parts! Don't wear loose clothing and take care not to let long hair get entangled in the moving parts.*

STROBOSCOPIC TIMING

50A. The most accurate way of setting the ignition timing is dynamically, using a stroboscopic test light such as the Gunson's model shown here. This method is easier and more accurate, as the test light enables you to see the timing mark on the crankshaft pulley as the engine is running, and automatically takes into account any wear and slackness in the ignition timing mechanisms.

Even at tick-over, the sparks and, therefore, the flashes are so frequent that the light appears to be continuous and when it is pointed at the engine's ignition timing marks it has the effect of 'freezing' the moving mark, so that the latter's relationship with the fixed mark can easily be seen.

50A

If you don't already possess a strobe light, your accessory shop will stock various models at an affordable price. The easiest to use are those with a xenon light (brighter than neon) and an inductive pick-up that simply clamps over the plug's HT lead. Most are simply powered via clip-on leads to the car battery, although there are models that use their own internal batteries.

Disconnect the vacuum advance pipe at the distributor and plug the end of the pipe with a suitable 'bung' such as a pencil. The engine needs to be running at idling speed, so if it has been started from cold, allow ten minutes running for it to warm-up and the idle speed to stabilise. Stop the engine before going on to the next section.

50B

50B. The timing marks will be found at the left-hand side of the engine (as you look towards the rear of the car), one on the rim of the crankshaft pulley, the other a pointer fixed to the engine 'block'. Before starting the engine it is a good idea to apply a spot of white paint, chalk or typists' correction fluid to the two marks to make them stand out in the brief flashes of the timing light.

6,000 MILE SERVICE

50C. Connect the timing light to the No. 1 plug lead as shown in the maker's instructions. This Gunson's Tachostrobe uses an adaptor to clip over the No. 1 spark plug lead - other types are interposed between the plug lead and distributor cap or plug. With the engine running, each spark 'pulse' triggers the strobe lamp causing a flash, which when directed at the pulley, illuminates the notch (arrowed) and pointer. You will see that the rapid flash of the strobe lamp appears to 'freeze' the timing marks.

If the notch and pointer align at tickover speed, the timing is correct but if not, the timing will require adjustment as follows:

50D. Switch off the engine and slacken the distributor clamp nut as shown. Start the engine and, while shining the timing light on the marks, rotate the distributor slightly one way or the other until the marks align. Cut the engine and tighten the clamp nut, being careful not to disturb the position of the distributor. Make a final check by starting the engine and checking the marks with the timing lamp - if all's well, switch off again and disconnect the timing light and reconnect the vacuum pipe.

INSIDE INFORMATION: If when within the rev range of 1,000 to 2,000 rpm the dwell angle varies by more than plus or minus one degree, the distributor bearings are probably excessively worn and the distributor should be changed for a new or reconditioned unit (the latter being quite a bit less expensive!).

50C

50D

☐ Job 51. Accelerator controls.

51A. Lubricate the accelerator control linkage at the injection system in the engine bay. Also lubricate, the throttle pedal pivot in the footwell recess. Use a spray lubricant like Castrol DWF or white silicone grease in the footwell, so as not to spoil your shoes with dripping oil - it stains leather!

51B. There are rather more lubrication points on a carburettor. With air filter removed, oil every spring, moving part and joint in the linkages.

☐ Job 52. Check clutch adjustment.

Check clutch pedal travel and adjust if necessary.

52A. With the clutch pedal in its normal 'at rest' position, measure the distance between the pedal's rubber pad and the lower inside-edge of the steering wheel, as shown. Now take another measurement with the pedal fully depressed: The difference between the two measurements should be 138mm (or 5.4") - any deviation greater than 5mm requires the cable to be adjusted. (Illustration, courtesy Vauxhall Motors Limited)

52B. The clutch cable adjuster is situated on the end of the cable in the engine bay (just above the gearbox on the right-hand side when looking to the rear of the car - arrowed) where it adjoins the clutch operating arm. The adjuster nut is held by an outer locknut which must first be slackened; screwing the adjuster nut up or down will alter the clutch pedal measurement to that required. When the measurement is correct, tighten the locknut and operate the pedal a couple of times then take a final measurement.

51A

51B

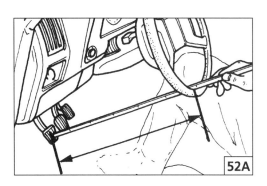

52A

52B

INSIDE INFORMATION: Note that the correctly-adjusted clutch pedal will come to rest at a higher position than the brake pedal - this is normal. If the pedals are level, then adjustment may be required, otherwise difficulty may be encountered in gear selection.

SPECIALIST SERVICE: If the clutch pedal position cannot be obtained or if the clutch action is stiff, noisy or ineffective (difficulty in engaging/changing gear) then have the clutch checked by a specialist garage. Replacing the clutch is beyond the capabilities of most owners due to the requirement for certain facilities and tools.

☐ Job 53. Cooling system.

Check the cooling system for leaks and all hoses for condition and tightness. Look at the ends of hoses for leaks - check clamps for tightness, if necessary and pinch the hoses to ensure that they are not starting to crack and deteriorate. If you don't want a hose to burst and let you down in the worst possible place, change any hose that seems at all suspect.

It is also worth checking there is no build up of leaves or other debris in the radiator matrix, that could restrict airflow through it.

☐ Job 54. Coolant check.

SAFETY FIRST!
i) The coolant should only be checked WHEN THE SYSTEM IS COLD. If you remove the pressure cap when the engine is hot, the release of pressure can cause the water in the cooling system to boil and spurt several feet in the air with the risk of severe scalding. ii) Take precautions to prevent anti-freeze being swallowed or coming in contact with the skin or eyes and keep it away from children. If this should happen, rinse immediately with plenty of water. Seek immediate medical help if necessary.

Use a hydrometer to check the specific gravity of the coolant. The tester will show by way of a reading or possibly with coloured balls. If the level is below the recommended amount, top up the system with anti-freeze until the correct specific gravity is obtained. Of course the engine will have to be run for the newly introduced anti-freeze to mix thoroughly otherwise a false reading will be had. If you have any doubt over the period that the old mix has been in the car, drain and refill with fresh.

54. The tester shown is readily available from accessory shops and acceptably accurate. In use, a small quantity of coolant is drawn into the glass 'dropper' and an indication of the strength of antifreeze is given. Similar testers are available and all work by measuring the specific gravity of the coolant in the manner of a battery hydrometer.

It is important that all engines have the correct proportion of anti-freeze in the coolant. This not only helps prevent freezing in the winter, but also overheating in summer temperatures. In addition, anti-freeze also helps prevent internal engine corrosion and is particularly necessary in engines fitted with alloy cylinder heads, i.e. all Cavaliers! See Job 2.

☐ Job 55. Check waterpump.

The water pump on all models is situated on the left-hand side of the engine (as you look to the rear of the car) beneath the alternator. It is driven by - and provides tension for - the camshaft drive belt, and its toothed pulley is hidden behind the cam-belt cover. As such, the pump is seldom likely to be seen by most owners, but as this is generally a very reliable unit, the need to see it is unlikely to arise!

However, while conducting these other checks it is worth visually examining the engine block around the water pump mountings for any sign of a leak. Leaks are characterised by a white, powdery deposit, sometimes tinged with the colour of the antifreeze, and may be seen in 'runs' down the side of the block. If any evidence of such a leak is present, first make sure the coolant hoses, connections and thermostat housing are not the cause, otherwise the car should be taken to a competent garage for investigation.

☐ Job 56. Check manual gearbox oil.

MANUAL CHANGE TRANSMISSION ONLY.

INSIDE INFORMATION: i) A number of gearbox types have been fitted to the Cavalier during its production life. However, the oil level plug on all of them is in one of two positions, see 56A. i) To check the oil level, you will have to add a quantity of new oil. This is because simply removing the level plug and checking that oil issues from the hole will not determine the contents of the gearbox proper. The level plug is located on the differential casing which, while an integral part of the gearbox, contains oil that is kept at a higher level than that in the main gearbox, with the result that oil may well be present in the differential casing, but not in the gearbox adjacent to it, thereby giving a false indication of the level.

56A. The gearbox level plug will be in one of these two positions (depending on type) adjacent to a driveshaft on the differential casing, either on the right or left-hand side of the casing.

Remove it using a 17mm spanner, turned anti-clockwise. Some oil will ooze from the hole as the plug is removed, so have a drip tray ready to catch it. (Illustration, courtesy Vauxhall Motors Limited)

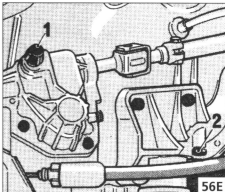

56B. Looking down into the engine bay right-hand side, the oil filler also doubles as a vent for the gearbox, and as such may not readily be recognisable. It is removed with a 17mm open-ended spanner, as above.

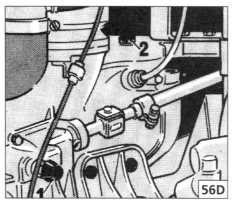

56C. Place the nozzle or pipe of the oil bottle into the hole and have an assistant squeeze the bottle gently so that oil flows into the gearbox, while you watch the level outlet for signs of oil starting to flow. When this occurs, replace the plug and stop filling - the level is now correct. Tighten the level plug and replace the vent/filler. Finally, wipe any excess or spilt oil from the gearbox casing with rag.

56D. As an extra point of reference, these are the filler/vent plug (1) and level plug (2) on the 1600 engine...

56E. ...and this on the 1300 engine. (Illustrations, courtesy Vauxhall Motors Limited)

FOUR WHEEL DRIVE ONLY

56F. Check the rear axle oil level by removing this plug - a 7mm Hex Allen key will be required. The oil level should be level to the bottom of the hole. Add the recommended lubricant (see Appendix 1 - Recommended Castrol Lubricants) until it just begins to flow from the hole, then replace the plug.

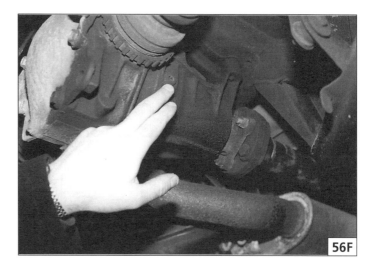

☐ **Job 57. Automatic transmission fluid.**

INSIDE INFORMATION: The auto. transmission fluid is checked with the engine running and the drive selector in the 'P' or PARK position. Depending on the temperature of the engine and transmission the reading is taken from one or other side of the dipstick. On a cold transmission, the level is checked using the side of the dipstick marked '+20 C.', while at normal operating temperature the reading is taken from the side marked '+94 C.'. Normal operating temperature is only reached after ten to fifteen miles driving, so allowing the car to 'warm-up' for five or ten minutes is not enough to warm the fluid sufficiently.

IMPORTANT: Absolute cleanliness is essential when dealing with the automatic transmission as even tiny particles of dirt or grit can have an adverse, and expensive! effect on the delicate, precision components within it.

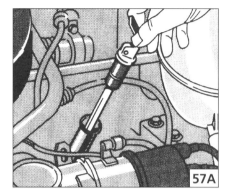

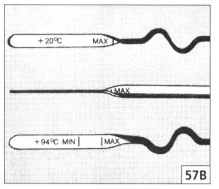

57A. The dipstick is positioned towards the right-hand side of the engine (as you look to the rear of the car). For early models up to 1987, it is placed just behind the distributor, while on later models it is in front. The handle of the dipstick is coloured red to distinguish it from the engine oil dipstick. (Illustration, courtesy Vauxhall Motors Limited)

Withdraw the dipstick, wipe it clean and replace it, pushing fully home up to the handle. Withdraw again and note the reading on the side of the dipstick relevant to the temperature of the fluid (see above - INSIDE INFORMATION).

57B. As explained above, the dipstick has level marks on both sides, which one is used depending on the temperature of the fluid. (Illustration, courtesy Vauxhall Motors Limited)

making it easy! **Fluid is added by pouring into the mouth of the dipstick tube. Make sure you buy the transmission fluid that is sold in bottles with a small spout, especially for this purpose.**

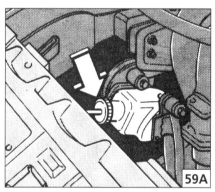

☐ Job 58. Four wheel drive transmission.

58. The four wheel drive gearbox fluid shares a reservoir combined with that of the power steering. IMPORTANT: Before reading the dipstick, switch on the ignition and depress the brake pedal until the fluid in the reservoir no longer rises - typically 10 to 15 'presses'. The level is clearly marked on a short dipstick - see Job 59B for details of this. The reservoir is situated in the engine bay on the right-hand side, immediately behind the battery.

Top up with Castrol Dexron R III if necessary, but if fluid loss occurs on a regular basis or shows a sudden drop between services, have the cause investigated by a Vauxhall dealer as soon as possible. (Illustration, courtesy Vauxhall Motors Limited)

☐ Job 59. Power steering.

If your model is fitted with power steering, check the fluid level in the reservoir.

PRE 1988 MODELS

59A. The reservoir is situated low down on the left-hand front of the engine. Remove the cap by turning anti-clockwise, wipe the small dipstick fixed to the cap and replace it - withdraw and note the fluid level. With the engine at operating temperature the fluid level should be at the FULL mark, while on a cold engine the level shouldn't fall below the ADD mark. (Illustration, courtesy Vauxhall Motors Limited)

POST 1988 MODELS (INCLUDING FOUR WHEEL DRIVE - see Job 58)

59B. The power steering fluid reservoir is situated on the right-hand side of the engine bay (as you look towards the rear of the car). Check the level by unscrewing the cap which has a short dipstick attached to it. There are two marks on the dipstick, the lower '20 deg.C' mark is used when the fluid is cold, and the upper '80 deg.C' when at operating temperature.

Top-up using Castrol Dexron R III, as specified in *Appendix 1 - Recommended Castrol Lubricants.*

☐ ## Job 60. Lubricate carburettor linkage.

60. Apply a few drops of Castrol Everyman light oil to the carburettor linkages and operating arm, allowing it to soak through the coil springs fitted to the spindles.

☐ ## Job 61. Lubricate throttle cable.

Place a dab of Castrol LM grease on the throttle cable where the inner cable exits the outer sleeve, at the carburettor linkage to help prevent water working its way in. Check the cable for any frayed strands or sharp kinks - if present the cable will need to be replaced as there is a danger of the throttle sticking 'open' when least expected.

☐ ## Job 62. Check exhaust emission.

Exhaust emissions became part of the British MoT test in 1991 and are always likely to be the subject of change, so check for the latest requirements. *See also, Chapter 7, Getting through the MoT.*

62. At present there are no DIY machines capable of measuring diesel smoke emissions, but the Gunson's Gastester MKII, shown in use here and also in *Chapter 9, Tools & Equipment*, can measure petrol engine CO (Carbon monoxide) levels very accurately. It comes with comprehensive instructions and data for most vehicles including of course, the Cavalier! Otherwise, it's a SPECIALIST SERVICE job.

60

62

> **SAFETY FIRST!**
> *Carbon monoxide is extremely poisonous and can kill within minutes - even when a catalytic converter is fitted. ALWAYS carry out emissions testing in the open - NEVER in your garage or other confined space.*

☐ ## Job 63. Adjust carburettor.

> **SAFETY FIRST!**
> *Carburettor adjustment has to be carried out with a warm, running engine. Therefore: i) Watch out for rotating cooling fan and belt and do not wear loose clothing or jewellery and tie back long hair. ii) Take care that you do not burn yourself on the hot engine parts and/or exhaust manifolds. iii) Always work out of doors. DO NOT perform this check in your garage or any confined space - exhaust gases are highly poisonous and can kill within minutes! iv) Apply a strict No Smoking! rule whenever you are servicing your fuel system. Remember, it's not just the petrol that's flammable, it's the fumes as well. Overall, if you're not (justifiably) confident, give the job to someone who is fully competent. Some manufacturers recommend that only trained mechanics should carry out work on a vehicle's fuel system. Read **Chapter 1, Safety First!***

FACT FILE - CARBURETTOR OR FUEL INJECTION?

Carburettor Models

Two types of carburettor have been used on petrol-engined Cavaliers, the GM 'Varajet II' and the Pierburg 2E3. Dates and applications are as follows:
Varajet II - 1300cc (1981-84), 1600cc (1981 -88).

Pierburg 2E3 - 1300cc (1985-88), 1400cc (1988 - on), 1600cc (1988 - on), 1800cc (1989 - on).

Identification is helped by the Varajet using a single, central nut to secure the air cleaner housing to the top of the carburettor, while the Pierburg uses three Phillips-type set screws. With the air cleaner removed, both types are clearly marked as to type.

Fuel Injection Models

Various types of fuel injection systems have been used, all made by Bosch:
LE-Jetronic - 1800cc (1982 - 86).

L3-Jetronic - 1800cc (1987 - 88).

Motronic - 2.0i (1987 - 88), SRi (1987 - 88).

Motronic ML4.1 - 2.0i (1988 - 92), SRi (1988 - 89), 2.0i 4WD - (1989 - on).

Motronic M1.5 - all models from 1990 (except 4WD, GSi 2000, V6)

Motronic M2.5 - GSi 2000 (1989 - on).

INSIDE INFORMATION: i) This Job requires the use of gas testing equipment and a tachometer to check idle speed, if any meaningful results are to be obtained. Indeed, attempting to 'tune' a carburettor without this equipment is likely to result in increased fuel consumption and poor performance, except in the hands of experienced mechanics although, it has to be said, even they tend to use them anyway, for speed of use and accuracy! ii) The carburettor should be the last part of the engine tune-up procedure, as the general settings will be affected by the condition efficiency of the other engine components such as the ignition system.

63A. In order to 'get at' the carburettor, you'll have to remove the air cleaner, disconnecting it from the air intake...

63B. ...and the carburettor top. Some have a single through-bolt sticking upwards.

First familiarise yourself with the carburettor fitted to your car, either the GM Varajet or Pierburg 2E3 as stated previously, paying particular attention to the location of the 'idle' (tick-over speed) and 'mixture' adjusting screws. Use the accompanying diagrams to determine where each screw is positioned.

63C. As we said earlier adjustments will be made without air filter housing in place: here's what the unit looks like with the air filter removed. Also, make sure you have a screwdriver of a length suitable for working in the confined space most adjustments are made in.

63D. This is the Idle Speed (Tick-over Speed) adjustment screw on the GM Varajet carburettor...

63E. ...and this the Mixture Adjustment screw.

Tamper-proof caps may be fitted to the adjusting screws - remove them either with a pair of pliers or a sharp instrument, depending on the type of seal. In the UK it isn't necessary to replace the seals, but in certain EC countries it is a legal requirement that they be replaced after adjustment.

63F. These are the adjustment screws on the Pierburg carburettor: 1 is the Idle Speed (Tick-over Speed) adjustment; 2 is the Mixture Adjustment screw. (Illustration, courtesy Vauxhall Motors Ltd.)

Before connecting up the gas analyser and tachometer the engine needs to be at operating temperature, so take the car for a short drive (five miles will do) or allow it to run at a fast idle speed for fifteen minutes or so. It is important the engine is at working temperature, not only for the accuracy of the gas analyser but also to make sure the choke control is off and the many fine tolerances found in the engine and its components are at their operating norm.

Once the engine is thoroughly warmed, connect up the gas analyser and tachometer, making sure all electrical accessories are switched off and, if an automatic transmission is fitted, that the drive selector is in the 'P' or 'PARK' position.

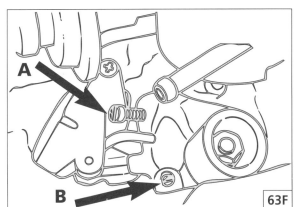

First check the idle speed on the tachometer - see *Chapter 8, Facts & Figures* for your model - and adjust the idle-speed screw if necessary. Turning the screw clockwise increases the speed, anti-clockwise reduces it.

Next, read the gas analyser to check for CO level and adjust the mixture screw if the reading is above or below the specification. Turning the screw 'in' or clockwise weakens the mixture and lowers the CO, while turning it 'out' richens and increases the CO reading. Only small movements of the screw are normally necessary, so turn it a quarter-turn at a time and check the readings, allowing the effects of each adjustment to register on the analyser - around thirty seconds may be necessary.

Generally, the newer the car the more accurately this can be set, but with older cars it may be necessary to allow an increase in the CO setting to ensure the engine runs smoothly in use. For instance, the specified CO level may be 1% plus or minus 0.5%, which is fine on an engine in perfect condition, but an older engine may need a CO level of 2.5% or 3% in order for it to run smoothly and efficiently. Some trial and error may be necessary to balance the lowest desirable CO content with smooth running. *See Chapter 7, Getting Through the MOT,* for the maximum allowable CO readings.

Once the desired richness level/CO setting has been obtained, you will invariably have to readjust the tick-over speed as it will have been affected by the change in mixture.

When all adjustments have been made, disconnect the gas analyser and tachometer and take the car for a test drive, checking that it doesn't stall, pulls smoothly and doesn't overheat.

☐ Job 64. Idle speed and mixture.

FUEL INJECTION PETROL ENGINES ONLY

SPECIALIST SERVICE: Due to the need for an accurate tachometer to check idle speed, and an exhaust gas analyser to check the mixture (and the knowledge to use them and interpret the readings) it is recommended these checks be carried out by a specialist tuning firm or reputable garage. However, for the keen DIY mechanic these items of equipment are available from Gunson's (see *Chapter 9, Tools & Equipment*) together with full instructions and data. Also, see Job 62.

> **FACT FILE: ENGINE CONDITION**
>
>
> If a reading within the 'legal' range proves difficult or impossible to achieve consistent with smooth running, some other factor may be affecting the combustion process of the engine such as air leaks, poor valve condition, choked or leaking exhaust. Have the car checked by a reputable garage or Vauxhall dealer if necessary. Running the engine for any length of time on a 'weak' mixture (very low CO reading) is likely to lead to internal engine damage, while driving it on a 'rich' or 'high' reading is illegal, environmentally unfriendly and a waste of expensive fuel!

☐ Job 65. Replace fuel filter.

> **SAFETY FIRST!**
> *Whenever you are dealing with diesel fuel, it's essential to protect your hands by wearing plastic gloves.*

DIESEL ENGINES ONLY

The diesel fuel filter is located on the rear bulkhead of the engine bay, just to the left of centre. Before proceeding, make sure a container is at hand in which to catch the fuel contained in the filter, together with a quantity of absorbent rag to mop up any spillages. A one-litre container will be sufficient.

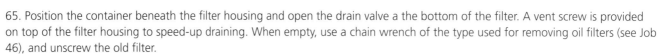

65. Position the container beneath the filter housing and open the drain valve a the bottom of the filter. A vent screw is provided on top of the filter housing to speed-up draining. When empty, use a chain wrench of the type used for removing oil filters (see Job 46), and unscrew the old filter.

INSIDE INFORMATION: Fill the diesel filter body as much as you can - the engine has to suck all the air out of the system before it is fed with diesel fuel, and this will save a lot of engine churning.

Before screwing on the new filter, lubricate the rubber sealing ring with a smear of clean diesel fuel and ensure the retainer ring in the centre of the filter is in place. Fit the new filter firmly by hand, close the drain valve and vent screw, then run the engine at a fast idle for a minute or so to vent the system. Finally check around the filter for leaks, tightening a little further if necessary.

6000 miles - Around the Car

☐ Job 66. Check seat belts.

66. Make sure the seat belts are clean and are not showing any signs of fraying or other damage. Ensue that if you pull slowly, the belt unreels smoothly; but also make sure that if you pull sharply the belt locks up. Check the buckles latch securely and that the reel mounting is secure.

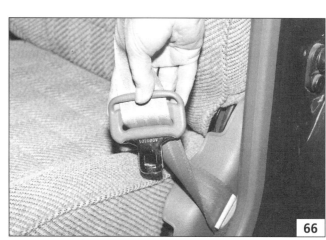

67A

67B

Job 67. Locks and hinges.

OIL CAN LUBE

It doesn't always figure highly, if at all, in service schedules, but there are a fair few moving parts on the motor car which would benefit from occasional oil-can lubrication. They will then work more smoothly, probably more quietly, and will certainly last longer. Here are just a few examples - but if you get into the habit of regularly 'carrying the can' around your car, you'll probably spot a few more!

67C

67A. Door hinges are a prime area of neglect - the hinge-pins of Cavalier doors are hollow, similar to those shown, and require a plastic cap to be removed before a squirt of oil is added; replace the cap afterwards!

67B. Sometimes you can use grease or oil, as here on a door check strap, which if left unlubricated, dries out, rusts up, and not only retards smooth door opening and closing, but also causes those strident 'graunching' noises which are always an embarrassment - particularly in your drive-way late at night! An occasional smear of grease works wonders.

INSIDE INFORMATION: On older, or previously neglected door hinges, it could be beneficial to first douse them with penetrating fluid, following up with the oil can a little later, when the penetrating stuff has done its work.

67C. Castrol's easing fluid, using the can's slim 'accessory tube', is handy for penetrating key lock mechanisms, or door lock push-buttons.

67D. Estate and hatchback tailgate hinges will benefit from a drop or two of oil as well, as will the tailgate lock and latch. Be careful not to put too much oil on the hinges, as it could seep past the seal and stain the headlining. (Illustration, courtesy Vauxhall Motors Limited)

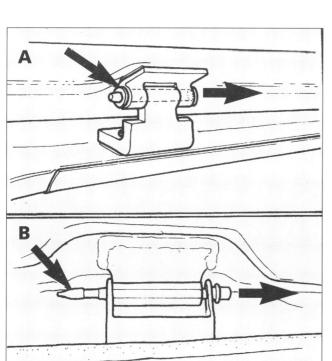

A

B

67D

Job 68. Bonnet release mechanism.

68. While you've got the oil can in your hand, go back under the bonnet. If the bonnet latch is not kept lubricated one day you may find you can't, in fact, get under the bonnet, because the latch has rusted and seized. There are possible 'emergencies' that could arise from this, but even more horrific is when a bonnet that has not closed securely flies open when you are driving! Lubricate the bonnet release, the release cable and the safety catch using clean silicone grease where it is easy to make contact with it, so that you won't soil clothes when you're leaning into the engine bay. Lubricate the bonnet hinges too.

68

☐ Job 69. Check seats.

69. Check the condition and security of the seats. The front ones should slide smoothly on their runners and latch securely as well as being securely mounted. Clean the runners of any dirt or grit that might have built up.

☐ Job 70. Test shock absorbers.

Bounce each corner of the car in turn in order to check the efficiency of the shock absorbers. If the car 'bounces' at all, the shock absorbers have had it. They should be replaced in pairs and efficient shock absorbers can make an enormous difference to your car's safety and handling.

69

☐ Job 71. Check/renew front disc brake pads.

SAFETY FIRST! AND SPECIALIST SERVICE
Obviously, your car's brakes are among its most important safety related items. Do NOT dismantle or attempt to perform any work on the braking system unless you are fully competent to do so. If you have not been trained in this work, but wish to carry it out, we strongly recommend that you have a garage or qualified mechanic check your work before using the car on the road. See also the section on BRAKES AND ASBESTOS in Chapter 1, Safety First! for further information. Always start by washing the brakes with a proprietary brand of brake cleaner but never use compressed air to clean off brake dust. Always replace the disc pads in sets of four - never replace the pads on one wheel only. After fitting new pads, avoid heavy braking - except in an emergency - for the first 150 to 200 miles (250 to 300 km).

GENERAL INFORMATION

All Cavalier models are fitted with disc brakes at the front. These brakes adjust themselves automatically as the pads wear down and so manual adjustment is not required or, indeed, possible. Wear on the pads is the reason that the brake fluid level will go down slightly between services, even though there's no sign of brake fluid leakage.

Slacken the wheelnuts before jacking-up the car, then make sure it is safely supported - see *Raising The Car Safely* at the beginning of this chapter. After the wheel is removed, the front brake caliper and disc are exposed. The pad friction-lining material is visible through the caliper 'window'. The brake 'pads' can be distinguished as fitting either side of the steel brake disc, visible in or near the centre of the window.

71A. It's important to ensure that there is plenty of 'meat' on the pads. This can be seen looking down into the caliper with the wheel removed. The manufacturers recommend that the minimum permissible brake pad thickness is around 7mm (including the steel backing-plate) but you should allow for the fact that you won't be checking the brakes again for a further 9,000 miles or twelve months. Also bear in mind that it is common for one pad to wear down more quickly than the other and you should always take the thickness of the most worn-out pad as your guide. As ever with your braking system, replace sooner rather than later.

71B. This pad has been removed to show the friction material and where to gauge its thickness. A minimum of 7mm (including the metal backing plate) is specified by the manufacturer, but if the pads measure less than 10mm it is as well to change them as soon as possible if the brakes are to be regarded as totally dependable.

71A

71B

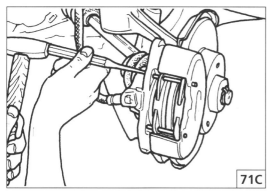

71C

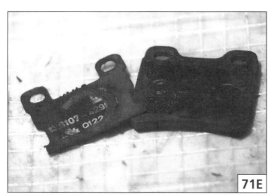

71E

71F

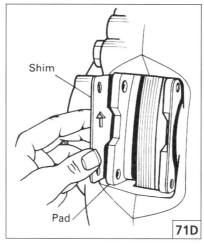

Shim

Pad

71D

FRONT BRAKE PAD RENEWAL.

ALL MODELS EXCEPT 2.O LITRE 1988-ON

(See Page 60 for details on 2.0 models from 1988-on)

INSIDE INFORMATION: i) A special pin-punch will be required to drift the pad retaining pins from the calipers. Because the pins are hollow, the punch requires a small 'step' to be included at the 'business' end that locates inside the pin, thereby keeping the punch central. These special punches are available from most good accessory shops and are worth purchasing - do not try to use a conventional 'straight' punch as there is a risk it will damage the retaining pin or become firmly and irretrievably jammed, requiring expert help. ii) ALWAYS replace disc pads in sets of four across the car: that is, both front wheels or both rear wheels at the same time. Failure to do this will result in unequal and dangerous braking, due to the imbalance in efficiency.

71C. Drive out the upper pad retaining pin, using the special punch, from the inside of the caliper as shown. The pins may well be corroded and stiff to move - if so, apply a little penetrating oil to the pins but, if the pads are to be used again, make absolutely sure no oil gets on to the pad surface.

As the upper pin is moved across, the two anti-rattle springs will be freed - be ready for this and take note of their position in relation to the pads and pins, then remove the lower pin. (Illustration, courtesy Vauxhall Motors Limited)

71D. By levering the outer pad away from the disc slightly, the pads can be removed from the caliper with pliers, along with their respective shims...

71E. ...which must be retained for re-fitting. Scrape away any rusty scale from the pad housings using an old screwdriver, brushing away any loose debris afterwards with a small brush, but remember - DO NOT BREATHE IN ANY DUST as it will contain potentially dangerous irritants.

INSIDE INFORMATION: In preparing to re-fit or renew the pads, wash any oil or grease from your hands so that you can't get it onto the friction materials. Also, wipe the disc surface with methylated spirit to remove any traces of oil, grease or dirt.

71F. Check the disc itself for signs of corrosion, scoring, uneven wear, and ridges at the inner and outer edges. Some wear and light scoring is inevitable of course, but if more than a few thousandths-of-an-inch deep then the disc will need renewing.

SPECIALIST SERVICE: Consult your Vauxhaul dealer and have them examine the disc and measure it with a micrometer if scoring is evident.

Badly scored or badly ridged discs will seriously reduce braking efficiency even with fully bedded-in pads. New pads would take for ever to bed-in on them and meanwhile braking efficiency could be virtually nil!

A light ridge, perhaps mostly a build-up of rust, can be carefully removed with a file - it's possible to feed the file (or a hefty old screwdriver) through a pad aperture, then steadying the file (or screwdriver blade) firmly against the ridge while you spin the disc.

SAFETY FIRST!
If you are in any doubt as to the condition of the disc or discs, seek professional advice immediately. Corroded or pitted areas of the disc's working surface indicates a possible problem with the caliper, which may be partially seized. Additionally, deep scoring causes the pad friction material to contract only onto the 'peaks' of the ridges, thereby drastically reducing the area of contact and subsequent braking efficiency.

In order to make room for new (obviously much thicker) disc pads, the caliper piston must be pushed back into the cylinder bore - one good reason why you have to be sure a piston's exposed circumference is absolutely clean, since it's vital that abrasive dirt doesn't get pushed back into the cylinder bore along with the piston.

making it easy! As the pistons are pushed back into their bores the brake fluid level in the reservoir will rise accordingly, often to the point of over-flow! Be prepared for this by removing a quantity of fluid first, the easiest way of which is to draw-off the fluid using an old battery hydrometer, to 'suck' the fluid a little at a time from the reservoir.

Before reassembly lightly smear a little special brake grease (*NOT* ordinary grease) around the top and bottom edges of the steel backing plate of the pads, being extra careful not to allow the grease to get onto the pads' friction material - use just a small amount of grease on each edge. Brake grease is available from your auto accessory store.

On reassembly, position the pads and shims in the caliper housing and fit the bottom pin first, followed by the anti-rattle springs, then the top pin. The springs will need to be tensioned as the top pin is tapped home. Remember to fit the pins from the outside of the caliper i.e. tap them home TOWARDS the engine side of the caliper, to finish flush with the caliper sides.

CAVALIERS EQUIPPED WITH PAD WEAR INDICATORS

INSIDE INFORMATION: When buying new disc pads, note that pads bought from Vauxhall agents or dealers may not come equipped with new wear sensors - these will be a separate 'extra'. However, pads bought from independent (or 'third-party') suppliers may well come with the sensor wires already fitted: it may be that you are replacing the pads before the wear sensors have contacted the disc and become damaged, in which case there is strictly no need to replace the sensors but as the cost of new ones is relatively small, you might want to replace them regardless.

2.0 LITRE MODELS FROM 1988

making it easy! A 7mm Allen or hexagonal key will be required for this job, to release the caliper guide bolts - these are usually very tight and will often have been fitted with a thread-locking compound on assembly, therefore a 'heavy-duty' tool is called for. Most 'ordinary' Allen keys are neither strong enough nor long enough, so the purchase of a purpose-made key is essential to the success of the job, and instrumental in preventing skinned knuckles!. High tensile tools with extended handles are available from most good accessory shops.

The larger-engined and high-performance Cavaliers use a different pattern of caliper which uses larger pads and has the advantage of providing more surface area to be forced into contact with the disc, hence more efficient braking. Additionally, the GSi 2000 and V6 have wear indicators fitted to the pads which illuminate a warning lamp on the dashboard when the pads are near the end of their life. While the caliper and pads are different in detail to those previously described, the general operation is the same.

71G. Lever the anti-squeal/pad retaining spring away from the caliper (also see 71J for alternative type) using a screwdriver, being careful not to bend it if it sticks; a little penetrating oil and careful levering will release a stubborn spring. Remove the wear indicator wire, if fitted, taking care not to pull the wire from the connector on the end of the wire.

71H. The caliper securing/guide bolts are protected from the elements by a rubber sleeve topped by a plastic cap which is easily pulled off. Insert the Allen key fully and apply tension - WARNING: Caliper guide bolts are notoriously tight, but they also have the habit of suddenly 'giving' as pressure on the tool mounts - be extra careful not to apply pressure to the tool in a way that the vehicle becomes unstable; direct effort downwards and be ready for the point of 'give' when the bolt may suddenly release and offer little or no resistance without warning. (These photographs were taken with the components off the car, for ease of illustration.)

71I. With the bolts (safely!) removed, it will probably be necessary to retract the piston sufficiently to allow the pads to clear any wear-ridge on the outer edge of the disc. Use a large pair of 'grips' (as

71J

71K

shown in 72E), or lever the inside pad away from the disc slightly using a flat lever. DO NOT apply excessive pressure to the outer edge of the disc, which can distort and be ruined.

71J. Lift-off the caliper: The inner pad is fixed to the piston by way of a spring clip and will come away with it, while the 'free' pad may remain with the caliper - simply lift it out. This, incidentally, illustrates an alternative type of retainer spring used on the Cavalier.

71K. This shows the pads and the spring clip which secures the inner pad to the (hollow) piston. It's a good idea when you collect the new pads from your supplier, to check that the box contains two pads of each type, otherwise you'll be unable to finish the job completely.

If wear indicators are fitted to your car, renew them along with the pads, even if they look to be in good condition.

Reassembly follows the guidelines above, but note the tightening torque of the guide bolts is 30 Nm (22ft/lb)   nothing like as tight as the struggle of removal would suggest! The use of a thread-locking compound is advisable, just a 'spot' on the threads of each bolt being sufficient. Fit the 'inboard' pad (with the spring clip) to the piston and the 'free' pad to the caliper, before replacing the latter. Don't forget to fit the wear indicators if necessary.

Job 72. Check/replace rear disc pads.

SAFETY FIRST! AND SPECIALIST SERVICE
Obviously, your car's brakes are among its most important safety related items. Do NOT dismantle or attempt to perform any work on the braking system unless you are fully competent to do so. If you have not been trained in this work, but wish to carry it out, we strongly recommend that you have a garage or qualified mechanic check your work before using the car on the road. See also the section on BRAKES AND ASBESTOS in Chapter 1, Safety First! for further information. Always start by washing the brakes with a proprietary brand of brake cleaner never use compressed air to clean off brake dust. Always replace the disc pads in sets of four - never replace the pads on one wheel only. After fitting new pads, avoid heavy braking - except in an emergency - for the first 150 to 200 miles (250 to 300 km).

2.0 LITRE AND V6 ENGINE MODELS

This procedure is similar to that covered in Job 71 for the front brake pads, but note that a different size of punch (3mm) will be necessary to remove the pad retaining pins if the pads are to be replaced.

72A. Loosen the rear wheel bolts, raise and support the rear of the car and remove the wheels. Examine the disc surface for signs of scoring, pitting or corrosion. Check also for wear ridges at the inner and outer limits of pad contact.

72B. The pads are clearly visible through the 'window' once the wheel has been removed. Check the pad thicknesses, which should be no less than 7mm including the backing plate. Check also that both pads display a similar degree of wear - one pad worn substantially more than the other indicates a sticking caliper piston, which should be investigated immediately by a reputable garage or Vauxhall dealer.

72A

72B

If the pads are fit for further service, spray brake cleaner liberally around the caliper to remove dust and debris (hold a rag beneath the caliper to catch the dirty fluid as it falls), wire-brushing first if the caliper, spring and pads are corroded.

6,000 MILE SERVICE

BRAKE PAD REPLACEMENT

72C. Drive out the upper pin, drifting it inwards, using the 3mm punch.

72C

72D. As the upper pin and the drift are withdrawn the anti-squeal spring will come free and can be removed, followed by the lower pin.

INSIDE INFORMATION: Wear cotton gloves - or at least use barrier cream - because brake dust is very hard to shift from nails and cracks in the skin.

72E. As the caliper is fixed, the pistons will usually need to be retracted in order for the pads to be removed past the inevitable wear-ridge - use a pair of grips as here, or a lever, to clear the pads but DON'T lever against the disc. Note that on these calipers there are two pistons, rather than the single one fitted to the front brakes.

72D

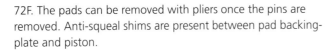
72E

72F. The pads can be removed with pliers once the pins are removed. Anti-squeal shims are present between pad backing-plate and piston.

72G. These pads show unequal wear, that from the inner side of the disc indicating a sticking piston on that side.

72H. Clean the pad housings, using a screwdriver to scrape away any corrosion...

72F

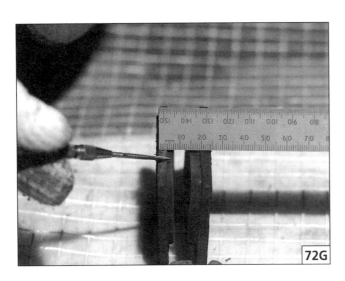
72G

72H

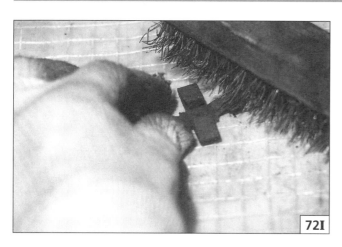

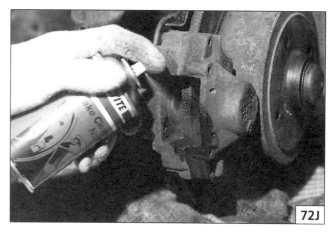

72I. ...and wire-brush the anti-rattle spring and pad retaining pins.

making it easy! 72J. Aerosol brake cleaner does a superb job if shifting brake dust and other 'gunge'.

72K. On reassembly, replace the pads and fit the bottom pin first, followed by the anti-rattle spring which has to be tensioned 'inwards' so that the top pin can be fitted.

72L. Tap the pins fully home, so that they are flush with the caliper.

72M. On Cavaliers with rear disc brakes, the parking (handbrake) brake mechanism and linings are within the disc hub, making in effect a drum brake. Check the lining thickness of the parking brake shoes visually through the inspection hole provided. A small torch might be useful to see them clearly; turn the disc so that the whole lining surface can be checked.

72N. Don't forget to lubricate the operating mechanism (behind the backplate) with a dab of brake grease where the handbrake cable hooks onto the actuating lever.

SPECIALIST SERVICE: If the handbrake shoes are worn or prove ineffective due to oil contamination, have them examined or changed by a reputable garage or Vauxhall dealer.

☐ **Job 73. Check/adjust/renew rear drum brakes.**

SAFETY FIRST! AND SPECIALIST SERVICE
Obviously, your car's brakes are among its most important safety related items. Do NOT dismantle or attempt to perform any work on the braking system unless you are fully competent to do so. If you have not been trained in this work, but wish to carry it out, we strongly recommend that you have a garage or qualified mechanic check your work before using the car on the road. See also the section on BRAKES AND ASBESTOS in Chapter 1, Safety First! for further information. Always start by washing the brakes with a proprietary brand of brake cleaner - brake drums removed, where appropriate - never use compressed air to clean off brake dust. Always replace the disc pads and/or shoes in sets of four - never replace the pads/shoes on one wheel only. After fitting new brake shoes or pads, avoid heavy braking - except in an emergency - for the first 150 to 200 miles (250 to 300 km).

73A

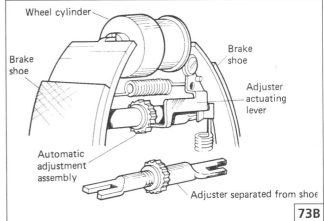

73B

ALL MODELS EXCEPT 2.0 LITRE AND V6

See *Job 72. SAFETY FIRST!* regarding raising the rear of the car, and also *Job 71* for precautions regarding brake dust.

73A. With the rear of the car raised and the wheel removed, undo the drum retaining screw, release the handbrake and pull the drum off.

73B. If the drum fails to pass over the shoes and 'sticks' part-way, insert a thin screwdriver and engage the automatic adjustment cog wheel, turning it with the screwdriver on the downward stroke. The arrangement of this is shown in the drawing.

73C

73C. Place a rag beneath the wheel and use a proprietary brake cleaning spray to 'flood' away all loose dust and dirt. Do the same with the inner surfaces of the drum.

73D. Examine the brake lining surfaces for wear, meaning that the friction lining should be a uniform thickness around the shoe, at least 2mm thick (not including the backing) or 1.5mm above the rivet heads, if the shoes are rivetted, and not display any signs of scoring or damage. Bear in mind that it will be another 9,000 miles before you check again, so err on the cautious side. Check also for traces of oil, grease or brake fluid - if present the shoes will need replacement.

73D

You can learn a lot about the condition of an engine from looking at the spark plugs. The following information and photographs, reproduced here with grateful thanks to NGK, show you what to look out for.

1. Good Condition

If the firing end of a spark plug is brown or light grey, the condition can be judged to be good and the spark plug is functioning at its best.

4. Overheating

When having been overheated, the insulator tip can become glazed or glossy, and deposits which have accumulated on the insulator tip may have melted. Sometimes these deposits have blistered on the insulator's tip.

6. Abnormal Wear

Abnormal electrode erosion is caused by the effects of corrosion, oxidation, reaction with lead, all resulting in abnormal gap growth.

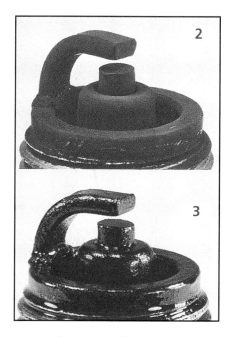

2. Carbon Fouling

Black, dry, sooty deposits, which will eventually cause misfiring and can be caused by an over-rich fuel mixture. Check all carburettor settings, choke operation and air filter cleanliness. Clean plugs vigorously with a brass bristled wire brush.

3. Oil Fouling

Oily, wet-looking deposits. This is particularly prone to causing poor starting and even misfiring. Caused by a severely worn engine but do not confuse with wet plugs removed from the engine when it won't start. If the "wetness" evaporates away, it's not oil fouling.

5. Normal Wear

A worn spark plug not only wastes fuel but also strains the whole ignition system because the expanded gap requires higher voltage. As a result, a worn spark plug will result in damage to the engine itself, and will also increase air pollution. The normal rate of gap growth is usually around 'half-a-thou.' or 0.0006 in. every 5,000 miles (0.01 mm. every 5,000 km.).

7. Breakage

Insulator damage is self-evident and can be caused by rapid heating or cooling of the plug whilst out of the car or by clumsy use of gap setting tools. Burned away electrodes are indicative of an ignition system that is grossly out of adjustment. Do not use the car until this has been put right.

73E. Examine the hydraulic wheel cylinder, in particular the rubber gaiters at each end. Pull each gaiter back slightly and check for any sign of dampness, which would indicate the internal seals of the cylinder are worn and require urgent replacement - seek professional help immediately.

BRAKE SHOE REPLACEMENT

making it easy! 73F. Before dismantling brake shoes, but after the drum has been removed, make a careful record of where everything goes, especially brake shoe return springs. Make a careful sketch, take a couple of photographs (a Polaroid would be ideal!) or 'video' the assembly - it could turn out to be a life saver - literally! Also, only work on one side at a time, so that you've always got the other one to refer to.

73G. Release the spring clips on the shoe steady pins by holding the pin at the rear of the brake backplate and pushing against the spring with pliers...

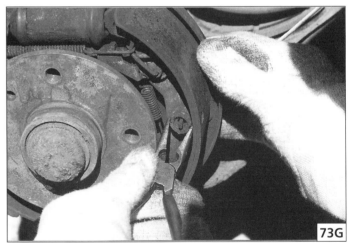

73H. ...with the spring compressed, turn it through 90 degrees and allow it to pass over the holding-pin head.

73I. Lever the bottom of one shoe away from the anchor plate, which will relieve the spring tension and allow the other shoe to be released.

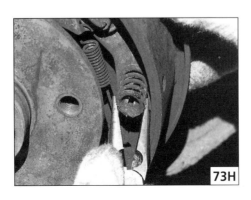

73J. Unhook the handbrake cable from the operating arm on the back of the backplate.

73K. The two shoes will still be joined by the top spring and the auto adjuster mechanism; unhook the top spring as shown here...

73L. ...and the shoes will separate and can be lifted away.

INSIDE INFORMATION: Try to remove the shoes in as near 'assembled' state as possible, to aid renewal. Place the assembly flat on the ground and build-up the new shoes a step at a time, transferring springs and adjuster in sequence. In this way you will avoid any confusion as to what part goes where, and can clean each part as it is dealt with.

73M. As soon as the shoes are lifted away, tie a loop of wire or cord around the hydraulic cylinder to prevent the pistons popping out of their bores, which would require the brakes to be bled. Clean the backplate and cylinder with spray and a rag before fitting the new shoes. Remember to attach the handbrake cable connector to the respective shoe before assembling the components; otherwise the installation operation is a reversal of the above procedure. Take care not to allow oil or grease to contaminate the new shoes!

73N. Pre-1984 Cavaliers have a basically similar layout, with the exception of the auto-adjuster of course! - but they do have shoe retaining clips (arrowed). These might be of the same type as in 73G and 73H; they might be those shown here, which you squeeze together and remove; or they might be a curved spring from under which the shoe has to be slid, the spring staying in place. The adjuster is a hexagonal nut on the back of the backplate. (Illustration, courtesy Vauxhall Motors Ltd.)

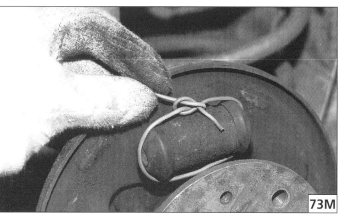

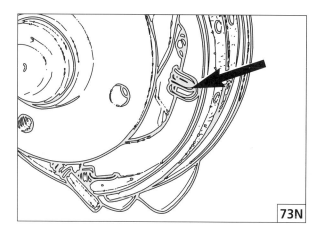

730. If there is less than 3mm of friction material on the brake shoes, or if there is any contamination from oil, grease or brake fluid, scrap them and replace with new.

On completion, operate the handbrake several times, followed by the foot brake, to centralise the shoes and allow the automatic adjuster to take up any slack.

730

☐ Job 74. Check brake proportioning valve.

This component is fitted to the rear underside of the car, its purpose being to control the flow of hydraulic fluid to the rear brakes, depending on the load carried by the vehicle. It does this by a connection to the bodywork in the form of a sprung arm which is deflected at varying angles depending on the load - the greater the load, the more fluid is allowed to pass and therefore the greater braking effort applied to the rear wheels.

SPECIALIST SERVICE: Have this component checked by a reputable garage or Vauxhall dealer.

Every 12,000 Miles or Every Twelve Months, whichever comes first

12,000 miles - The Engine Bay

☐ Job 75. Read stored engine codes.

INJECTION MODELS FROM 1987 ONLY

SPECIALIST SERVICE: Have your Vauxhall dealer or tuning specialist read the engine stored fault codes (which includes faults in the auto transmission, where applicable) with their specialist code reader and act accordingly. Do note that Gunsons now produce a 'Fault Code Reader' suitable (and affordable!) for the DIY user. It only identifies faults, of course; it doesn't correct them!

☐ Job 76. Check camshaft belt.

UP TO 1987 ONLY

Check camshaft drivebelt tension and condition.

INSIDE INFORMATION: The camshaft drivebelt, or 'cam-belt' is driven by the crankshaft and transmits power to the camshaft and water pump by way of toothed pulleys (the cambelt itself being 'toothed'). As such the belt plays a vital part in the operation of the engine, for without it the engine cannot run. It is obviously important that the belt must be in good condition at all times, especially as a breakage of the belt while the engine is running can cause serious damage to the pistons and/or valve gear, as well as stopping the vehicle.

SPECIALIST SERVICE: The manufacturer recommends changing the belt every four years or 36,000 miles, whichever comes first. There is no recommended period of inspection, but many owners prefer to have the tension and overall condition of the belt checked at 12,000 miles or every two years, if only for peace of mind. Most reputable garages will be happy to carry out these checks for a small charge. Special tools are required to change and tension the cambelt, as well as a strict procedure, so we recommend the job be undertaken by a proficient mechanic or Vauxhall agent.

☐ Job 77. Emission control equipment.

CAVALIERS FROM 1991-ONLY

SPECIALIST SERVICE: The emission control systems fitted to cars from 1991 form part of the engine management systems and to test them requires special Vauxhall test instruments and a procedure that takes into account numerous other components, many of which cannot be tested individually. We therefore recommend the emission control equipment is tested by a Vauxhall agent or dealer.

78A

☐ **Job 78. Air cleaner element.**

CARBURETTOR ENGINED MODELS UP TO 1988

78A. The air filter housing is secured either by a single central nut, or cross-head screws as shown. Remove either the nut or screws to release the housing from the carburettor.

78B. Release the spring clips placed around the edge of the housing, plus the small cross-head screw near the front, and lift off the upper casing, exposing the filter which can now be removed.

78C. Carefully remove any dust or debris (leaves, flies etc.) from the lower casing, taking care that none enters the carburettor intake situated in the centre of the housing - a vacuum cleaner with hose and nozzle is ideal for this task, if available. Fit the new filter and replace the housing top cover clips. Before replacing the top cover screws or nut, lift the front of the filter housing to expose the hot-air flap in the "snout" of the casing. On types fitted with a vacuum capsule, on a cold engine the flap should be "closed" to allow only cold air from the front of the snout, but with the engine running the flap should raise to allow hot air from around the exhaust manifold to enter the housing via the downward facing port. If no vacuum capsule is fitted, the flap is controlled by a thermostat and should be in the "open" position when cold, but closing the flap against the hot-air port when the engine reaches operating temperature. Check also the condition of the short connecting hose between the intake and the exhaust manifold shroud; replace if damaged.

FUEL INJECTION AND POST-1988 CARBURETTOR MODELS

78D. The filter housing is situated in the lower front corner of the engine bay, to the left as you look to the rear of the vehicle. The top cover is secured by four spring clips (arrowed) and, on later models, a cross-head screw. Remove the clips and screw (if fitted).

Lift the top cover as far as the air intake hose will allow, as much as is necessary to remove the old filter. Clean the lower housing of debris, with a vacuum cleaner hose and nozzle if possible.

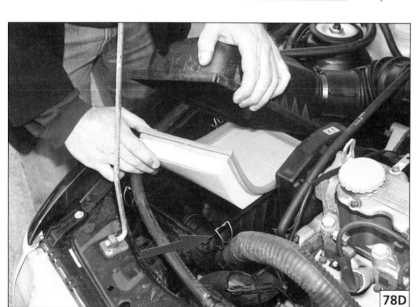

Place the new filter in position, ensuring the latex seal on the upper edge of the filter seats properly in the groove on the lower housing - the upper casing will not fit properly if the filter is mis-placed. Refit the top cover, clips and screw (if fitted).

DIESEL ENGINED MODELS ONLY

78F. The air filter housing on both types of diesel engine is situated in the centre of the engine bay, above the engine. To remove the filter, undo the two cross-head screws on the straps that secure the housing, undo two further screws that secure the air scoop to the front engine-bay panel. (Illustration, courtesy Vauxhall Motors Limited)

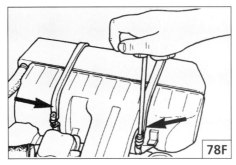

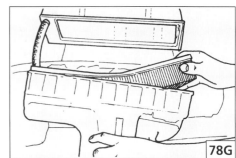

78G. The filter housing can now be parted and the filter removed; clean the lower housing, fit the new filter element and replace the air scoop and straps. (Illustration, courtesy Vauxhall Motors Limited)

☐ Job 79. Air cleaner intake.

PETROL ENGINES ONLY

79. The automatic air intake valve balances cold air taken from the front of the car, with hot air taken from a shroud surrounding the exhaust manifold. To check it is working, simply remove the air intake ducting and check that the valve plate moves freely and returns to its original position.

☐ Job 80. Check/renew fuel filter.

CARBURETTOR ENGINES

MODELS UP TO 1985 ONLY

SAFETY FIRST!
A small amount of fuel is likely to be lost with this job, so position a rag beneath the fuel pump to catch it. Disconnect the battery before disconnecting the filter - see FACT FILE on page 24.

80A. The fuel filter is contained within the fuel pump and consists of a fine screen through which the fuel is drawn from the tank. To remove the filter for cleaning, remove the screw in the centre of the fuel pump and lift away the lid, revealing the screen filter and sealing rubber. Clean the filter in fresh fuel and replace, taking care that the sealing rubber is not distorted and is positioned correctly.

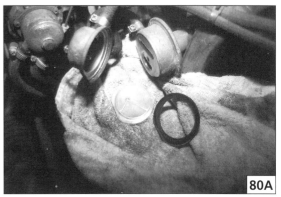

MODELS AFTER 1985 ONLY

80B. The in-line fuel filter is located at the top of the engine, just behind the cam/valve cover. It is placed in the fuel supply line between pump and carburettor. It is non-cleanable and must be replaced. First undo the two fuel pipe securing clips at the filter.

80C. The filter is held in place on a small bracket and secured by two screws - remove these and discard the filter, fitting a new one in place. After tightening the fuel pipe clips run the engine and check for leaks.

INSIDE INFORMATION: Ensure that the arrow on the filter points in the direction the fuel will flow through it. Some filters work in either direction, in which case there will be no arrow.

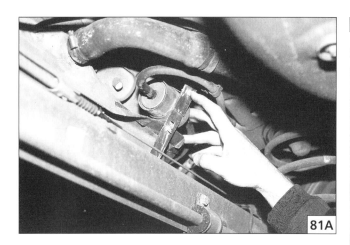

81A

Job 81. Renew fuel microfilter.

FUEL INJECTION ENGINES ONLY

SAFETY FIRST!
*This job requires the rear of the car to be raised sufficiently to give good working clearance beneath the fuel tank, necessitating the use of ramps or axle stands. Be doubly careful to ensure the stability of the car before venturing beneath it - see **Raising the Car Safely** at the beginning of this chapter for how to do this safely. Also, see **SAFETY FIRST!** on page 70. Fuel injection systems remain pressurised even when the engine is switched off and require special procedures to make them safe - UNDER NO CIRCUMSTANCES loosen or remove fuel pipes on a fuel injection system. If pipework requires repair, take the car to a fuel injection specialist or your Vauxhall dealer.*

81B

81A. The fuel filter is positioned at the rear of the fuel tank beneath the car. Position a container to catch the small amount of fuel that will inevitably be spilt and undo the two hose clips, one at each end of the filter. On models up to 1992 the filter is free-hanging, while on later cars it is fixed by a bracket, as shown. A single screw holds the filter and bracket.

81B. Before removing the hoses note which way the arrow stamped on the filter casing is pointing - in most cases it will be visible and pointing towards the pump, in the direction of travel. If there are no markings and the filter is to be replaced, mark one end so that it can be refitted correctly. If fitting a new filter, make sure its arrow points the same way as the original.

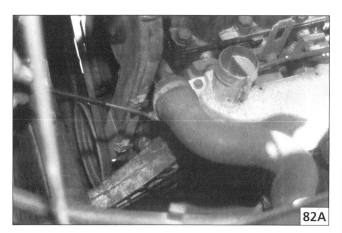

82A

SAFETY FIRST!
i) The coolant level should only be worked on WHEN THE SYSTEM IS COLD. If you remove the pressure cap when the engine is hot, the release of pressure can cause the water in the cooling system to boil and spurt several feet in the air with the risk of severe scalding. ii) Take precautions to prevent anti-freeze being swallowed or coming in contact with the skin or eyes. If this should happen, rinse immediately with plenty of water. Seek immediate medical help if necessary. Keep anti-freeze away from children and pets.

82B

Job 82. Check coolant hoses.

82A. Certainly once a year, and before adding anti-freeze as described shortly, check the condition of all coolant hoses and the security of their clips. But beware of tightening a clip on a leaking elderly hose - renewing both hose and clip is the wiser option.

82B. Examine the hoses for signs of cracking (carefully bending the straights and straightening the bends) and squeeze them to feel for any softening, perhaps caused by oil contamination. Don't overlook minor hoses, such as a feed to a water-heated inlet manifold.

Old hoses become very set in their ways, and should you need to renew one you may find that, even with its clips fully slackened off, it will be reluctant to budge.

making it easy! 82C. Rather than employ too much force, particularly on a radiator, where there's a high risk of fracturing the hose stub, simply slide the clip out of the way and use a strong, sharp knife to carefully slit the hose until you can open it up and peel it off the stub. Replace it with new.

82C

Thoroughly clean the stubs, carefully using a file and emery cloth if necessary, to remove the lumpy corrosion often found on elderly alloy cooling system components.

Position new clips (preferably of the flat, 'worm-drive' type) on the new hose, ensuring their tightening screws are best placed for easy screwdriver access when the hose is fitted. A smear of washing-up fluid will help the hose slide fully home on the stubs. Tighten the clips firmly, but don't 'bury' them in the hose.

☐ Job 83. Anti-freeze.

Arguably, once your cooling system contains anti-freeze your car is protected for ever more from the dangers of freezing up, since it is widely held that the strength of the anti-freezing element in the mixture will never wane.

However, whether this is entirely true or not, there is the danger that over a long period casual topping-up of the coolant with plain water will have weakened the mixture. On top of that, we are told that while the anti-freeze constituents live on, the beneficial 'all the year round' anti-corrosion inhibitors built into the mixture do not.

83A

Hence a general recommendation that the anti-freeze/coolant mixture is changed at least every two years, while many motorists are happier to still regard the job as an annual pre-winter precaution.

83A. First remove the bottom hose from its connection with the radiator, after positioning a container to catch the old coolant. When all has drained, refit the hose.

83B. Pour the antifreeze into the header tank to give a 50-50 dilution; see *Chapter 8, Facts and Figures* for capacity of the cooling system.

☐ Job 84. Check power steering hose and belt.

84. The power steering rack is hidden down at the back of the engine and the pipes that connect to it can be difficult to spot, especially if the engine is as dirty as this one! Carefully trace the power steering pipes from the pump to the rack, checking for any sign of leaks, including the unions and pipe connectors. If a leak is suspected, have the car checked by a reputable garage as soon as possible. Check the drive belt as for alternator, Job 23. Slacken the mounting bolts; re-tension if necessary.

83B

POWER STEERING DRIVE BELT
On 1.6 litre models the pump is driven by the alternator drive belt and is adjusted by way of the alternator.

On 1.8 and 2.0 litre models the pump has its own belt and is adjusted by slackening the mounting bolts and lengthening or shortening the treaded-rod adjuster beneath the pump body. Belt deflection should be no more than 10mm when tested by hand.

☐ Job 85. Check air conditioning.

Check all connections to the air conditioning compressor and look for signs of corrosion and leaks. However, the first sign of something amiss (for most owners!) is when the system fails. **SPECIALIST SERVICE:** Problems with air conditioning equipment must be referred to a Vauxhall dealer or specialist, due to the equipment needed to test it and the precautions necessary in handling the ozone-damaging gas with which it is filled. Under no circumstances should you attempt to disconnect pipework or components.

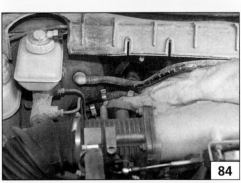

84

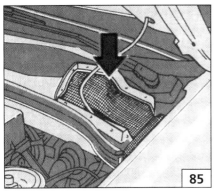

85

85. One job you must do yourself is to check regularly that the leaf grilles in the far left - and right-hand sides of the engine bay are free of leaves. Also, run the unit at least once a month. Another is to check the drive belt for obvious signs of cracking or other deterioration. (Illustration, courtesy Vauxhall Motors Limited)

☐ Job 86. Battery terminals.

Provided the battery is kept clean and dry and is not topped-up over generously, its terminals should also remain clean and sound unless a generator fault is causing it to be over-charged, with consequent heavy 'gassing' from the cells.

Generally speaking, it is electrolyte spillage or this excess vapour which leads to the 'fungal growth' noted on the terminals of neglected batteries. It is a condition which, as well as the highly corrosive effect on nearby metals, such as the battery clamp and the battery tray, also causes poor electrical contact. In the extreme, the starter may fail to operate, or all electrics may apparently fail.

86A

86A. If you have inherited a secondhand vehicle suffering from this problem, simply pouring hot water (or a mixture of hot water and domestic washing soda) over the terminals and any other affected parts, such as the battery strap or clamp, and the battery tray, will usually prove remarkably effective.

Take care that you don't pour the hot water into the battery cells or onto nearby vulnerable components.

If necessary, the hot water treatment can be followed by use of a wire brush and/or emery cloth to bring the battery lead connectors and the battery terminal posts back to clean and bright condition. A slim knife blade or half-round file can be useful to clean inside the lead connectors.

86B

SAFETY FIRST!
Be very careful to guard against 'short circuits' when working on battery terminals. The gas ensuing from the cells, particularly when the battery is being charged, is extremely explosive and ignition by a careless spark can cause a truly horrific battery explosion. (A typical cause of accidental short-circuit is the bristles of a wire brush touching a battery terminal and a battery strap at the same time, or, similarly, a spanner being used to tighten a terminal nut also touching this strap or the car bodywork).

86B. Once all connections are clean and dry, a smear of petroleum jelly (such as 'Vaseline') or a proprietary battery jelly, will guard against further corrosion and help to maintain good electrical contact. Badly affected metals should be treated with a rust killer and re-painted.

86C. Finally, terminal connections should be tight but not 'murdered'.

☐ Job 87. Glow plug maintenance.

Rarely will you see any mention of the glow plugs or pre-heating system made on service schedules. This is because manufacturers regard the cold-starting system as one that either works or doesn't... and if it doesn't, you can probably set things right by renewing all the glow plugs.

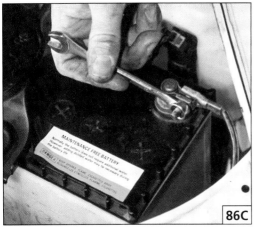

86C

However, as a keen DIYer you'll no doubt want to keep an eye on the condition of the plugs, which can be a handy indicator of injector problems. Our recommendation is that you remove all glow plugs at each major service (typically the annual service), wipe the soot from them, check there's no erosion, and refit them. It's best to catch worn-out plugs before you start experiencing starting difficulties.

GLOW PLUG REMOVAL

87. Before removing a glow plug from the cylinder head, disconnect the battery earth lead. Next, disconnect the wire or connecting strap from the plug and unscrew it from the cylinder head by just a couple of turns using a ring spanner or socket. Clean away dirt from around the plug so that none finds its way into the engine once the plug is removed, then fully unscrew the plug (and its sealing washer, if fitted). It's a good idea to blank off the plug hole with a piece of cloth to prevent dirt from entering.

REFITTING THE GLOW PLUG

Where a plug sealing washer is fitted this should be renewed before refitting the plug. If a plug tightening torque is specified in your handbook, it is important to observe it, as overtightening can cause damage. Admittedly, it isn't very easy gauging a tightening torque when you're using a spanner; the important thing is not to overtighten, as this can damage the plugs. This is because an annular gap between the screw body and the element sheath will close up if overtightened, so altering the plug's heating characteristics, causing it to draw excessive current and burn out all the sooner. Make sure that the electrical connection to each plug is clean and corrosion-free, then refit the supply wire or strap before reconnecting the battery.

12,000 Miles - Around the Car.

☐ Job 88. Toolkit and jack.

Inspect the toolkit, wipe tools with an oily rag to stop them rusting and lubricate the jack, checking that it works smoothly. Also, check that the spare wheel retaining bolt hasn't rusted in. Remove it and lubricate the threads with a dab of grease.

☐ Job 89. Lamp seals.

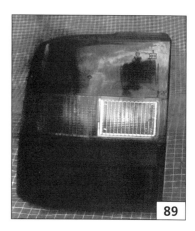

89. Check the headlamps, front indicators and rear lamp clusters for signs of water ingress, usually apparent as condensation on the inside of the lens. If present, either the weather seal has failed or mechanical damage such as stone chips is letting water in. Remove lenses so that you can check the seals. Renew them where possible and/or replace lenses.

☐ Job 90. Alarm sender unit.

If an alarm is fitted to your car, replace the battery in each alarm sender unit. Otherwise, it is all too easy to be banished from your own car, if the battery 'dies' at an inopportune moment.

☐ Job 91. Adjust headlights.

It is possible to adjust your own headlights but not with sufficient accuracy. Badly adjusted headlights can be very dangerous if they don't provide you, the driver, with a proper view of the road ahead or if they dazzle oncoming drivers. Older drivers and those with poor eyesight can become disorientated when confronted with maladjusted headlights. SPECIALIST SERVICE: Have the work carried out for you by a garage with beam measuring equipment. Any MoT testing station in the UK will be properly equipped.

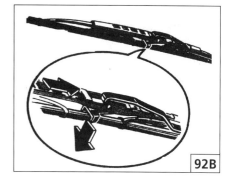

☐ Job 92. Renew wiper blades.

92A. Wiper blades don't last for ever, even though some people seem to think they do! It's a good policy to change them every year at least, not only on safety grounds but because a clear screen makes driving, especially at night, so much more comfortable. Refer to Job 13 for details of how to change them.

92B. A more economical way is to change just the rubber blades, as shown. (Illustration, courtesy Vauxhall Motors Limited)

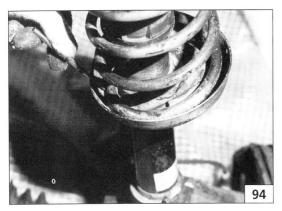

Job 93. Check hub bearings.

SPECIALIST SERVICE: Other than simply spinning the wheels and listening for a rumbling or grating noise from the bearings, there is little the inexperienced mechanic can do to test them. We therefore recommend this job be undertaken by a reputable garage or Vauxhall dealer, who will be able to test the pre-load of the bearings with accuracy and check for other faults.

Job 94. Check steering and suspension.

Test the steering column by grasping the steering wheel and rocking it up-and-down and sideways. Excessive play needs to be investigated - seek professional advice.

94. Check the front spring/shock absorber units (correctly termed 'Macpherson struts'), looking for badly corroded or broken springs. Make sure the drain holes in the lower spring seat-pan are clean and clear. Check the damper inside the spring for signs of oil staining, indicating a failed unit - have it investigated and always renew dampers in pairs, one each side of the car. Check the rear springs and dampers in a similar way, but note the springs are separate. Grasp each damper and try to rock it- there should be little or no free play, but if some is present, check the damper mounting bolts are secure, otherwise seek professional help. Check that all rubber bushes are in good condition. Lever each one with a stout screwdriver and look for movement. Check to see if any are spread or missing - replace if necessary.

Job 95. Check soft-top frame.

CONVERTIBLE CARS ONLY

Check the soft-top frame for security of all nuts, bolts and riveted joints. Tighten where necessary (if possible) and check that the locking mechanism hooks are properly adjusted and not coming loose.

12,000 Miles - Under the Car

Job 96. Engine/gearbox mounts.

All models have three mountings, two on the gearbox and one on the engine. All are difficult to see as they are enclosed in steel brackets. Test by 'rocking' the engine - if undue slackness, seek **SPECIALIST SERVICE**.

Job 97. Inspect underside.

When dry, inspect the underside of the car for rust and damage. Renew paint, underbody sealant and wax coating locally as necessary. Old-fashioned bitumen type underseal goes brittle and comes loose anyway, this only makes the problem worse. Water will soon penetrate this area and form a breeding ground for corrosion. Scrape off any such loose underseal and paint on wax coating in its place, when dry. Use an old screwdriver or light hammer to test for unsound and corroded areas of bodywork beneath the car, including the inner panels of the boot and engine bay. Investigate areas of loose paint and flaking rusty metal.

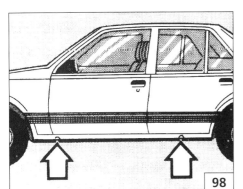

Job 98. Clear drain holes.

98. Check and clear drain holes in doors, sills, boot etc. Use a thin probe to poke the holes clear, although for a lasting job a vacuum and nozzle will clear most debris. Check also the bulkhead well at the rear of the engine bay, especially for leaves in winter - your vacuum cleaner is possibly the only thing that will shift them! (Illustration, courtesy Vauxhall Motors Limited)

Job 99. Check prop shaft U.J.s

FOUR WHEEL DRIVE ONLY

Grasp the propellor shaft and 'twist' it while holding the axle input flange, to test for any play or slackness in the joints of which there should be none. Also examine the rubber couplings for signs of damage, splitting or perishing. Have them replaced if in any doubt.

Job 100. Renew brake fluid.

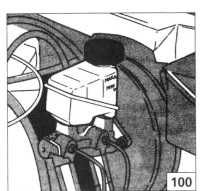

100. SPECIALIST SERVICE: Vauxhall now recommend the brake fluid be changed annually on all models and ages of their cars. This is best done by a garage or Vauxhall agent, who will have the necessary facilities and equipment to carry out the work quickly and safely. (Illustration, courtesy Vauxhall Motors Limited)

CHAPTER THREE

Every 24,000 Miles - or Every Two Years, whichever comes first

☐ Job 101. Radiator pressure cap.

Renew the radiator pressure cap - the rubber seal perishes which allows the coolant to boil at a lower temperature.

☐ Job 102. Check brake discs/drums and calipers.

102. SPECIALIST SERVICE: It is advisable to have a specialist or Vauxhall dealer inspect brake drums/callipers at this longer period, where they can be tested for run-out (a slight wobble of the disc), ovality (excessive wear in the drums that leaves them slightly oval) and sticking pistons in the calipers. The specified minimum dimensions for discs and/or drums can also be measured with great accuracy.

Every 36,000 Miles - or Every Three Years - whichever comes first

☐ Job 103. Renew camshaft belt.

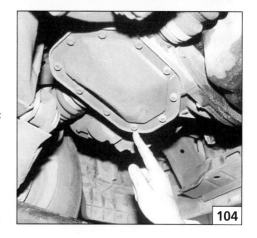

SPECIALIST SERVICE & INSIDE INFORMATION: Vauxhall recommend the cambelt be changed at 36,000 miles or FOUR years for all petrol engined cars, with diesels at 72,000 miles or eight years. We would recommend playing safe and sticking to 36,000 miles or THREE years for all cars. A cambelt breaks without warning and, if it does so, an engine can be very severly damaged as the pistons hit the valves. This job is best entrusted to a reputable garage or Vauxhall agent, who will have the necessary facilities and skills to carry out the work.

☐ Job 104. Change gearbox oil/transmission transmission fluid.

MANUAL TRANSMISSION
INSIDE INFORMATION: Although Vauxhall do not specify this job (to the extent that no drain plug is provided!) we consider it wise.

104. To drain the old oil it is necessary (in the absence of a drain plug) to unbolt this plate from the gearbox differential housing. Remove all the bolts (but two, left loose), starting with the lowest one and working up; this will allow the plate to maintain its seal with the gasket until a drip tray can be positioned beneath it, when a sharp tap from a soft-faced hammer or block of wood, struck sideways, will free the plate and allow the oil to drain. This can be messy! Always use a new gasket when refitting the plate, after draining is complete. Top-up the gearbox with the recommended fluid (See *Appendix 1, Lubrication Chart*) following the procedure set out in Job 56.

AUTOMATIC TRANSMISSION
When you've removed the sump pan (very similar to the manual pan but with 18 bolts instead of 10) the next thing you come to, once the fluid is drained, is a large flat filter screen. Wash the pan and screen meticulously in white spirit before reassembling with a new gasket.

☐ Job 105. Rustproofing.

Corrosion cost car owners far more then mechanical wear. Completely rustproofing your car every three years can save you a small fortune - see *Chapter 5, Rustproofing*.

☐ Job 106. Renew HT leads.

Replacing the HT leads and distributor cap now will reduce winter starting problems with petrol engines. See Job 48.

Every 63,000 Miles

☐ Job 107. Replace glow plugs.

Poor starting can be the bane of life for owners of older diesel engines. Replacing the glow plugs at this stage can make a major difference. See Job 87 for details.

CHAPTER 4 - BODYWORK

In this Chapter, we show you how to make your car look its best. First, we demonstrate that your car's appearance can be improved beyond recognition by a couple of hours of work on a Sunday morning. Then, just in case a passing gate post should leap out at you, we explain how to carry out simple bodywork repairs at home.

PART I: THE BODY BEAUTIFUL

Have you ever looked in amazement at the condition of cars on a dealer's forecourt and wondered why your car doesn't look like that? Well, it can! It's all a matter of know-how and a bit of hard work - and using the techniques described in this Chapter, you'll find that your car can be made to look almost like new again, without using too many cans of elbow grease!

☐ I.2 Weekend trips in your car are likely to be cursed by the 'bugs on the bumper' syndrome, as well as black tar on the bodywork. Soak all the bug-splatted areas with soapy water first, while you wash the rest of the car, then come back later, when they've been softened. Rub off with cloth, rather than a sponge. Use a proprietary brand of tar remover to wipe off tar splash.

☐ I.1 Apply a thin coat of modern car polish, to give a far longer-lasting shine than old-fashioned waxes (though we've yet to find one that lasts as long as claimed!). Cover just one section of the car at a time and then, as soon as the wax dries

to a haze, buff off for a superb shine. You'll see the dull paint and oxides come off on the cloth as you buff.

I.1

SOFT-TOP SPORTS CARS: If your vinyl soft-top has ingrained dirt, scrub it gently all over with a nail brush and soapy water. When dry, apply a good quality vinyl cleaner to bring the appearance back

I.2

like new. Fabric soft-tops should only be washed, not scrubbed, but can be hosed off to shift the dirt.

making it easy!
• As you polish, keep turning the cloth, always presenting a clean face to the surface of the paint - that's the secret of obtaining a clear shine with no rub marks. You'll need several clean cloths for polishing a whole car!

• Try removing a bug splat with a kitchen abrasive pad - the gentler sort made for non-stick pans - but only on glass and chrome; it'll ruin the shine on paintwork.

☐ I.3 It's easy to forget that around a fifth of your car's 'bodywork' is in fact glass. Use purpose-made glass cleaner, or a clean wash leather, for sparkling results. Clouding on the inside (said to be the vapour from upholstery plastics!) cleans off in the same way.

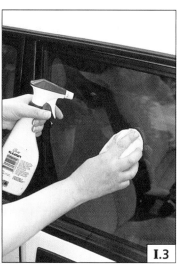

I.3

☐ I.4 Tyres are one of the most 'visual' parts of your car. There are proprietary tyre polishes and paints available, but be warned that the improvement in appearance goes the first time you drive on a wet road! A good cleaning with the wash sponge - *after* you've washed the rest of the car - is usually enough. Alloy wheels need a spray-on alloy wheel cleaner to shift stuck-on brake dust.

I.4

☐ *I.5 INSIDE INFORMATION: Many people just don't know what to do about dull plastic bumpers. Use a colourless trim cleaner and you'll find that just wiping it on will bring about a magical improvement. Several coats may be needed. (The old, black-coloured bumper polish makes a real mess of your hands, by the way!)*

☐ I.6 Even when an engine bay is clean, it often looks dirty. Use a spray-on cleaner to remove the heavy dirt and grease - best if you let it soak in to the worst areas. Use an old paintbrush in nooks and crannies. A vinyl protectant will then bring up a wonderful sheen to all of your hoses and pipes as well as all underbonnet paintwork.

I.5

> *making it easy!* If your engine is very oily, ask a local garage with a steam cleaner to hose off the worst of the 'grunge' before starting to clean up the engine bay. Paint any bare metal exposed by the steam cleaning, before it starts to rust.

☐ I.7 Choose a vinyl cleaner designed to put back the suppleness into vinyl and protect it from fading, as well as to remove dirt and grime and restore the appearance. If you hate the 'tacky' high gloss shine produced by some of them, look out for the low-gloss variety, giving a more natural finish.

INSIDE INFORMATION: If you can't get hold of low-gloss vinyl cleaner, try wiping over with a damp cloth before the cleaner has fully dried. This also 'wipes' away the worst of the gloss.

Rubber seals will last far longer if they are protected against the elements, by regular treatments with vinyl and rubber protectant. Scrape out dirt and grit from around the lower door seals then treat them all with several coats.

☐ I.8 Fabric seats and carpets will certainly benefit from cleaning with a proprietary brand of spray-on car upholstery cleaner - or a household upholstery cleaner. Follow the instructions carefully, take care not to soak cloth trim (it could cause shrinking) and the result will be carpets and cloth seats that look like new.

I.6

You can make leather more supple, and keep it cleaner and longer lasting by using a purpose-made brand of leather care. After use, the leather will feel soft and supple, because of the lanolin and mois-turisers that you will have added. At first, you may be surprised to see the colour of your leather go much darker but don't worry; that will pass as the leather cleaner dries out naturally.

I.7

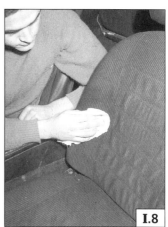

I.8

PART II: REPAIRING BODYWORK BLEMISHES

However well you look after your car, there will always be the risk of car park accident damage - or even worse! The smallest paint chips are best touched up with paint purchased from your local auto. accessory shop. If your colour of paint is not available, some auto. accessory shops offer a mixing scheme (including aerosols, in some cases) or you could look for a local paint factor in Yellow Pages. Take your car along to the paint factor and have them match the colour and mix the smallest quantity of cellulose paint that they will supply you with. Larger body blemishes will need the use of body filler.

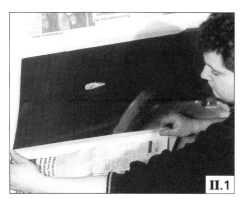

II.1

SAFETY FIRST!
Always *wear plastic gloves when working with body filler, before it has set. Always wear a face mask when sanding filler and wear goggles when using a power sander.*

☐ II.1 The rear of this car's bodywork has sustained a nasty gash, the sort of damage for which you will certainly need to use body filler. The first stage is to mask off. Try to find "natural" edges such as body mouldings or styling stripes and wherever you can, mask off body trim rather than having to remove it.

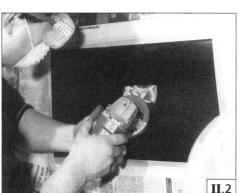

II.2

☐ II.2 Remove all paint from the damaged area and for about 25mm (1 in.) around the damaged area. Roughen the bare metal or surface with coarse abrasive paper - a power sander is best. Wipe over the area with white spirit (mineral spirit) and then wash off with washing-up liquid in water - *not* car wash detergent.

INSIDE INFORMATION: Rub the surrounding paintwork with cutting compound so that the new paint has a better chance of matching the old.

☐ II.3 Mix the filler and hardener, following the instructions on the can. It's best to use a piece of plastic or metal rather than cardboard because otherwise, the filler will pick up fibres from the surface of the card. Mix thoroughly until the colour is consistent and no traces of hardener can be discerned.

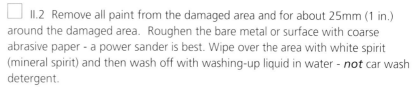

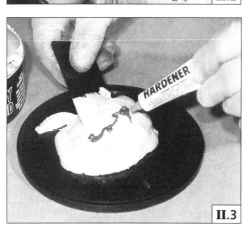

II.3

☐ II.4 You can now spread the filler evenly over the repair. If the damage is particularly deep, apply the paste in two or more layers, allowing the filler to harden before adding the next layer. The final layer should be just proud of the level required, but do not overfill as this wastes paste and will require more time to sand down.

☐ II.5 It is essential when sanding down that you wrap the sanding paper around a flat block. You can see from the scratch marks that this repair has been sanded diagonally in alternate directions until the filler has become level with the surrounding panel, but you have to take care not to go deeply into the edges of the paint around the repair.

INSIDE INFORMATION: There will invariably be small pin holes even if the right

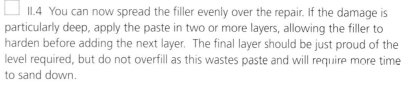

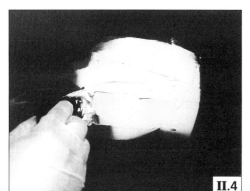

II.4

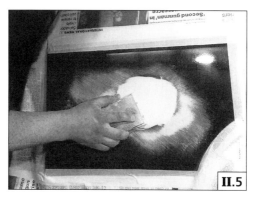

II.5

amount of filler was applied first time. Use a tiny amount of filler scraped very thin over the whole repair, filling in deep scratches and pin holes and then sanding off with a very fine grade of sand paper - preferably dry paper rather than wet-or-dry because you don't want to get water on to the bare filler.

☐ II.6 You can now use an aerosol primer to spray over the whole area of the repair but preferably not right up to the edges of the masking tape...

☐ II.7 ...and now use wet-or-dry paper, again on a sanding block, to sand the primer paint.

INSIDE INFORMATION: Don't sand fresh primer paint - leave it up to a day to harden off.

The filler is now protected from the water by the paint. If you do apply paint right up to the edge of the tape, be sure to 'feather' the edges of the primer, so that the edges blend in smoothly to the surrounding surface, with no ridges.

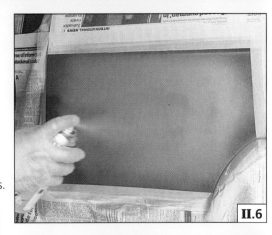

II.6

SAFETY FIRST!
Always wear an efficient mask when spraying aerosol paint and only work in a well-ventilated area, well away from any source of ignition, because spray paint vapour, even that given off by an aerosol, is highly flammable. Ensure that you have doors and windows open to the outside when using aerosol paint but in cool or damp weather, close them when the vapour has dispersed, otherwise the surface of the paint will "bloom", or take on a milky appearance. In fact, you may find it difficult to obtain a satisfactory finish in cold or damp weather.

II.7

☐ II.8 Before starting to spray, ensure that the nozzle is clear. Note that the can must be held with the index finger well back on the aerosol button. If you let your finger overhang the front of the button, a paint drip can form and throw itself on to the work area as a paint blob.

making it easy! • One of the secrets of spraying paint which doesn't run, is to put a very light coat of spray paint on to the panel first, followed by several more coats, allowing time between each coat for the bulk of the solvent to evaporate.

• Alternate coats should go on horizontally, followed by vertical coats as shown on the inset diagram.

☐ II.9 After allowing about a week for the paint to dry, you will be able to polish it with a light cutting compound, blending the edges of the repair into the surrounding paintwork.

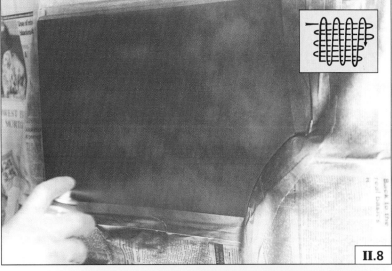

II.8

*INSIDE INFORMATION: Do note that if your repairs don't work out first time and you have to apply more paint on top of the fresh paint that you have already used, allow a week to elapse otherwise there is a strong risk of pickling or other reactions to take place. Also note that a prime cause of paint failure is the existence of silicones on the surface of the old paint before you start work. These come from most types of polish and are not all that easy to remove - they **won't** sand off!. Thoroughly wipe the panel down with white spirit before starting work and wash off with warm water and washing-up liquid to remove any further traces of the polish and the white spirit - but don't use the sponge or bucket that you normally use for washing the car otherwise you will simply introduce more silicones onto the surface!*

II.9

CHAPTER 5 - RUSTPROOFING

When mechanical components deteriorate, they can cost you a lot of money to replace. But when your car's bodywork deteriorates, it can cost you the car, if corrosion goes beyond the point where repairs are economical to carry out. Rust prevention should be regarded as a regular maintenance job, one which enables you to extend the life of your car by many years - and that will save you *real* money!

If you want to prolong its life, you'll have to inject rustproofing fluid into all the enclosed box sections and 'chassis' sections on your car. In many cases, you'll find holes already in place; in others, you'll be able to take off a cover, a piece or trim or a door lock in order to gain access. But in quite a few cases, you'll need to drill holes to gain an entry.

Don't be a drip!

*INSIDE INFORMATION: i) Place **lots** of newspaper beneath the car to catch the inevitable drips. ii) Some seat belts retract into a cavity that you will want to spray with fluid. Pull each belt out and hold it there until you have finished spraying the fluid. iii) All electric motors should be covered up with plastic bags so that none of the rustproofing fluid gets in and all windows should be fully wound up.*

iv) Ensure that all drain channels are clear so that any excess rustproofing fluid can drain out and also check once again that they are clear after you have finished carrying out the work to ensure that your application of the fluid has not caused them to be clogged up, otherwise water will become trapped, negating much of the good work you have carried out.

making it easy! Decide on your drill size with reference to the size of the injector nozzle and the size of grommets that you can obtain for blanking the holes off again afterwards. You'll feel a bit foolish if you drill first, only to find that they don't make grommets to fit the holes you've drilled!

Choose Your Weapon

Those hand pump injectors that you can buy from DIY shops are often worse than useless. They don't usually make a proper spray, but simply squirt a jet of fluid that does nothing to give the all-over cover required. Make a dummy 'box section' out of a cardboard box - cut it and fold to make it about 10 or 15 cm square - and try a dummy run. Open up and see if it has worked. If you haven't obtained full misting of the fluid, you could be making the problem worse.

INSIDE INFORMATION: Rust strikes even harder in those areas that aren't properly covered!

Consider taking your car to a garage with suitable equipment and having them do the work for you. Full, professional injection equipment, as shown in the following picture sequence, will make the fluid reach much further and deeper than amateur equipment, and if you enlist the services of the best experts as featured here, you'll be able to benefit from their experience.

> **SAFETY FIRST!**
> **Before using rustproofer, read the manufacturer's safety notes. Keep rustproofing fluid off the exhaust or any other components where it could be ignited. Keep it away from brake components, covering them up with plastic bags before starting work. Follow *Chapter 1, Safety First!*, and advice at the start of *Chapter 3, Servicing Your Car* especially with regard to safe working beneath a car raised off the ground. Rustproofers all contain solvents. In a confined space, such as a garage, solvents can build up, creating both a health and a fire hazard. Wear an efficient face mask so that you don't inhale vapour and work out of doors, keeping out of confined spaces. Wear gloves and goggles, but if you do get any fluid in your eyes, wash out with copious amounts of water and immediately seek medical advice if necessary. If any welding has to be carried out on the vehicle within a few months of rustproofing being carried out, you must inform those who are carrying out the work because of the fire risk.**

Our thanks are due to Dinol Ltd. for carrying out the work, using Dinitrol rustproofing fluid.

RUSTPROOFING

☐ Job 1. Clean underbody.

You will have to hose off the underside of the body, paying particular attention to the undersides of the wings and wheel arches, before you can start to apply new rustproofing. Scrape off any hard, thick deposits of mud, and any old flaking body sealant under the car. One of the quickest ways to do the job is to use a power washer with a long lance. Many garages have this equipment for customer use in a wash bay and this is a very efficient way of doing the job. You will, however, still have to go underneath with a scraper afterwards as even a power jet won't take off flaking body sealant. You will also have to wait up to a week for the underside of the car to dry thoroughly (in warm, dry weather) before applying new rustproofing.

☐ Job 2. Equipment.

2. Gather together all the materials you need to do the job before you start. You will also need lifting equipment and axle stands.

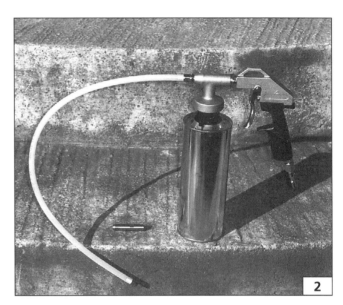

> *making it easy!* A compressor-driven gun of this type won't break the bank - try your local motor trade parts factors - but you'll need to buy or hire a compressor. Results will be perfect.

Bear in mind the safety equipment you will need - referred to in *Safety First!* - see page 81. You will need copious amounts of newspaper to spread on the floor because quite a lot of rust-proofing fluid will run out of the box sections and other areas under the car and you may have to park your car over newspaper for a couple of days after carrying out this treatment. Remember that the vapour given off by the materials will continue for several days, so park your car in the open for a week or so if you can, rather than in an enclosed garage.

INSIDE INFORMATION: Tip from Dinol, the manufacturers of Dinitrol: Except in a heat wave, it is essential to stand the container of rustproofer in a tub of hot water to keep it fluid. Top up the tub from time to time with more hot water while you are working. Not only will warm rustproofer penetrate seams better, it will flow through the applicator better and not clog so easily. Some people thin the rustproofer with white spirit, but warming it is better. Wash the gun and lances out with white spirit afterwards. If you let the rustproofer set, it is almost impossible to clean them.

Around the Car

☐ Job 3. Chrome trim and seams.

Some rustproofing fluids in aerosol cans are thin enough for injecting behind chromium trim strips and badges but some people find that they are inclined to leave a stain on the paintwork around the trim. As an alternative to a rustproofing fluid, you can use a water dispersant or a thin oil.

☐ Job 4. Doors.

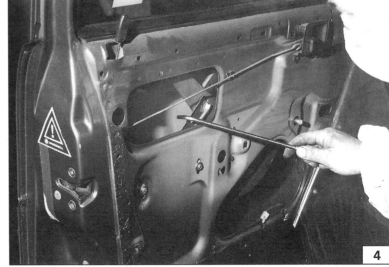

4. Remove the trim panel and carefully "peel" away the clear plastic membrane that covers the door inner cavity. Insert the nozzle to cover all the inside of the door, making sure you get plenty of 'creeping' fluid into the steel joints, where water could collect and corrosion could occur. Naturally, the main problem is that moisture collects in the bottom of the doors and rots them out from the inside - use plenty of fluid here. If you don't want to remove the door trims, then fluid can be sprayed through the lower drain slots, but note that this will only provide protection for the lower surfaces and seams.

☐ Job 5. The "A" post.

5. The "A" post box-section is that part of the body immediately behind the front wings to which the front doors are hinged. Access is gained by unscrewing the courtesy light switch and inserting a flexible nozzle as far as it will go, spraying as it is withdrawn. Feed the nozzle in both directions (up and down) so that all inner surfaces are covered, paying particular attention to the bottom of the post.

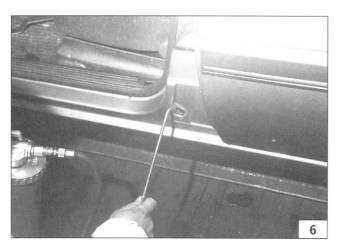

☐ Job 6. The "B" post.

6. Cavaliers made from 1988 will have a grommet fitted to the lower "B" post (the box section that connects the roof to the floor and to which the rear doors are hinged) which gives adequate access if a flexible nozzle is inserted and worked up into the post. Earlier models will need a hole drilled in a similar position to that shown - be sure to cover the hole with a grommet afterwards.

INSIDE INFORMATION: Think carefully before drilling holes to insert rustproofing fluid, especially in the "chassis", where there are numerous holes already. If you do drill a hole in steel, make sure that you file off the rough burrs and then apply an anti-rusting agent, followed by a coating of paint followed by a layer of wax. Make sure the area you drill into is indeed hollow and not the inside of the car or luggage bay! Spend time looking out for wires or pipes. Disconnect the car's battery.

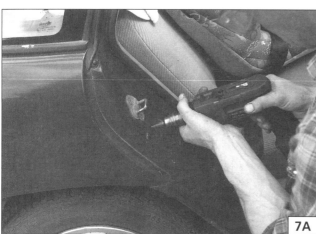

☐ Job 7. The "C" post.

7A. The "C" post is that section of the bodywork up to which the rear doors close. A hole can be drilled here as shown...

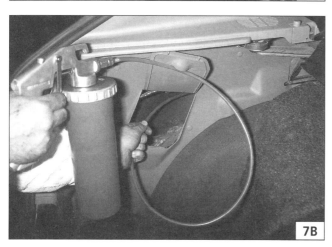

7B. ...or it is possible to insert a flexible nozzle through the boot area, behind the trim, which gives access to most of the "C" post section. Pay particular attention to the lower edges, where the rear wing forms a double skin with the post, a common "rot-spot" on all cars - make sure this area is adequately treated with fluid.

RUSTPROOFING

☐ Job 8. Tailgate/boot lid.

8. Remove the trim panel from the tailgate (the boot lid on some models, while others are "open" already) and work the flexible nozzle into all the strengthening ribs and seams, spraying as the nozzle is drawn out. On tailgates, "wiggle" the nozzle up into the sides of the 'gate around the rear screen aperture. When spraying is complete, close the door/tailgate so that fluid drains down into the bottom seam. Make sure the drain holes remain clear on the bottom edge.

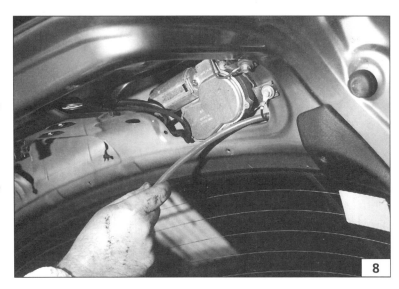

☐ Job 9. Boot/luggage bay area.

9. Remove the pull-away side trims and work the nozzle into the space between the outer wing and the boot/luggage bay "floor", paying particular attention to the lower joint which forms the wheel arch. It is a good idea to remove the rear lamps also, in order to reach the box section beneath them and to adequately treat the upper corners of the wing. Insert the flexible nozzle into the box section that crosses the boot at the rear - holes provided for the wiring harness will give access to this section. Spray the spare wheel compartment (after removing the wheel!) but remember to wipe the excess fluid away before replacing it.

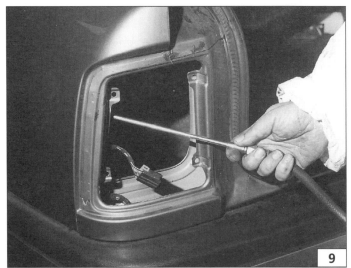

☐ Job 10. Bonnet.

10. Apply fluid into all strengthening ribs and channels on the underside of the bonnet. Some models have a fibre-board insulation cover clipped to the underside - remove this first. Pay attention to the front, rear, and side-seams of the bonnet, making sure sufficient fluid is applied to penetrate the layers of metal. As with the tailgate, close the bonnet after application so that fluid runs down to the front seam.

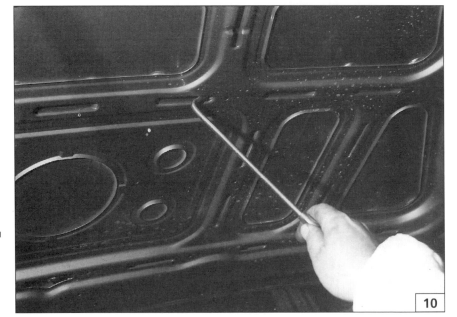

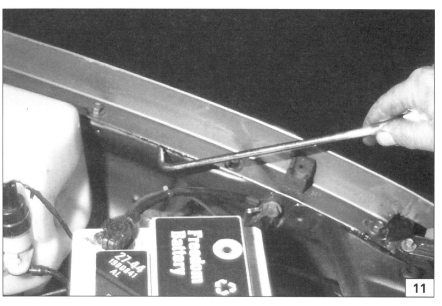

☐ Job 11. Engine bay.

11. Apply fluid to the joints between wings and body and to the wing fixing bolts/washers. Also apply fluid to the suspension tops, behind and beneath the front "slam" panel, down the seams between inner wing and bulkhead. Insert a flexible nozzle to the "apron" at the rear of the engine bay, reaching the seam beneath the panel where the windscreen is fixed, and around the wiper motor and heater blower box. At each end of the rear apron, work the nozzle up into the windscreen pillars, spraying as it is withdrawn.

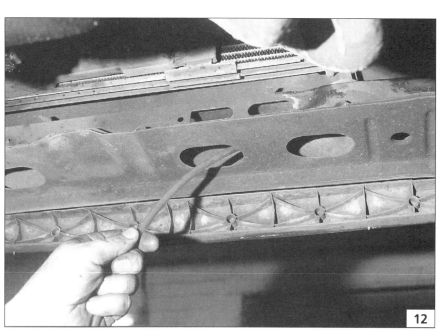

Under the Car

☐ Job 12. Front cross member.

12. Work the flexible nozzle along the cross-member and spray as it is withdrawn, paying particular attention to the end-seams where they join the inner wing "out-riggers" that travel forwards through the engine bay; use the flexible nozzle to treat these sections too, gaining access through the many drain holes already provided.

☐ Job 13. Sills.

13. The sills are arranged with a central strengthening membrane so it is necessary to drill two holes to ensure coverage of the whole sill inner area. Work the flexible nozzle into each hole, in both fore and aft directions, each time spraying as it is withdrawn. Small drainage holes are present on the sill panels - make sure these are clear by poking with a short length of stiff wire. Fluid should issue from all such holes, if you've applied it sufficiently!

RUSTPROOFING

☐ Job 14. Rear 'chassis' sections.

14. Use the flexible nozzle, inserted through the existing drainage/lightening holes and gaps, to treat all enclosed areas of chassis and body box-sections, for instance, the boot floor strengthening ribs, the rear cross member behind the bumper, the coil spring mounts, etc.

☐ Job 15. Spray underside and wheel arches.

THE UNDERSIDE

15. Get yourself prepared for this job! Disposable overalls or old clothes are a necessity and none more so than some form of headgear to protect your hair. Gloves and a face-mask are also essential.

First of all, the thinner, 'creeping' type of fluid is sprayed into and onto every seam. (This would was away if not covered over.) Then, it's time to cover the entire surface with the tougher type of protectant. For this process the thicker, black underbody fluid is used - note that this needs to be warmed by standing in a bucket of very hot water for twenty minutes or so before use. Make doubly sure that the car is safely raised and stable - this is no time to take chances - and ensure any floor protection is in place and secure. Spray the fluid while it is still warm and "thin", taking care to ensure an even coverage with no gaps. When spraying over fuel and brake pipes make at least two passes with the spraygun, at different angles, so that the fluid isn't masked by the pipes which would leave an unprotected "shadow"

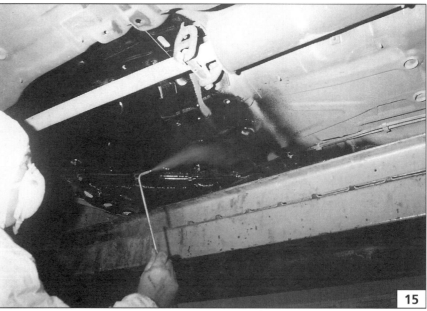

behind them. Start at the front of the car and work backwards, ending with the boot underside and spare wheel well.

THE WHEEL ARCHES

Remove all four wheels and wrap plastic bags around the brake discs or drums. If your car is fitted with plastic "inner splash-guards" it's a good idea to remove them so that the fluid can be applied to the "hidden" seams and surfaces, because they can still get damp, if not wet, and consequently will corrode. Pay particular attention to the outer wheel arch seams - spray "outwards" from inside the wheelarch to ensure good penetration and sealing. Spray also up into the coil spring recesses (suspension tops), varying the angle of the spray gun as the fluid is applied.

Finally, clean any fluid "overspray" from the body work, including the door sills where fluid will have dripped from the door drain holes. Use a good glass cleaner if fluid has found its way onto the windows (it usually does!), especially the windscreen. Also, clean the windscreen wiper blades, as traces of fluid will be smeared across the screen when the wipers are next used and you're unlikely to see much through it! The last job is to fit any grommets into holes you may have drilled - soak them in fluid before fitting, which will provide a very effective seal when the fluid turns to wax over the next week or so.

CHAPTER 6 - FAULT FINDING

This Chapter aims to help you to overcome the main faults that can affect the mobility or safety of your vehicle. It also helps you to overcome the problem that has affected most mechanics - amateur and professional - at one time or another... Blind Spot Syndrome!

It goes like this: the vehicle refuses to start one damp Sunday morning. You decide that there must be no fuel getting through. By the time you've stripped the fuel pump and fuel lines and "unblocked" the fuel tank, it's time for bed. And the next day, the local garage finds that your main HT lead has dropped out of the coil! Something like that has happened to most of us!

Don't jump to conclusions: if your engine won't start or runs badly, if electrical components fail, follow the logical sequence of checks listed here and detailed overleaf, eliminating each "check" (by testing, not by "hunch") before moving on to the next. And remember that the great majority of failures are caused by electrical or ignition faults: only a minor proportion of engine failures come from the fuel system. Follow the sequences shown here - and you'll have a better chance of success in finding that fault. Before carrying out any of the work described in this Chapter please read carefully *Chapter 1, Safety First!*

Engine won't start.

1. Starter motor doesn't turn.

2. Is battery okay?

3. Check battery connections for cleanliness/tightness.

4. Have battery 'drop' test carried out by specialist.

5. Test battery with voltmeter or, preferable, with a hydrometer.

6. Can engine be rotated by hand?

7. If engine cannot be rotated by hand, check for mechanical seizure of power unit, or pinion gear jammed in mesh with flywheel - 'rock' car backwards and forwards until free, or apply spanner to square drive at front end of starter motor.

8. If engine can be rotated by hand, check for loose electrical connections at starter, faulty solenoid, or defective starter motor.

9. Starter motor turns slowly.

10. Battery low on charge or defective - re-charge and have 'drop' test carried out by specialist.

11. Internal fault within starter motor - e.g. worn brushes.

12. Starter motor noisy or harsh.

13. Drive teeth on ring gear or starter pinion worn/broken.

14. Main drive spring broken.

15. Starter motor securing bolts loose.

16. Starter motor turns engine but car will not start. See 'Ignition System' box.

Ignition system.

> **SAFETY FIRST!**
> It is essential that you read **Chapter 1, Safety First!, The Ignition System** before carrying out work on this part of the car.

(Carry out the following checks as appropriate. For example, some vehicles have contact breaker ignition while the majority of modern cars have electronic ignition. Only Step 17 can be carried out on cars with electronic ignition. If any faults are found - **SPECIALIST SERVICE**.)

17. Check for spark at plug (remove plug and prop it with threads resting on bare metal of cylinder block). Do not touch plug or lead while operating starter.

MODELS WITHOUT ELECTRONIC IGNITION ONLY

18. If no spark present at plug, check for spark at contact breaker points when 'flicked' open (ignition 'on'). Double-check to ensure that points are clean and correctly gapped, and try again.

19. If spark present at contact breaker points, check for spark at central high tension lead from

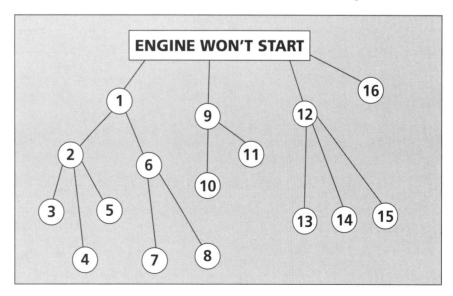

coil. NOTE: Don't carry out this check with electronic ignition systems. An uncontrolled spark can, in some cases, seriously damage the ECU (Electronic Control Unit).

20. If spark present at central high tension lead from coil, check distributor cap and rotor arm; replace if cracked or contacts badly worn.

21. If distributor cap and rotor arm are okay, check high tension leads and connections - replace leads if they are old, carbon core type suppressed variety.

22. If high tension leads are sound but dirty or damp, clean/dry them.

23. If high tension leads okay, check/clean/dry/re-gap sparking plugs.

24. Damp conditions? Apply water dispellant spray to ignition system.

25. If no spark present at contact breaker points (cars without electronic ignition only), examine connections of low tension leads between ignition switch and coil, and from coil to contact breaker (including short low-tension lead within distributor).

26. If low tension circuit connections okay, examine wiring.

27. If low tension wiring is sound, is capacitor okay? If in doubt, fit new capacitor.

28. If capacitor is okay, check for spark at central high tension lead from coil. NOTE: DON'T carry out this check with electronic ignition systems. An uncontrolled spark can, in some cases, seriously damage the ECU (Electronic Control Unit).

29. If no spark present at central high tension lead from coil, check for poor high tension lead connections.

30. If high tension lead connections okay, is coil okay? If in doubt, fit new coil.

31. If spark present at plug, is it powerful or weak? If weak, see '27' (non-electronic ignition models only).

32. If spark is healthy, check ignition timing.

33. If ignition timing is okay, see 'Fuel System' box.

Fuel system.

FUEL INJECTED ENGINES ONLY

34. Do not disconnect fuel pipes to check fuel flow, as system is pressurised; check fuel pump operation by listening for "buzz" when ignition is switched on - buzz should last no more than 1 or 2 seconds; if longer, suspect fuel pump. If no buzz, suspect fuel pump relay - seek professional help.

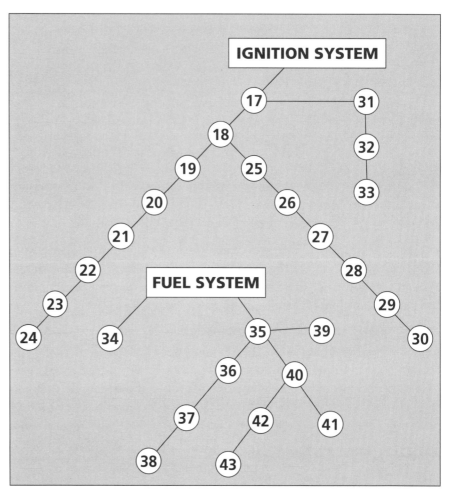

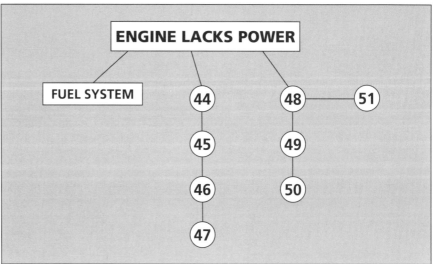

NON FUEL INJECTED ENGINES ONLY

35. Check briefly for fuel at feed pipe to carb. See 36. If no fuel present at feed pipe, is petrol tank empty? (Rock car and listen for 'sloshing' in tank, as well as looking at gauge).

36. Check for a defective fuel pump. With outlet pipe disconnected AND AIMED AWAY FROM HOT EXHAUST COMPONENTS, ETC. as well as your eyes and clothes, and into a suitable container, turn the engine over (manual

*SAFETY FIRST! Before working on the fuel system, read **Chapter 1, Safety First!** Take special care to 1) only work out of doors, 2) wear suitable gloves and goggles and keep fuel out of eyes and away from skin: 3) if fuel does come into contact with skin, wash off straight away, 4) if fuel gets into your eyes, wash out with copious amounts of clean, cold water. Seek medical advice if necessary, 5) when testing for fuel flow, pump into a sufficiently large container, minimising splashes, 6) don't smoke, work near flames or sparks or work when the engine or exhaust are hot.*

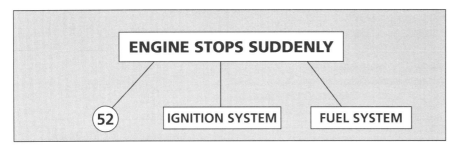

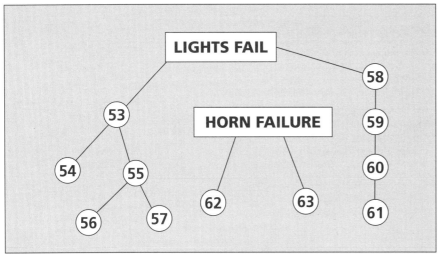

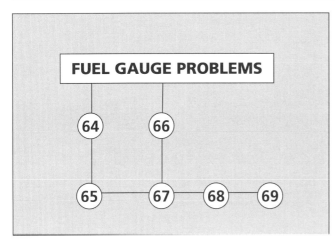

47. If oil level okay, check for slipping fan belt, cylinder head gasket 'blown', partial mechanical seizure of engine, blocked or damaged exhaust system.

48. If engine temperature is normal, check cylinder compressions.

49. If cylinder compression readings low, add a couple of teaspoons of engine oil to each cylinder in turn, and repeat test. If readings don't improve, suspect burnt valves/seats.

50. If compression readings improve after adding oil as described, suspect worn cylinder bores, pistons and rings.

51. If compression readings are normal, check for mechanical problems, for example, binding brakes, slipping clutch, partially seized transmission, etc.

Engine stops suddenly.

52. Check for sudden ingress of water/snow onto ignition components, in adverse weather conditions. Sudden failure is almost always because of an ignition fault. Check for simple wiring and connection breakdowns.

Lights fail.

53. Sudden failure - check fuses.

54. If all lamps affected, check switch and main wiring feeds.

55. If not all lamps are affected, check bulbs on lamps concerned.

56. If bulbs appear to be okay, check bulb holder(s), local wiring and connections.

57. If bulb(s) blown, replace!

58. Intermittent operation, flickering or poor light output.

59. Check earth (ground) connections(s).

60. If earth(s) okay, check switch.

61. If switch okay, check wiring and connections.

Horn failure.

62. If horn does not operate, check fuse, all connections (particularly earths/grounds) and cables. Remove horn connections and check/clean. Use 12v test lamp to ascertain power getting to horn.

63. If horn will not stop(!), disconnect the horn and check for earthing of cable between button and horn unit and the wiring and contacts in the horn switch housing. **SPECIALIST SERVICE.** Horn wiring and connections are more complex than they appear at first. If necessary, have them checked by a specialist.

pump) or switch on ignition (electric pump) and fuel should issue from pump outlet.

37. If pump is okay, check for blocked fuel filter or pipe, or major leak in pipe between tank and pump, or between pump and carb.

38. If the filter is clean and the pump operates, suspect blocked carburettor jet(s) or damaged/sticking float, or incorrectly adjusted carburettor.

39. If there is petrol in the tank but none issues from the feed pipe from pump to carburettor, check that the small vent hole in the fuel filler cap is not blocked and causing a vacuum. NOTE: On some cars there is no vent hole in the filler cap. Other arrangements are made for venting the tank. There are many systems - **SPECIALIST SERVICE.**

40. If fuel is present at carburettor feed pipe, remove spark plugs and check whether wet with unburnt fuel.

41. If the spark plugs are fuel-soaked, check that the choke is operating as it should and is not jammed 'shut'. Other possibilities include float needle valve(s) sticking 'open' or leaking, float punctured, carburettor incorrectly adjusted or air filter totally blocked. Clean plugs before replacing.

42. If the spark plugs are dry, check whether the float needle valve is jammed 'shut'.

43. Check for severe air leak at inlet manifold gasket or carburettor gasket. Incorrectly set valve clearances.

Engine lacks power.

44. Engine overheating. Check oil temperature gauge (where fitted). Low oil pressure light may come on.

45. Air cleaner intake thermostat not opening/closing at the correct temperatures. Replace or free-off as necessary.

46. If thermostat okay, check oil level. BEWARE - DIPSTICK AND OIL MAY BE VERY HOT.

Fuel gauge problems.

64. Gauge reads 'empty' - check for fuel in tank!

65. If fuel is present in tank, check for earthing of wiring from tank to gauge, and for wiring disconnections.

66. Gauge permanently reads 'full', regardless of tank contents. Check wiring and connections as in '65'.

67. If wiring and connections all okay, sender unit/fuel gauge defective.

68. With wiring disconnected, check for continuity between fuel gauge terminals. Do

NOT test gauge by short-circuiting to earth. Replace unit if faulty.

69. If gauge is okay, disconnect wiring from tank sender unit and check for continuity between terminal and case. Replace sender unit if faulty.

FACT FILE: EMERGENCY STARTING

Pushing or Towing

NOTE: This is not possible for vehicles with automatic transmission. Diesel engines: only attempt in warm weather or with a warm engine.

Turn off all unnecessary electrical load; switch on ignition and depress the clutch pedal. Select second of third gear; release the clutch when the car reaches a person's running speed.

Starting with Jump Leads

> **Safety First!**
> This process can be dangerous and the following instructions must be followed to the letter. Also see **Chapter One, Safety First!** and the relevant part of **Chapter 3** for information on safe handling of car batteries.

Ensure that the battery providing the jump start has the same voltage (12 volt) as the

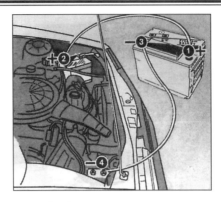
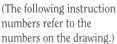

battery fitted to your car.

Do not lean over the battery during jump starting.

Switch off all unnecessary electrical loads and apply the hand brake. Auto. Transmission: Place gear selector in 'P'. Manual Transmission: Place gear shift lever in neutral.

Note that on some batteries and on battery connections, '+' (positive) terminals are coloured red and '-' (negative) terminals are coloured blue or black.

Run the engine of the vehicle providing the

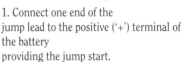
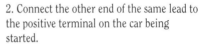

jump start (if battery fitted to vehicle).

(The following instruction numbers refer to the numbers on the drawing.)

1. Connect one end of the jump lead to the positive ('+') terminal of the battery providing the jump start.

2. Connect the other end of the same lead to the positive terminal on the car being started.

3. Connect one end of the other jump lead to the negative ('-') terminal on the 'slave' battery...

4. ...and the other end to the negative battery lead on the car, or to some bare metal in the car's engine bay.

Now try to start the car as quickly as is reasonably possible.

IT IS IMPORTANT that the leads are removed in the exact reverse sequence to that shown above. Keep hands, hair and loose clothing away from moving parts in both engine bays.

Supplementary information - diesel engines

The following fault finding chart covers only those parts of the system that can be checked at home. If a simple solution is not found, it will be necessary to call on the services of a main dealer or diesel injection specialist.

1. No fuel. *If the tank is allowed to run dry, the system will have to be bled.*

2. Fuel blockages from the tank to the pump can be checked at home. *However, see Safety First! below...*

> **SAFETY FIRST!**
> It is most important that any checks on the fuel system from the pump to the engine are carried out by a specialist. The high pressure means that a blockage is unlikely but also means that there is a safety hazard involved in working on this part of the system. Very high pressure can remain in the system even when the engine is not running.

3. Air in fuel system. *Bleed as described in Chapter 3, Servicing Your Car.*

4. Glow plugs (cold engine). These only fail after a very high mileage and usually one at a time. The usual symptom is an engine which starts, misfires and smokes badly until warmed up. *Proper checking is usually a SPECIALIST SERVICE job.*

5. Slow cranking speed. *Can be caused by bad electrical connections or a flat battery.*

6. Worn bores will affect a diesel engine more severely than a petrol engine. *A worn out engine is less likely to start or run properly.*

7. Stop control faulty. *Check that the solenoid in the stop control "clicks" when the solenoid is switched on or off, in which case you can assume it is*

working. If a manually-controlled valve is fitted, check that the valve at the pump operates when the knob is moved. Otherwise this is also a SPECIALIST SERVICE job.

8. Injection pump faulty. **SPECIALIST SERVICE**

9. Injector faulty. **SPECIALIST SERVICE**

10. Injector feed pipe leaking. **SPECIALIST SERVICE**

	1	2	3	4	5	6	7	8	9	10
Engine will not start	✓	✓	✓	✓	✓	✓	✓	✓		
Engine will not stop							✓			
Engine misfires	✓						✓		✓	✓
Excessive (black) smoke from exhaust								✓	✓	

CHAPTER 7
GETTING THROUGH THE MOT

This Chapter is for owners in Britain whose vehicles need to pass the 'MoT' test. The Test was first established in 1961 by the then Ministry of Transport and it attempts to ensure that vehicles using British roads reach minimum standards of safety. Approximately 40 per cent of vehicles submitted for the test fail it, but many of these failures could be avoided by knowing what the vehicle might 'fall down on', and by taking appropriate remedial action before the test 'proper' is carried out.

It is true that the scope of the test has been considerably enlarged in the past few years, with the result that it is correspondingly more difficult to be sure that your vehicle will reach the required standards. In truth, however, a careful examination of the relevant areas, perhaps a month or so before the current certificate expires, will highlight components which require attention, and enable any obvious faults to be rectified before you take the vehicle for the test.

Getting Ahead

It is also worth noting that a vehicle can be submitted for a test up to a month before the current certificate expires - if the vehicle passes, the new certificate will be valid for one year from the day of expiry of the old one, provided that the old certificate is produced at the time of the test.

PART I: THE BACKGROUND

Keeping Up To Date

Alterations are being made to the Test on a regular basis - almost always making it tougher than it was before. It is MOST IMPORTANT that UK owners find out for themselves about any changes in the requirements that might have been made since this book was written. Your local MoT Testing Station should be able to help - if not, take your custom elsewhere! Also, non-UK owners should obtain information on the legal requirements in their own territory - and act accordingly.

Making A Good Impression

If your vehicle is muddy or particularly dirty (especially underneath) it would be worth giving it a thorough clean a day or two before carrying out the inspection so that it has ample time to dry. Do the same before the real MoT test. A clean vehicle makes a better impression on the examiner, who can refuse to test a vehicle which is particularly dirty underneath.

On the other hand, a clean vehicle makes a better impression and it will help the examiner to see what he is supposed to be examining. Generally, this will work in the owner's favour. For example, if a component or an area of underbody or chassis is particularly difficult to examine due to a build-up of oily dirt etc., and if the examiner is in doubt about its condition, he is entitled to fail that component because it was not possible for him to conclude that it reached the required standard. Had it been clean, it might well have been tested, and passed!

MoT testers do not dismantle assemblies during the test but you may wish to do so during your pretest check-up for a better view of certain wearing parts, such as the rear brake

SAFETY FIRST!
The MoT tester will follow a set procedure and we will cover the ground in a similar way, starting inside the vehicle, then continuing outside, under the bonnet, underneath the vehicle, etc. When preparing to go underneath the vehicle, do ensure that it is jacked on firm level ground and then supported on axle stands or ramps which are adequate for the task. Wheels which remain on the ground should have chocks in front of and behind them, and while the rear wheels remain on the ground, the hand brake should be firmly ON. For most repair and replacement jobs under your vehicle these normal precautions will suffice. However, the vehicle needs to be even more stable than usual when carrying out these checks. There must be no risk of it toppling off its stands while suspension and steering components are being pushed and pulled in order to test them. Read carefully Chapter 1, Safety First! and the first part of Chapter 3, Servicing Your Car for further important information on raising and supporting a vehicle above the ground.

shoes for example. See *Chapter 3, Servicing Your Car* for information on how to check the brakes.

Buying And Selling

This chapter provides a procedure for checking your vehicle's condition prior to its official MoT test. The same procedure could be equally useful to UK and non-UK owners alike when examining vehicles prior to purchase (or sale for that matter). However, it must be emphasised that the official MoT certificate should not be regarded as any guarantee of the condition of a vehicle. All it proves is that the vehicle reached the required standards, in the opinion of a particular examiner, at the time and date it was tested.

Pass The MoT!

The aim of this chapter is to explain what is actually tested on a vehicle and (if it is not obvious) how the test is done. This should enable you to identify and eliminate problems before they undermine the safety or diminish the performance of your vehicle and long before they cause the expense and inconvenience of a test failure.

Tool Box

Dismantling apart, few tools are needed for testing. A light hammer is useful for tapping panels underneath the vehicle when looking for rust. If this produces a bright metallic noise, then the area being tapped is solid metal. If the noise produced is dull, the area contains rust or filler. When tapping sills and box sections, listen also for the sound of debris (that is, rust flakes) on the inside of the panel. Use a screwdriver to prod weak parts of panels. This may produce holes of course, but if the panels have rusted to that extent, you really ought to know about it. A strong lever (such as a tyre lever) can be useful for applying the required force to suspension joints etc. when assessing whether there is any wear in them.

You will need an assistant to operate controls and perhaps to wobble the road wheels while you inspect components under the vehicle.

Age Related Checks

Two more brief explanations are required before you start your informal test. Firstly, the age of the vehicle determines exactly which lights, seat belts and other items it should have. Frequently in the next few pages you will come across the phrase "Cars first used ..." followed by a date. A vehicle's "first used" date is either its date of first registration, or the date six months after it was manufactured, whichever was earlier. Or, if the vehicle was originally used without being registered (such as a vehicle which has been imported to the U.K. or an ex-H.M. Forces model, etc.) the "first used" date is the date of manufacture.

Rust And Load Bearing Areas

Secondly, there must not be excessive rust, serious distortion or any fractures affecting certain prescribed areas of the bodywork. These prescribed areas are load-bearing parts of the bodywork within 30 cm (12 in.) of anchorages or mounting points associated with testable items such as seat belts, brake pedal assemblies, master cylinders, servos, suspension and

steering components and also body mountings. Keep this rule in mind while inspecting the vehicle, but remember also that even if such damage occurs outside a prescribed area, it can cause failure of the test. Failure will occur if the damage is judged to reduce the continuity or strength of a main load-bearing part of the bodywork sufficiently to have an adverse effect on the braking or steering.

The following notes are necessarily abbreviated, and are for assistance only. They are not a definitive guide to all the MoT regulations. It is also worth mentioning that the varying degrees of discretion of individual MoT testers can mean that there are variations between the standards as applied. However, the following points should help to make you aware of the aspects which will be examined. Now, if you have your clipboard, checklist and pencil handy, let's make a start...

The 'Easy' Bits

Checking these items is straightforward and should not take more than a few minutes - and could avoid an embarrassingly simple failure...

Lights

Within the scope of the test are headlights, side and tail lights, brake lights, direction indicators, and number plate lights (plus rear fog lights on all cars first used on or after 1 April, 1980, and any earlier cars subsequently so equipped, and also hazard warning lights on any vehicle so fitted). All must operate, must be clean and not significantly damaged; flickering is also not permitted. The switches should also all work properly. Pairs of lights should give approximately the same intensity of light output, and operation of one set of lights should not affect the working of another - such trouble is usually due to bad earthing.

Front fog and spot lights are not part of the MoT test (although their use is covered by *Construction and Use* regulations so that, for instance, spot lights should go out when headlights are turned off main beam) and won't be tested, provided they're not a physical hazard. Rear fog lights are part of the Test however. See later in this Chapter for details.

Indicators should flash at between 60 and 120 times per minute. 'Rev' the engine to encourage them, if a little slow (although the examiner might not let you get away with it!) Otherwise, renew the (inexpensive) flasher unit and check all wiring and earth connections.

Interior 'tell-tale' lights, such as for indicators, rear fog lights and hazard warning lights should all operate in unison with their respective exterior lights.

Headlight aim must be correct - in particular, the lights should not dazzle other road users. An approximate guide can be obtained by shining the lights against a vertical wall, but final adjustment may be necessary by reference to the beam checking machine at the MoT station. Most testers will be happy to make slight adjustments where necessary but only if the adjusters work. Make sure before you take the vehicle in that they are not seized solid!

Reflectors must be unbroken, clean, and not obscured - for example, by stickers.

Wheels And Tyres

Check the wheels for loose nuts, cracks, and damaged rims. Missing wheel nuts or studs are also failure points, naturally enough!

There is no excuse for running on illegal tyres. The legal requirement is that there must be at least 1.6 mm of tread depth remaining, over the 'central' three-quarters of the width of the tyre all the way around. From this it can be deduced that there is no legal requirement to have 1.6 mm (1/16 in.) of tread on the 'shoulders' of the tyre, but in practice, most MoT stations will be reluctant to pass a tyre in this condition. In any case, for optimum safety - especially 'wet grip' - you would be well advised to change tyres when they wear down to around 3 mm (1/8 in.) or so depth of remaining tread.

Visible 'tread wear indicator bars', found approximately every nine inches around the tread of the tyre, are highlighted when the tread reaches the critical 1.6 mm point.

Tyres should not show signs of cuts or bulges, rubbing on the bodywork or running gear, and the valves should be in sound condition, and correctly aligned.

Old-fashioned cross-ply and radial-ply tyre types must not be mixed on the same axle, and if pairs of cross-ply and radial-ply tyres are fitted, the radials must be on the rear axle.

Windscreen

The screen must not be damaged (by cracks, chips, etc.) or obscured so that the driver does not have a clear view of the road. Permissible size of damage points depends on where they occur. Within an area 290 mm (nearly 12 in.) wide, ahead of the driver, and up to the top of the wiper arc, any damage must be confined within a circle less than 10 mm (approx. 0.4 in.) in diameter. This is increased to 40 mm (just over 1.5 in.) for damage within the rest of the screen area swept by the wipers.

Washers And Wipers

The wipers must clear an area big enough to give the driver a clear view forwards and to the side of the vehicle. The wiper blades must be securely attached and sound, with no cracks or 'missing' sections. The wiper switch should also work properly. The screen washers must supply the screen with sufficient liquid to keep it clean, in conjunction with the use of the wipers.

Mirrors

Your vehicle must have at least two, one of which must be on the driver's side. The mirrors must be visible from the driver's seat, and not damaged or obscured so that the view to the rear is affected. Therefore cracks, chips and discolouration can mean failure.

Horn

The horn must emit a uniform note which is loud enough to give adequate warning of approach, and the switch must operate correctly. Multi-tone horns playing 'in sequence' are not permitted, but two tones sounding together are fine.

Seat Security

The seats must be securely mounted, and the sub-frames should be sound.

Seat Belts

Seat belts must be in good condition (i.e. not frayed or otherwise damaged), and the buckles and catches should also operate correctly. Inertia reel types, where fitted, should retract properly.

Belt mountings must be secure, with no structural damage or corrosion within 30 cm (12 in.) of them.

Number (Registration) Plates

Both front and rear number plates must be present, and in good condition, with no breaks or missing numbers or letters. The plates must not be obscured, and the digits must not be repositioned (to form names, for instance).

Vehicle Identification Numbers (VIN)

Vehicles first used on or after 1 August, 1980 have to have a clearly displayed VIN - Vehicle Identification Number (or old-fashioned 'chassis numbers' for older cars) which is plainly legible. See *Chapter 2, Buying Guide* for the correct location on your vehicle.

Exhaust System

The entire system must be present, properly mounted, free of leaks and should not be noisy - which can happen when the internal baffles fail. 'Proper' repairs by welding, or exhaust cement, or bandage are acceptable, as long as no gas leaks are evident. Then again, common sense, if not the MoT, dictates that exhaust bandage should only be a very short-term emergency measure. For safety's sake, fit a new exhaust if yours is reduced to this!

PART II: THE CHECKLIST

You've checked the easy bits - now it's time for the detail! Some of the 'easy bits' referred to above are included here, but this is intended as a more complete check list to give your vehicle the best possible chance of gaining a First Class Honours, MoT Pass!

Inside The Vehicle

☐ 1. The steering wheel should be examined for cracks and for damage which might interfere with its use, or injure the driver's hands. It should also be pushed and pulled along the column axis, and also up and down, at 90 degrees to it. This will highlight any deficiencies in the wheel and upper column mounting/bearing, and also any excessive end float, and movement between the column shaft and the wheel. Look, too, for movement in the steering column couplings and fasteners (including the universal joint if applicable), and visually check their condition and security. They must be sound, and properly tightened.

GETTING THROUGH THE MOT

In the case of cars (the majority) with steering racks, rotate the steering wheel in both directions to test for free play at the wheel rim - this shouldn't exceed approximately 13 mm. (0.5 in.), assuming a 380 mm. (15 in.) diameter steering wheel.

In the case of the smaller number of cars with steering boxes, free play at the wheel rim shouldn't exceed approximately 75 mm (3.0 in.), assuming a 380 mm (15 in.) diameter steering wheel.

In both cases where the steering wheel is larger or smaller the amount of permissible free play should be raised or lowered accordingly.

☐ 2. Check that the switches for headlights, sidelights, rear fog lights direction indicators, hazard warning lights, wipers, washers and horn, appear to be in good working order and check that the tell-tale lights or audible warnings are working where applicable.

☐ 3. Make sure that the windscreen wipers operate effectively with blades that are secure and in good condition. The windscreen washer should provide sufficient liquid to clear the screen in conjunction with the wipers.

☐ 4. Check for windscreen damage, especially in the area swept by the wipers. From the MoT tester's point of view, Zone A is part of this area, 290 mm (11.5 in.) wide and centred on the centre of the steering wheel. Damage to the screen within this area should be capable of fitting into a 10 mm (approx. 0.4 in.) diameter circle and the cumulative effect of more minor damage should not seriously restrict the driver's view. Windscreen stickers or other obstructions should not encroach more than 10 mm (approx 0.4 in.) into this area. In the remainder of the swept area the maximum diameter of damage or degree of encroachment by obstructions is 40 mm (approx. 1.6 in.) and there is no ruling regarding cumulative

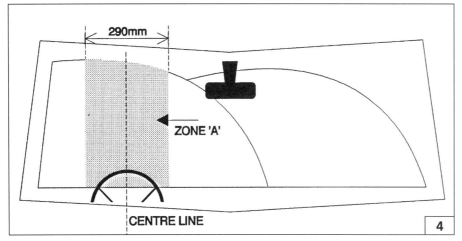

multi-tone horns (which alternate between two or more notes) are not permitted at all. On cars first used after 1 August 1973, the horn should produce a constant, continuous or uniform note which is neither harsh nor grating.

☐ 6. There must be one exterior mirror on the driver's side of the vehicle and one other mirror - either an exterior mirror fitted to the passenger's side or an interior mirror. The required mirrors should be secure and in good condition.

☐ 7. Check that the hand brake operates effectively without coming to the end of its working travel. The lever and its mechanism must be complete, securely mounted, unobstructed in its travel and in a sufficiently good condition to remain firmly in the "On" position even when knocked from side to side. The 30 cm rule on bodywork corrosion applies in the vicinity of the hand brake lever mounting.

☐ 8. The foot brake pedal assembly should be complete, unobstructed, and in a good working condition, including the pedal rubber (which should not have been worn smooth). There should be no excessive movement of the pedal at right angles to its normal direction. When fully depressed, the pedal should not be at the end of its travel. The pedal should not feel spongy (indicating air in the hydraulic system), nor should it tend to creep downwards while held under pressure (which indicates an internal hydraulic leak).

☐ 9. Seats must be secure on their mountings and seat backs must be capable of being locked in the upright position.

☐ 10. The law requires all models to be fitted with seatbelts for the driver and front passenger. These have to be three-point lap and diagonal belts. Rear seat belts are a requirement for vehicles first used after 31 March 1987 with three anchorage points for the 'outer' passengers, and at least a lap belt only for the centre passenger position. Examine seat belt webbing and fittings to make sure that all are in good condition and that anchorages are firmly attached to the vehicle's structure. Locking mechanisms should be capable of remaining locked, and of being released if required, when under load. Flexible buckle stalks (if fitted) should be free of corrosion, broken cable strands or other weaknesses. Note that any belts fitted which are not part of a legal requirements may be examined by the tester but will not form part of the official test.

damage. Specialist windscreen companies can often repair a cracked screen for a lot less than the cost of replacement. Moreover, the cost of repair is often covered by comprehensive insurance policies. DIY repair kits are also available.

☐ 5. The horn control should be present, secure and readily accessible to the driver, and the horn should be loud enough to be heard by other road users. Gongs, bells and sirens are not permitted (except as part of an anti-theft device) and

☐ 11. On inertia reel belts, check that on retracting the belts, the webbing winds into the retracting unit automatically, albeit with some manual assistance to start with.

☐ 12. Note the point raised earlier regarding corrosion around seat belt anchorage points. The MoT tester will not carry out any dismantling here, but he will examine floor mounted anchorage points from underneath the vehicle if that is possible.

☐ 13. Before getting out of the vehicle, make sure that both doors can be opened from the inside.

Outside The Vehicle

☐ 14. Before closing the driver's door, check the condition of the inner sill. Usually the MoT tester will do this by applying finger or thumb pressure to various parts of the panel while the floor covering remains in place. For your own peace of mind, look beneath the sill covering, taking great care not to tear any covering. Then close the driver's door and make sure that it latches securely and repeat these checks on the nearside inner sill and door.

Now check all of the lights, front and rear, (and the number plate lights) while your assistant operates the light switches.

☐ 15. As we said earlier, you can carry out a rough and ready check on headlight alignment for yourself, although it will certainly not be as accurate as having it done for you at the MoT testing station. Drive your vehicle near to a wall, as shown. Check that your tyres are correctly inflated and the vehicle is on level ground.

Draw on the wall, with chalk:
• a horizontal line about 2 metres long, and at same height as centre of headlight lenses.
• two vertical lines about 1 metre long, each forming a cross with the horizontal line and the same distance apart as the headlight centres.
• another vertical line to form a cross on the horizontal line, midway between the others.

Now position your vehicle so that:
• it faces the wall squarely, and its centre line is in line with centre line marked on the wall.
• the steering is straight.
• headlight lenses are 5.0 metres (16 ft.) from the wall.

Switch on the headlights' 'main' and 'dipped' beams in turn and measure their centre points. You will be able to judge any major discrepancies in intensity and aim prior to having the beams properly set by a garage with beam measuring equipment.

Headlights should be complete, clean, securely mounted, in good working order and not adversely affected by the operation of another lamp, and these basic requirements affect all the lights listed below. Headlights must dip as a pair from a single switch. Their aim must be correctly adjusted and they should not be affected (even to the extent of flickering) when lightly tapped by hand. Each headlight should match its partner in terms of size, colour and intensity of light, and can be white or yellow.

☐ 16. Side lights should show white light to the front and red light to the rear. Lenses should not be broken, cracked or incomplete. Stop lights must be red, of course.

☐ 17. Check your indicators, doing what the MoT tester will do: turn on side lights and apply the brake lights while ensuring that the indicators still work properly, and that none of the lights interfere with each other, causing dimness or intermittent failure. Check side repeater lights, too.

☐ 18. Vehicles first used before 1 April 1986 do not have to have a hazard warning device, but if one is fitted, it must be tested, and it must operate with the ignition switch either on or off. The lights should flash 60-120 times per minute, and indicators must operate independently of any other lights.

☐ 19. There must be two red rear reflectors - always fitted by the manufacturers, of course! - which are clean and are securely and symmetrically fitted to the vehicle.

☐ 20. Your vehicle must have at least one rear fog light fitted to the centre or offside of the vehicle. If there are two, they must be spaced an equal distance from the centre. It must comply with the basic requirements (listed under headlights) and emit a steady red light. Its tell-tale light, inside the vehicle, must work to inform the driver that it is switched on.

☐ 21. There must be registration number plates at the front and rear of the vehicle and both must be clean, secure, complete and unobscured. Letters and figures must be correctly formed and correctly spaced and not likely to be misread due to an uncovered securing bolt or whatever. The year letter counts as a figure. The space between letters and figures must be at least twice that between adjacent letters or figures.

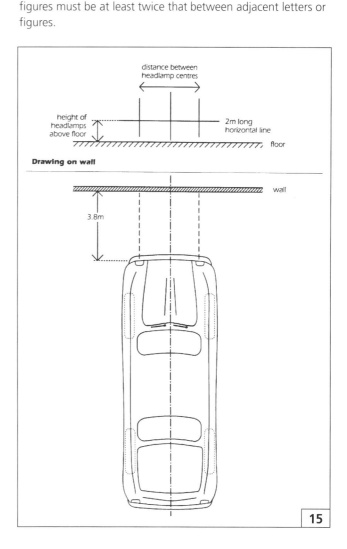

distance between headlamp centres

height of headlamps above floor

2m long horizontal line

floor

Drawing on wall

wall

3.8m

15

☐ 22. Number plate lights must be present, working, and must not flicker when tapped by hand, just as for other lights. Where more than one light or bulb was fitted as original equipment, all must be working.

Wheels And Tyres

The MoT tester will examine tyres and wheels while walking around the vehicle and again when he is underneath it.

☐ 23. Front tyres should match each other and rear tyres should match each other, both sets matching in terms of size, aspect ratio and type of structure. For example, you must never fit tyres of different sizes or types, such as cross-ply or radial, on the same 'axle' - both front wheels counting as 'on the same axle' in this context. If cross-ply or bias belted tyres are fitted to the rear of the car, you must not fit radial-ply tyres to the front. If cross-ply tyres are fitted to the rear, bias belted tyres should not be fitted to the front. (We recommend that you do not mix tyre types anywhere on the car.)

☐ 24. Failure of the test can be caused by a cut, lump, tear or bulge in a tyre, exposed ply or cord, a badly seated tyre, a re-cut tyre, a tyre fouling part of the vehicle, or a seriously damaged or misaligned valve stem which could cause sudden deflation of the tyre. To pass the test, the grooves of the tread pattern must be at least 1.6 mm deep throughout a continuous band comprising the central three-quarters of the breadth of tread, and round the entire outer circumference of the tyre.

We are grateful to Dunlop/SP Tyres for the photographs and information in this section.

☐ 24A. Modern tyres have tread wear indicators built into the tread groves (usually about eight of them spread equidistantly around the circumference). These appear as continuous bars running across the tread when the original pattern depth has worn down to 1.6 mm. There will be a distinct reduction in wet grip well before the tread wear indicators start to show, and you should replace tyres before they get to this stage, even though this is the legal minimum in the UK.

NEW TYRE   ILLEGAL TYRE   24A

☐ 24B. Lumps and bulges in the tyre wall usually arise from accidental damage or even because of faults in the tyre construction. You should run your hand all the way around the side wall of the tyre, with the vehicle either jacked off the ground, or moving the vehicle half a wheels revolution, so that you can check the part of the tyre that was previously resting on the ground. Since you can't easily check the insides of the tyres in day-to-day use, it is even more important that you spend time carefully checking the inside of each tyre - the MoT tester will certainly do so! Tyres with bulges in them must be scrapped and replaced with new, since they can fail suddenly, causing your vehicle to lose control.

24B

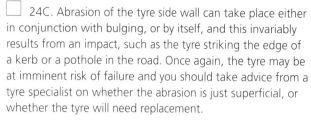

24C. Abrasion of the tyre side wall can take place either in conjunction with bulging, or by itself, and this invariably results from an impact, such as the tyre striking the edge of a kerb or a pothole in the road. Once again, the tyre may be at imminent risk of failure and you should take advice from a tyre specialist on whether the abrasion is just superficial, or whether the tyre will need replacement.

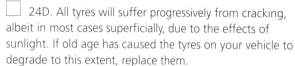

24D. All tyres will suffer progressively from cracking, albeit in most cases superficially, due to the effects of sunlight. If old age has caused the tyres on your vehicle to degrade to this extent, replace them.

24E. If the outer edges of the tread are worn noticeably more than the centre, the tyres have been run under inflated which not only ruins tyres, but causes worse fuel consumption, dangerous handling and is, of course, illegal.

Over-inflation causes the centre part of the tyre to wear more quickly than the outer edges. This is also illegal but in addition, it causes the steering and grip to suffer and the tyre becomes more susceptible to concussion damage.

24F. Incorrect wheel alignment causes one side of the tyre to wear more severely than the other. If your vehicle should hit a kerb or large pothole, it is worthwhile having the wheel alignment checked by a tyre specialist since this costs considerably less than new front tyres!

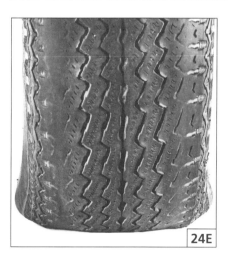

25. Road wheels must be secure and must not be badly damaged, distorted or cracked, or have badly distorted bead rims (perhaps due to "kerbing"), or loose or missing wheel nuts, studs or bolts.

26. Check the bodywork for any sharp edges or projections, caused by corrosion or damage, which could prove dangerous to other road users, including pedestrians.

27. Check that the fuel cap fastens securely and that its sealing washer is neither torn nor deteriorated, or its mounting flange damaged sufficiently to allow fuel to escape (for example, while the vehicle is cornering).

Under The Bonnet

28. The vehicle should have a Vehicle Identification Number fitted to the bodywork. This can be on a plate secured to the vehicle or, etched or stamped on the bodywork. See *Chapter 2, Buying Guide* for more information.

29. Check the steering rack or box for security by asking your assistant to turn the steering wheel from side to side (with the road wheels on the ground) while you watch what happens under the bonnet. Then, check for free play in the steering assembly as a whole. This is done by turning the steering wheel from side to side as far as possible without moving the road wheels - and

measuring how far the steering wheel can be moved in this way. More than 75 mm (approx. 3 in.) of free play, on a steering box system, or 13 mm (approx. 0.5 in.), on a steering rack, at the perimeter of the steering wheel, due to wear in the steering components, is sufficient grounds for a test failure. Note that the free play is based on a steering wheel diameter of 380 mm (approx 15 in) and will be less for smaller steering wheels - which all of them virtually are! Also check for the presence and security of retaining and locking devices in the steering column assembly.

☐ 30. While peering under the bonnet, check that hydraulic master cylinders and reservoirs are securely mounted and not severely corroded or otherwise damaged. Ensure that the caps are present, that fluid levels are satisfactory and that there are no fluid leaks.

☐ 31. Also check that the brake servo is securely mounted and not damaged or corroded to an extent that would impair its operation. Vacuum pipes should be sound, that is, free from kinks, splits and excessive chafing and not collapsed internally.

☐ 32. Still under the bonnet have a thorough search for evidence of excessive corrosion, severe distortion or fracture in any load bearing panelling within 30 cm (12 in.) of important mounting points such as the master cylinder/servo mounting, front suspension mountings etc.

Under The Vehicle - Front End

☐ **33. SAFETY FIRST! On some occasions there is no alternative but for your assistant to sit in the vehicle whilst you go beneath. Therefore: 1) Place ramps as well as axle stands beneath the vehicle's structure so that it cannot fall. 2) Don't allow your assistant to move vigorously or get in or out of the vehicle while you are beneath it. If either of these are problematical, DON'T CARRY OUT CHECK 34 - leave it to your garage.**

☐ 34. Have an assistant turn the steering wheel from side to side while you watch for movement in the steering mechanism. Make sure that the rack or box mountings are secure, that the ball joints show no signs of wear and that the ball joint dust covers are in sound condition. Ensure that all split pins, locking nuts and so on are in place and correctly fastened, throughout the steering and suspension systems.

☐ 35. With each wheel raised in turn, spin the wheel listening for roughness in the bearings. There must be none.

☐ 36. Under the vehicle, check the condition of the front springs. Wearing goggles, use a stuff brush to clean off the mud and other debris so that you don't miss a hidden 'crack'. Make sure that all suspension mountings are sound.

☐ 37. Inspect the front shock absorbers. Their upper shrouds (outer casing) tend to rust. Any sign of leaks will cause failure of the test - look for weeping hydraulic fluid just below the lower edge of the upper shroud. Take a firm grip on the upper and lower shroud in turn with both hands and try to twist the damper to check for deterioration in the top and bottom mounting bushes.

☐ 38. With all four wheels on the ground, push down firmly a couple of times on each front wing of the vehicle, then let go at the bottom of the stroke. The vehicle should return to approximately its original level within two or three strokes. Continuing oscillations will earn your vehicle a 'failure' ticket for worn front shockers!

Under The Vehicle - Rear Suspension

☐ 39. Check the operation of the rear shock absorbers in the same way as the front (Check 38).

☐ 40. Check the rear wheel bearings as described in check 35.

☐ 41. Check the condition of the rear springs and suspension components as described in check 36.

☐ 42. Check the condition of the rear shock absorbers as described in check 37.

Braking System

☐ 43. The MoT brake test is carried out on a special 'rolling road' set-up, which measures the efficiency in terms of percentage. For the foot brake, the examiner is looking for 50 per cent; the hand brake must measure 25 per cent. Frankly, without a rolling road of your own, there is little that you can do to verify whether or not your vehicle will come up to the required figures. What you can do, though, is carry out an entire check of the brake system, which will also cover all other aspects the examiner will be checking, and be as sure as you can that the system is working efficiently.

IMPORTANT! See *Chapter 3, Servicing Your Car* for important information, including *SAFETY FIRST!* information before working on your vehicle's brakes.

☐ 44. The MoT examiner will not dismantle any part of the system, but you can do so. So, take off each front wheel in turn, and examine as follows:

Disc Brakes

Check the front brake discs themselves, looking for excessive grooving or crazing, the calliper pistons/dust seals (looking for signs of fluid leakage and deterioration of the seals), and the brake pads - ideally, replace them if less than approximately 3mm (1/8th in.) friction material remains on each pad - but check the recommendations in *Chapter 3*.

Drum Brakes

Remove each brake drum and check the condition of the linings (renew if worn down to anywhere near the rivet heads), the brake drum (watch for cracking, ovality and serious scoring, etc.) and the wheel cylinders. Check the cylinder's dust covers to see if they contain brake fluid. If so, or if it is obvious that the cylinder(s) have been leaking, replace them or - ONLY if the cylinder bore is in perfect condition - fit a new seal kit.

☐ 45. Ensure that the drum brake adjusters (where fitted) are free to rotate (i.e. not seized!). If they are stuck fast, apply a little penetrating oil (but if possible, only from behind the backplate; if you have to work inside the brake drum, take great care to avoid the risk of getting oil on the brake shoes), and gently work the adjuster backwards and forwards with a brake adjuster spanner. Eventually the adjusters should free and a little brake grease can be applied to the threads to keep them in this condition. Now rotate the adjuster until the brake shoes contact the drum (preventing the road wheel from turning), then reverse the adjustment just enough to allow the wheel to turn.

☐ 46. A similar procedure can be applied to the handbrake adjustment. Check that the handbrake applies the brakes fully, well before it reaches the end of its potential range of movement. Ensure that the handbrake lever remains locked in the 'on' position when fully applied, even if the lever is knocked sideways.

☐ 47. Closely check the state of ALL visible hydraulic pipework. If any section of the steel tubing shows signs of corrosion, replace it, for safety as well as to gain an MoT pass. Look too for leakage of fluid around pipe joints, and from the master cylinder. The fluid level in the master cylinder reservoir must also be at its correct level - if not, find out why and rectify the problem! At the front and rear of the vehicle, bend the flexible hydraulic pipes (by hand) near each end of each pipe, checking for signs of cracking. If any is evident, or if the pipes have been chafing on the tyres, wheels, steering or suspension components, replace them with new items, rerouting them to avoid future problems. Note also that where the manufacturers fitted a clip to secure a piece of pipe, then it must be present and the pipe must be secured by it.

☐ 48. Have an assistant press down hard on the brake pedal while you check all flexible pipes for bulges. As an additional check, firmly apply the foot brake and hold the pedal down for a few minutes. It should not slowly sink to the floor (if it does, you have a hydraulic system problem). Press and release the pedal a few times - it should not feel 'spongy' (due to the presence of air in the system). Now check the operation of the brake servo by starting the engine while the brake pedal is being held down. If all is well, as the vacuum servo starts to work, the pedal should move a short distance towards the floor. Check the condition of the servo unit and its hoses - all MUST be sound. If there is the risk of any problems with the braking system's hydraulics, have a qualified mechanic check it over before using the vehicle.

☐ 49. A test drive should reveal obvious faults (such as pulling to one side, due to a seized calliper piston, for example), but otherwise all will be revealed on the rollers at the MoT station...

Bodywork Structure

A structurally deficient vehicle is a dangerous vehicle, and rust can affect many important areas, including the sills, any 'outriggers' and the floorpan. Examine these areas carefully.

☐ 50. Essentially, fractures, cracks or serious corrosion in any load bearing panel or member (to the extent that the affected sections are weakened) need to be dealt with. In addition, failure will result from any deficiencies in the structural metalwork within 30 cm (12 in.) of the seat belt mountings, and also the steering and suspension component attachment points. Repairs made to any structural areas must be carried out by 'continuous' seam welding, and the repair should restore the affected section to at least its original strength.

☐ 51. The MoT examiner will be looking for metal which gives way under squeezing pressure between finger and thumb, and will use his wicked little 'Corrosion Assessment Tool' (i.e. a plastic-headed tool known as the 'toffee hammer'!), which in theory at least should be used for detecting rust by lightly tapping the surface. If scraping the surface of the metal shows weakness beneath, the vehicle will fail.

☐ 52. Note that the security of doors and other openings must also be assessed, including the hinges, locks and catches. Corrosion damage or other weakness in the vicinity of these items can mean failure. All doors must latch securely. It must be possible to open both front doors from inside and outside the vehicle and rear doors from the outside only.

Exterior Bodywork

☐ 53. Look out for surface rust, or accident damage, on the exterior bodywork, which leaves sharp/jagged edges and which may be liable to cause injury. Ideally, repairs should be carried out by welding in new metal, but for non-structural areas, riveting a plate over a hole, bridging the gap with glass fibre/body filler or even taping over the gap can be legally acceptable, at least as far as the MoT test is concerned.

Fuel System

☐ 54. Another recent extension of the regulations brings the whole of the fuel system under scrutiny, from the tank to the engine. The system should be examined with and without the engine running, and there must be no leaks from any of the components. The tank must be securely mounted, and the filler cap must fit properly - 'temporary' caps are not permitted.

Emissions

☐ 55. In almost every case, a proper 'engine tune' will help to ensure that your vehicle is running at optimum efficiency, and there should be no difficulty in passing the test, unless your engine or its ancillaries are well worn.

All petrol engines are subject to the 'visual smoke emission' test. The engine must be fully warmed up, allowed to idle, then revved slightly. If smoke emitted is regarded by the examiner as being 'excessive', the vehicle will fail. Often smoke emitted during this test is as a result of worn valve stem seals, allowing oil into the combustion chambers during tickover, to be blown out of the exhaust as 'blue smoke' when the engine is revved. In practice, attitudes vary widely between MoT stations on this aspect of the test.

☐ 56. For diesel-engined vehicles a 'smoke' test also applies. Again, the engine must be fully warmed up, and allowed to idle, before being revved to around 2,500 rpm for 20 seconds (to 'purge' the system). If dense blue or black smoke is emitted for more than five seconds, the vehicle will fail. In addition, the exhaust smoke is tested. Problems will require **SPECIALIST SERVICE**.

FACT FILE: VEHICLE EMISSIONS

PETROL ENGINED VEHICLES WITHOUT CATALYSER

Vehicles first used before 1 August 1973
• visual smoke check only.

Vehicles first used between 1 August 1973 and 31 July 1986
• 4.5% carbon monoxide and 1,200 parts per million, unburned hydrocarbons.

Vehicles first used between 1 August 1986 and 31 July 1992
• 3.5% carbon monoxide and 1,200 parts per million, unburned hydrocarbons.

PETROL ENGINED VEHICLES FITTED WITH CATALYTIC CONVERTERS

Vehicles first used from 1 August 1992 (K-registration on).

All have to be tested at an MoT Testing Station specially equipped to handle cars fitted with catalytic converters whether or not the vehicle is fitted with a 'cat'. If the test, or the garage's data, shows that the vehicle was not fitted with a 'cat' by the manufacturer, the owner is permitted to take the vehicle to a Testing Station not equipped for catalysed cars, if he/she prefers to do so (up to 1998-only). Required maxima are - 3.5% carbon monoxide and 1,200 parts per million, unburned hydrocarbons. The simple emissions test (as above) will be supplemented by a further check to make sure that the catalyst is maintained in good and efficient working order.

The tester also has to check that the engine oil is up to a specified temperature before carrying out the test.

DIESEL ENGINES' EMISSIONS STANDARDS FROM 1 JANUARY 1996

The Tester will have to rev your engine hard, several times. If it is not in good condition, he is entitled to refuse to test it. This is the full range of tests, even though all may not apply to your car.

Vehicles first used before 1 August, 1979

Engine run at normal running temperature; engine speed taken to around 2500 rpm (or half governed max. speed, if lower) and held for 20 seconds. FAILURE, if engine emits dense blue or black smoke for next 5 seconds, at tick-over. (NOTE: Testers are allowed to be more lenient with pre-1960 vehicles.)

Vehicles first used on or after 1 August, 1979

After checking engine condition, and with the engine at normal running temperature, the engine will be run up to full revs between three and six times to see whether your engine passes the prescribed smoke density test. (For what it's worth - 2.5k for non-turbo cars; 3.0k for turbo diesels. An opacity meter probe will be placed in your car's exhaust pipe and this is not something you can replicate at home.) Irrespective of the meter readings, the car will fail if smoke or vapour obscures the view of other road users.

IMPORTANT NOTE: The diesel engine test puts a lot of stress on the engine. It is IMPERATIVE that your car's engine is properly serviced, and the cam belt changed on schedule, before you take it in for the MoT test. The tester is entitled to refuse to test the car if he feels that the engine is not in serviceable condition and there are a number of pre-Test checks he may carry out.

CHAPTER 8 - FACTS & FIGURES

This Chapter serves two main purposes. In *Part I,* we aim to provide you with a guide to all the major production changes that have taken place, and second, we supply the 'Facts & Figures' you will need when servicing your car. In fact, *Part II* of this chapter, *Capacities and Settings,* will make essential reading when you come to carrying out servicing, since you will then need to know things like the correct spark plug gap, torque settings and a whole host of other adjustments and measurements.

PART I - MAJOR MILESTONES

Soon after its introduction in 1981 the front-wheel-drive (FWD) Cavalier quickly established itself as a popular choice for both private and fleet buyers, and has consistently been at or near the top of the "best-sellers" list ever since.

The new design was a radical change from the previous model and virtually the only thing they have in common is the name, Cavalier! (The previous, rear wheel-drive car is not covered by this book, of course.)

The Engine is the four cylinder over-head camshaft engine design, which featured first in the Astra range the previous year. This engine was among the first mass-production units to feature hydraulic tappets, or valve-lifters, which require no adjustment and give quieter running.

Although obviously differing in physical size, the basic engine design has evolved to span the range from 1.2 to 2.0 litres capacity.

The Bodywork proved popular with buyers, especially the hatchback design, which had previously only been seen on smaller cars such as the Astra and its predecessor, the Chevette.

To the end, Vauxhall continued to up-grade the Cavalier and, although its replacement (Vectra in the UK and mainland Europe, where the Cavalier was known as Vectra, confusingly!), the Cavalier is just as popular today. Among numerous awards, the Cavalier SRi was voted "Tow-car of the year" in 1994 by the Caravan Club and also has won the "Fleet car of the Year" award in 1994, the eighth time it won it in nine years.

CHRONOLOGY

Aug. 1981 - "New" Cavalier with front-wheel-drive (FWD) introduced, replacing the earlier rear-wheel-drive model. Completely new design in all respects, including bodywork and engines. Initially available in two or four-door saloon or five-door hatchback. Engine sizes available at launch: 1.3, 1.6, 1.8 litres; 4-speed manual gear box standard, 3-speed automatic optional. (Known as 'Vectra', rest of Europe.)

Jul. 1982 - Diesel engine (designated 16D) introduced; based on the 1.6 petrol engine, which it closely resembles. 1600cc SR model launched in four door saloon form only.

Sep. 1982 - 1.3 engine fitted with electronic ignition, in line with other models. New 5-speed gearbox fitted to GLS and SR models. 2-door saloon version discontinued.

Oct. 1982 - SRi and CD models launched, powered by 1.8 fuel-injected engine and 5-speed gearbox as standard in four or five-door forms. 1600 SR discontinued.

Apr. 1983 - Diesel saloon and hatchback models now fitted with five-speed gearbox as standard.

Aug. 1983 - New version of 4-speed manual gearbox introduced on 1600cc models, while 5-speed 'box has revised ratios for improved performance.

Oct. 1983 - Estate (5 door) introduced, with 1600cc petrol engine and uprated suspension.

Feb. 1984 - 1600cc diesel engine now available in estate car, along with 5-speed gearbox.

Oct. 1985 - Two-door Convertible model introduced, fitted with 1.8 fuel-injection engine and 5-speed gearbox.

Jun. 1986 - Minor changes to diesel engine; (now 16DA).

Aug. 1986 - 2.0 litre engine with fuel injection now available, designated 20NE, fitted as standard to CD models, replacing the 1.8 engine.

Mar. 1987 - SRi "130" introduced with high-compression 2.0 litre fuel injection engine (designated 20SEH and developing 130 BHP), close-ratio 5-speed gearbox and alloy wheels.

Oct. 1987 - 1.6 LX and 1.8 LXi models introduced.

Oct. 1988 - Cavalier range up-dated with completely new body styling and other, more minor, changes. Engine range now includes 1.4 litre petrol version (replaplacing the 1.3), and a 1.7 diesel replaces 1.6. All engines have electronic ignition systems. Saloon and hatchback versions available, but estate and convertible models discontinued. 4-speed automatic transmission optional.

Jan. 1989 - Four wheel drive (4x4) 2.0i model launched, with 130 BHP engine and available in saloon form only.

Oct. 1989 - GSi 2000 16-valve and GSi 4x4 16-valve launched, with 150 BHP engine and ABS (anti-lock braking system);catalytic converter on 4x4. Both available in saloon form only.

Dec. 1990 - 2.0i 4x4 revised to include rear disc brakes, SRi-type interior, boot spoiler and alarm.

Mar. 1992 - 1.7 Turbo diesel launched, in L and GL versions.

Apr. 1992 - 2.0i Diplomat launched, with cross-spoked alloy wheels, leather trim, air conditioning.

Jun. 1992 - 2.0i models (except 4x4 and SRi) have catalytic converter fitted as standard. "Expression" limited edition continues into second production run of 4000.

Oct. 1992 - Range revised, with restyled body, grille; side-impact protection beams now standard. "Envoy" replaces former base models; LS replaces earlier L; GLS replaces GL.

Mar. 1993 - 2.5 litre V6 engine introduced, with 5-speed manual or four-speed automatic gearbox, ABS, traction-control, drivers' airbag. Limited edition "Colorado" launched, with 1.8i engine, production run - only 4500.

Oct. 1993 - Driver's airbag now fitted to all models.

Mar. 1994 - ABS now standard on all models. 2.0 SRi 16-valve engine uprated to 136BHP.

Aug. 1994 - Major equipment upgrades across whole range, including interior trim and alloy wheels, uprated front suspension, darkened rear lamps, black rear panel (except "Envoy" & SRi). The 2.0i 4x4 Turbo is discontinued.

Oct. 1994 - All models have revised "Omega" type grille with chrome "V" motif. Engine immobiliser fitted to all petrol engined models, except 1.6i "Concept" version.

Oct. 1995 - Vectra introduced. All-new replacement for Cavalier, which is now discontinued.

PART II - CAPACITIES AND SETTINGS

The following information is likely to be required when carrying out certain service jobs and also provides basic technical specifications. We have divided it into various sections of the car and have detailed the different models under each section.

PETROL ENGINES

PLEASE NOTE that just two models have different coolant capacities for auto. and manual transmission cars. All others have the same coolant capacity for both transmission types.

1.3 litre (1981 to '88)
Designation - 13S
Bore - 75.0mm
Stroke - 73.4mm
Capacity - 1297 cc
Compression Ratio - 9.2:1
BHP (DIN) - 55kw @ 5,800 rpm.
Fuel System - Carburettor: GM Varajet II up to '84: Pierburg 2E3 '86 to '88
Ignition system - CB points up to 1984; AC electronic to '88
Coolant Capacity - 6.3 litres (6.7 litres, auto. transmission)
Sump oil capacity - inc filter: 3.0 litres.

1.4 litre (1988 to '92)
Designation - 14NV
Bore - 77.6mm
Stroke - 73.4mm
Capacity - 1389 cc
Compression ratio - 9.4:1
BHP (DIN) - 55kw @ 5,600 rpm.
Fuel system - Carburettor: Pierburg 2E3
Ignition system - Bosch electronic.
Coolant Capacity - 5.6 litres.
Sump oil capacity - inc filter: 3.0 litres.

1.6 litre (1981 to '88)
Designation - 16S
Bore - 80.0mm
Stroke - 79.5mm
Capacity - 1598 cc
Compression ratio - 9.2:1
BHP (DIN) - 63kw @ 5,800 rpm.
Fuel system - Carburettor: GM Varajet II
Ignition system - Bosch electronic
Coolant Capacity - 7.7 litres.
Sump oil capacity - inc filter: 3.5 litres.

1.6 litre (1988 to '92)
Designation - 16SV
Bore - 79.0mm
Stroke - 81.5mm
Capacity - 1598 cc
Compression ratio - 10.0:1
BHP (DIN) - 60kw @ 5,400 rpm.
Fuel system - Pierburg 2E3
Ignition system - Lucas or Bosch electronic
Coolant Capacity - 5.8 litres.
Sump oil capacity - inc filter: 3.5 litres.

1.6 litre Injection (1991-on)
Designation - C16NZ
Bore - 79.0mm
Stroke - 81.5mm
Capacity - 1598 cc
Compression ratio - 9.2:1
BHP (DIN) - 75kw @ 5,200 rpm.
Fuel system - Rochester Multec single-point injection
Ignition system - Rochester electronic.
Coolant Capacity - 5.8 litres.
Sump oil capacity - inc filter: 3.5 litres.

1.8 litre (1983 to '88)

Designation - 18E; 18SE for 1987 to '88
Bore - 84.8mm
Stroke - 79.5mm
Capacity - 1796 cc
Compression ratio - 9.5:1 (10.0:1 for 1987 to '88)
BHP (DIN) - 82kw @ 5,600 rpm.
Fuel system - Bosch LE Jetronic (to '86): L3 Jetronic (87 to '88)
Ignition system - Bosch electronic.
Coolant Capacity - 7.6 litres (7.4 litres, with automatic transmission).
Sump oil capacity - inc filter: 3.55 litres: 4.0 litres 18SE eng.

1.8 litre (1988 to '92 Carburettor models)

Designation - 18SV
Bore - 84.8mm
Stroke - 79.5mm
Capacity - 1796 cc
Compression ratio - 10.0:1
BHP (DIN) - 66kw @ 5,400 rpm.
Fuel system - Pierburg 2E3
Ignition system - Lucas or Bosch electronic.
Coolant Capacity - 6.7 litres.
Sump oil capacity - inc filter: 3.5 litres.

1.8 litre (1990-on: Fuel injection models)

Designation - C18NZ
Bore - 84.8mm
Stroke - 79.5mm
Capacity - 1796 cc
Compression ratio - 9.2:1
BHP (DIN) - 90 @ 5,400 rpm.
Fuel system - Rochester Multec single-point injection.
Ignition system - Bosch electronic.
Coolant Capacity - 7.2 litres (7.1 auto. transmission).
Sump oil capacity - inc filter: 3.5-4.0 litres.

2.0 litre (1986 to '94)

Designation - 20 NE (C20 NE with catalyst)
Bore - 86.0mm
Stroke - 86.0mm
Capacity - 1998 cc
Compression ratio - 9.2:1
BHP (DIN) - 85kw @ 5,600 rpm.
Fuel system - Bosch Motronic injection.
Ignition system - Bosch Motronic electronic.
Coolant Capacity - 6.9 litres.
Sump oil capacity - inc filter: 4.0 litres: 3.5 from 1988-on

2.0 litre SRi (1986 to '94)

Designation - 20 SEH
Bore - 86.0mm
Stroke - 86.0mm
Capacity - 1998 cc
Compression ratio - 10.0:1
BHP (DIN) - 95kw @ 5,600 rpm.
Fuel system - Bosch Motronic up to '87: Motronic ML4,1 '88-on.
Ignition system - Bosch electronic.
Coolant Capacity - 6.9 litres (7.2 from 1988).
Sump oil capacity - inc filter: 3.5 litres.

2.0 litre 16-Valve (1989-on)

Designation - 20 XEJ: C20 XE from 1990
Bore - 86.0mm
Stroke - 86.0mm
Capacity - 1998 cc
Compression ratio - 10.5:1
BHP (DIN) - 150kw @ 6,000 rpm.
Fuel system - Bosch Motronic M2,5 injection.
Ignition system - Bosch electronic.
Coolant Capacity - 7.2 litres.
Sump oil capacity - inc filter: 4.5 litres.

2.0 litre Turbo 4x4 (1992-on)

Designation - C20 LET
Bore - 86.0mm
Stroke - 86.0mm
Capacity - 1998 cc
Compression ratio - 9.0:1
BHP (DIN) - 204kw @ 5,600 rpm.
Fuel system - Bosch Motronic M2,7 injection.
Ignition system - Bosch electronic.
Coolant Capacity - 7.2 litres.
Sump oil capacity - inc filter: 4.5 litres.

2.5 litre V6 (1992-on)

Designation - C25XE
Bore - N/A
Stroke - N/A
Capacity - 2498 cc
Compression ratio - 10.8:1
BHP (DIN) - 170kw @ 6,000 rpm
Fuel system - Bosch Motronic M2,8
Ignition system - Bosch electronic.
Coolant Capacity - 7.3 litres.
Sump oil capacity - inc filter: 4.5 litres.

DIESEL ENGINES

1.6 litre (1983 to '88)

Designation - 16D to 1985; 16DA to 1988
Bore - 80.0mm
Stroke - 79.5mm
Capacity - 1598 cc
Compression ratio - 23.0:1
BHP (DIN) - 40 kw @ 4,600 rpm.
Fuel system - Self-priming pump, driven from camshaft drive belt.
Coolant Capacity - 7.7 litres.
Sump oil capacity - inc filter: 5.0 litres.

1.7 litre (1988-on)

Designation - 17D to 1992: 17DR 1993-on.
Bore - 82.5mm
Stroke - 79.5mm
Capacity - 1699 cc
Compression ratio - 23.0:1
BHP (DIN) - 42kw (17D); 44kw (17DR).
Fuel system - Self-priming pump, driven from camshaft drive belt.
Coolant Capacity - 9.1 litres.
Sump oil capacity - inc filter: 4.75 litres.

1.7 litre Turbo (1992-on)
Designation - 17DT
Bore - 79.0mm
Stroke - 86.0mm
Capacity - 1686 cc
Compression ratio - 22.0:1
BHP (DIN) - 82kw @ 4,400 rpm.
Fuel system - Self-priming pump, driven from camshaft drive belt.
Coolant Capacity - 7.4 litres.
Sump oil capacity - inc filter: 4.5 litres.

GENERAL SPECIFICATIONS

All models (exc.V6):
4 cylinder in-line, overhead camshaft (twin camshafts on 16v models), with hydraulic valve lifters.

Firing order:
4 cyl. engines, 1-3-4-2: V6 engine, 1-2-3-4-5-6

Basic timing:
1.3, 1.6, 1.8, 2.0 litre - 10 deg BTDC. 1.4 litre - 5 deg BTDC. (Mark on pulley aligns with pointer on crankcase).
Note: On models from 1988 ignition timing is controlled by computer and is non-adjustable.

Spark plug types:

1.3, 1.4, 1.6, 1.8, 2.0 models:
Make - AC
Type - CR42XLS

2.0 litre 16v SRi from 1992:
Make - Bosch
Type - FR8 LDC

2.0 litre Turbo 4x4 from 1992:
Make - Vauxhall
Type - 90 44 25 14

2.5 litre V6 model:
Make - Bosch
Type - FR7 LDC

Plug electrode gap (all types) - 0.7 to 0.8mm

Tightening torque - 20 Nm.

COOLING SYSTEM.

System cap release pressure - 1.2 to 1.5 bar.
Electric fan on/off temperature - 100/95 deg.C. (1.6 diesel - 97/93 deg.C.)

ELECTRICAL SYSTEM.

Battery - 12volt, 44 Amp/hour (exc. V6 - 55 A/h: Diesel - 60 A/h)

Alternator output:
1.3, 45 amp

1.6, 1.8, 2.0 (up to 1988) 55 or 65 amp;
All other models - 70 amp.

Lamp Bulbs:
(All figures shown are watts. All bulbs are 12 volt.)

Headlamps - 65
Foglamps - 55
Sidelamps - 4
Indicators, front & rear - 21
Side indicator repeaters - 5
Combined stop/tail lamps - 21/5
Rear no. plate (single) - 10
Rear no. plate (estate) - 5
Reverse lamp - 21
Engine bay/boot interior - 10
Glove box - 5
Instrument warning (excl. alternator) - 1.2
Alternator warning lamp - 3
Cigar lighter - 1.2
Switch inner bulbs - 1.2
Switch symbols - 0.5
Rear fog lamps - 21

GEARBOX/TRANSMISSION CAPACITIES
(All capacities in litres)

4-speed manual g/box:
1.3 1981 to '84 - 1.7 litres: All other models - 3.5 litres

5-speed manual g/box:
1.3 1981 to '84: 1.8 litres: All other models - 2.1 litres

NOTE: Cavalier gearboxes are not fitted with drain plugs and draining is not an official service requirement, therefore the above quantities are for guidance only; follow the procedure for oil changing, checking the level and topping-up in *Chapter 3, Servicing Your Car*.

Automatic transmission:
All models: 7.0 litres

Tyre sizes and pressures:
(Optional tyre sizes shown in brackets).
All figures given front/rear in pounds per square inch (p.s.i.).

1.3 - 155R13; 29/26
1.4 & 1.6 - 163SR13; 28/25: (185/70HR13 - 29/26)
1.8 & 2.0 - 185/70R13; 29/26: (195/60HR14 - 32/29)
2.0 SRi - 195/60HR14; 32/29
2.0 16V - 195/60R15; 35/32: (205/55R15 - 33/30)
2.0 Turbo 4x4 - 205/50ZR16; 33/30
1.6 Diesel - 165TR13; 28/25
1.7 Diesel - 175/70R14; 29/26
1.7 Turbo Diesel - 174/70R14; 28/25: (196/60R14 - 32/29)

Wheel nut torque:
All models - 66ft/lb (90Nm).

CHAPTER 9 - TOOLS & EQUIPMENT

Although good tools are not cheap, if you reckon their cost against what you would otherwise spend on professional servicing and repairs, your arithmetic should show you that it doesn't take long to recoup your outlay - and then to start showing a profit!

In fact, there is no need to spend a fortune all at once - most owners who do their own servicing acquire their implements over a long period of time. However, there are some items you simply cannot do without in order to properly carry out the work necessary to keep your car on the road. Therefore, in the following lists, we have concentrated on those items which are likely to be valuable aids to maintaining your car in a good state of tune, and to keep it running sweetly and safely and in addition we have featured some of the tools that are 'nice-to-have' rather than 'must have' because as your tool chest grows, there are some tools that help to make servicing just that bit easier and more thorough to carry out.

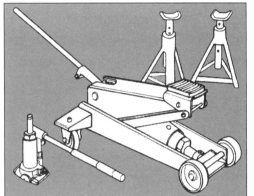

Two vital points - firstly always buy the best quality tools you can afford. 'Cheap and cheerful' items may look similar to more expensive implements, but experience shows that they often fail when the going gets tough, and some can even be dangerous. With proper care, good quality tools will last a lifetime, and can be regarded as an investment. The extra outlay is well worth it, in the long run.

Over the years, there have been various nut/bolt/spanner designations. For many years British cars standardised on 'AF', a designation referring to the measurement 'across the flats' of the hexagon nut or bolt head, while the 'foreigners' were 'Metric'. While there are still many 'AF' cars around, all modern cars are 'Metric' of course, apart from American cars. (For the record, 'metric' sizes are also measured across their flats!). Be sure you know which designation applies to your car before you start buying. Your local motor accessory store should be able to advise, or you could all your local main dealer to make sure, if necessary.

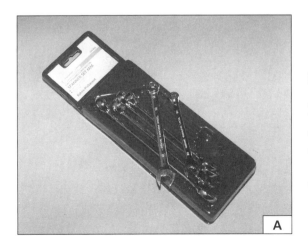

SPANNERS:

A. The two common types of spanner are the ring and the open-ended. The ring spanner grips practically all round the bolt, and is preferable where the bolt is really tight, for an open-ended spanner, merely straddling two flats of the bolt, could slip. On the other hand, the open-end is often quicker and easier to use - so this set of 'Combination' spanners, a ring at one end, open-ended the other, is a nice compromise!

All the tools featured here are available from your local High Street auto-accessory store or Super Store. Any special tools needed for your car are referred to in Chapter 3.

B. While the 'flatness' of the combination spanners (or of a conventional open-ended spanner) is often useful, there are occasions when only the offset, or 'swan neck' of the conventional ring spanner will do the job - like when having to operate over the top of one bolt in order to undo another.

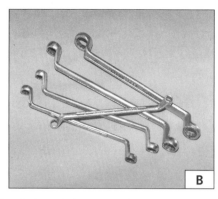

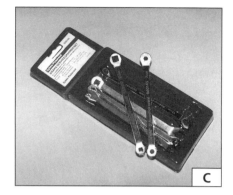

Unlike the combination spanners, the conventional ring and open-ended spanners will have a different size at each end.

Usually, the AF sizes will rise in sixteenths of an inch, and the metrics by one millimetre - the following sizes will probably cover most of your needs:
AF - 3/8 x 7/16, 1/2 x 9/16, 5/8 x 11/16, 13/16 x 7/8
Metric - 10 x 11, 12 x 13, 14 x 15, 16 x 17

C. The sturdy specialist brake spanner used, for brake adjusters or bleed nipples, is undeniably a wise buy, as mentioned in the brake servicing text. You might not need the set as shown here, but you can choose individual sizes to suit your car, such as 1/4 in. square x 11/32 in. square or 1/4 in. hexagonal x 5/16 in. AF, or perhaps 8 x 10mm hexagonal - there are others.

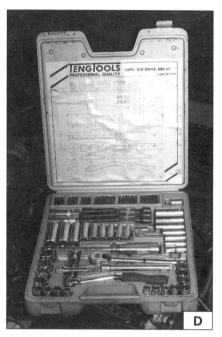

D. A basic socket set should figure highly on your shopping list, for it will cover your basic spanner sizes and can often solve difficult access or extra-leverage problems. This one is a fairly sophisticated set, and includes a number of useful extras, such as spark plug spanners and Allen key and screwdriver bits. Don't buy more than you need, however, and don't be tempted by cheap, nasty - and often dangerous - market stall socket sets.

E. A torque wrench was also once a luxury, but nowadays it's practically essential, with specific torque settings quoted for many of the nuts and bolts used in modern car engineering. The example shown will cater for most applications, including adjustable wheel-bearing hub nuts, but even the next size up (30-150 lb/ft) in the DIY range will still fall short of the 200-odd lb/ft specified for some hub nuts!

F. If you still need a plug spanner, and particularly if your engine features deep-set spark plugs, this Sykes-Pickavant 'extra long plug wrench', combining both 10mm and 14mm sizes, could be a boon. Some plugs are set deeper than the average length of a socket-set spark plug spanner, and if the socket set's extension bar is prone to leaving the spanner socket stuck on the plug, then you could have a problem ...

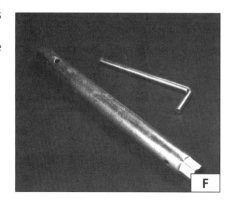

SCREWDRIVERS:

G. You will need a selection of screwdrivers, both flat-bladed and cross-headed, long ones, short ones, slim ones, fat ones ...

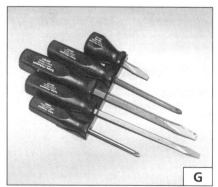

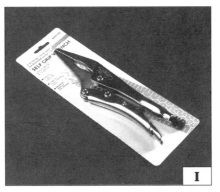

PLIERS:

H. Ordinary combination (or 'engineers') pliers are needed for general work, while a long-nosed pair are handy where access is tight. Their cutting edges are useful for stripping cable insulation, or for snipping wire or trimming split-pin lengths, but you might prefer a pair of specialist side-cutter pliers for such work.

I. Jolly useful as an extra pair of hands, or for gripping such as a rusty nut or bolt really tightly, is a self-grip wrench. This is a long-nose example, but there are also ordinary straight-jaw and round jaw versions.

SUNDRIES:

J. You'll need hammers, including the useful 1lb ball-pein type, plus a hefty copper hammer and maybe a soft (plastic-headed) hammer, too.

K. The wire brush should have brass bristles and as well as an ordinary set of feeler gauges, an 'ignition set' covers most plug and points gap sizes, and includes a points file and a spark plug gap setting tool.

L. You may need a grease gun (although virtually no modern cars have grease points) but you *will* want an oil can, and an oil funnel, and a container of sufficient capacity into which the engine oil can be drained.

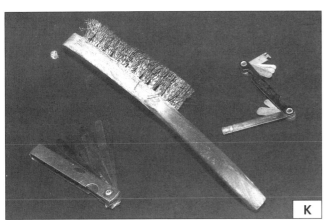

M. You may also need a drain plug 'key' suitable for your car unless all the drain plugs are 'bolt'-type hexagons.

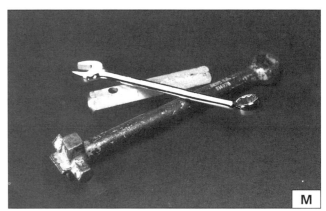

TOOLS & EQUIPMENT

N. Well worthwhile, since some oil filters can be cussedly tight, is some sort of oil filter wrench - this chain-type is a nice example. In extreme cases, even these wrenches can fail to get a grip, in which case, drive an old screwdriver right through the filter and twist it loose.

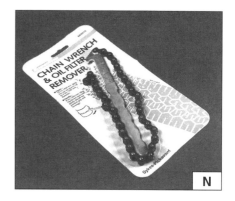

O. A separate set of hand-held Allen keys is a good idea (they come in metric or Imperial sizes), and an adjustable spanner and a 'Junior' hacksaw will have their uses.

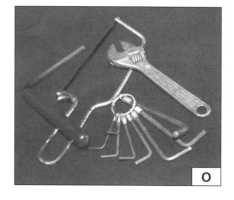

P. For your weekly maintenance checks, you'll need a tyre pressure gauge, tyre tread depth gauge and a footpump - which might, like the example here, have an integral pressure gauge. And whether you're wheel-changing at home or roadside, you will welcome the extremely useful Sykes-Pickavant 'Wheelmaster' wrench, which can be extended to give enough leverage to shift those wheel nuts or bolts that the average car-kit wheelbrace wouldn't even look at - see the wheel-change routine at the start of Chapter 3. Remember to carry the extendable wrench with you in the car!

LIFTING:

Q. While the jack supplied with the car *might* be OK for emergency wheel-changes, you would soon tire of trying to use it for servicing operations. Here, you need a good trolley jack, and one of the latest on the market is this 2-ton lifting capacity 'Lift and Lock' example which, as its name suggests, has a built-in fail-safe locking device in the event of hydraulic failure.

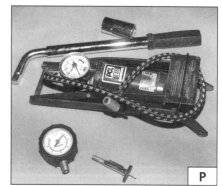

R. No matter what sort of jack you use, it is ESSENTIAL that you should not venture beneath a car supported on a jack alone. Having raised it, you need to support it safely and securely. What you need now is definitely NOT house bricks (or any other such potentially dangerous items!) but rather axle stands or wheel-ramps. Adjustable-height stands are essential and both axle stands and ramps should be produced by a 'name' manufacturer, for safety's sake. If you don't need the wheels off, it can be argued that the ramps offer better stability - though you'll benefit from some assistance when it comes to driving upon them. See the start of *Chapter 3*.

TUNING AIDS:

S. As we have said earlier in this chapter and within the servicing sections, the tuning aids that are now available to the DIY market have become practically invaluable 'musts' for the dedicated home mechanic. Any of the Gunson's collection shown here would soon prove their worth. Top of the tree, of course, is their 'Gastester Professional' - don't let its designation suggest that it's not for DIY use, for although it's expensive a group of friends sharing its cost would find their outlay well worth the benefits offered by the unit's Exhaust Gas 'CO' functions, plus its Voltage, Dwell and RPM modes. If it's pure 'multi-meter' you're after, then their 'Digimeter 320' is a tidy little hand-held unit, with clear digital read-outs for such as Volts (DC and household AC) and Amps, Ohms, rpm, and Dwell (degrees and per cent), and its sophistication extends to Frequency, Period and Pulsewidth testing (handy for fuel injection systems), as well as Diode, Resistance and Continuity testing. Also by Gunson's is the powerful 'Timestrobe' xenon timing light, the now not so new, but still novel 'Colortune' and (not shown) the 'Carbalancer'. The latter two devices are virtually invaluable when it comes to carburettor tuning.

APPENDIX 1
RECOMMENDED CASTROL
LUBRICANTS

Castrol offers a broad range of top-quality oils, greases and other essential fluids, and they will all figure in the 'Recommended' list appended to the handbooks issued by the major motor manufacturers.

ENGINE OIL.
PETROL ENGINES.

GTX (15W/50): A 'superior' multi-grade engine oil that is certainly suitable for newer vehicles requiring an SAE 15W/50 or 20W/50 viscosity oil, but which is particularly appropriate for older technology engines and high-mileage vehicles, where working clearances might be higher than average.

GTX2 (15W/40): Suits newer vehicles, including turbo-charged, where this viscosity is recommended.

GTX3 Lightec (10W/40): Specially formulated for multi-valve, high-technology engines, including turbos, where a light viscosity oil has been recommended.

Models up to 1987

Castrol GTX 15W/50

Models from 1988

Castrol GTX2 15W/40

Turbo, 16V & V6 engines

GTX3 Lightec 10W/40

DIESEL ENGINES.

GTD (15W/40): Specially formulated for the particular demands of all diesel engines, including turbo-charged.

All diesel models, including turbo

Castrol GTD 15W/40

GEARBOX OIL.
MANUAL TRANSMISSIONS

Castrol Syntrax Universal

AUTOMATIC TRANSMISSION

Castrol Dexron R III

POWER STEERING

Castrol Dexron R III

BRAKE FLUID
Vehicles without ABS

Castrol Universal Brake Fluid:

Vehicles fitted with ABS

Castrol Super Disc 5.1

WHEEL BEARINGS

Castrol LM grease

DOOR LOCKS & HINGES

Castrol Everyman

ELECTRICAL CONNECTIONS

Castrol DWF

NUT & BOLT RELEASE

Castrol Easing Oil

COOLING SYSTEM

Castrol Antifreeze & Summer Coolant

CASTROL ANTI-FREEZE: Recommended for use in petrol or diesel engine cooling systems, with aluminium or cast engines. Its formulation of mono ethylene glycol and corrosion inhibitors makes it suitable for all-year-round use, and because it contains no phosphate it is reckoned that the problems of deposits in some modern uprated engines are eliminated. A 33 per cent concentration will protect down to minus 17 degrees C.

SPECIALISTS & SUPPLIERS

APPENDIX 2
SPECIALISTS & SUPPLIERS
FEATURED IN THIS BOOK

All of the products and specialists listed below have contributed in various ways to this book. All of the consumer products used are available through regular high street outlets or by mail order from specialist suppliers.

Castrol (UK) Ltd, Burmah House, Pipers Way, Swindon, Wiltshire, SN3 1RE. Tel: 01793 452222
Contact Castrol's Consumer Technical Department Help Line on the above number for advice on lubrication recommendations.

NGK Spark Plugs (UK) Ltd, 7-8-9 Garrick Industrial Centre, Hendon, London, NW9 6AQ. Tel: 0181 202 2151.
Top quality spark plugs.

Dinol (GB) Limited, Dinol House, 98 Ock Street, Abingdon, Oxford, OX14 5DH. Tel: 01235 530677
Suppliers of Dinitrol rust proofing fluids, and are equipped to carry out rustproofing on vehicles.

Erringtons of Evington Limited, Main Street, Evington, Leicester, LE5 6DQ. Tel: 0116 273 0421
Extremely helpful Vauxhall dealership!

Gunson Ltd, Coppen Road, Dagenham, Essex, RM8 1NU. Tel: 0181 984 8855.
Electrical and electronic engine tuning equipment.

HPI Autodata, HP Information plc, Dolphin House, P O Box 61, New Street, Salisbury, Wiltshire, SP1 2TB Tel: 01722 422422
Before buying any used car, check it out with HPI Autodata.

Kamasa Tools, Saxon Industries, Lower Everland Road, Hungerford, Berkshire, RG17 0DX. Tel: 01488 684545.
Wide range of hand and power tools, some of which were used in this book.

SP Tyres UK Ltd, Fort Dunlop, Birmingham, B24 9QT. Tel: 0121 384 4444.
Manufacturers of Dunlop tyres.

Sykes-Pickavant Group plc, Kilnhouse Lane, Lytham St Annes, Lancs, FY8 3DU. Tel: 01253 721291
Wide range of hand tools and specialist equipment, some of which were used in this book.

Vauxhall Motors Limited, Griffin House, PO Box 3, Osborne Road, Luton, Bedfordshire, LU2 0SY. Tel: 01582 21122
See your local main dealer in Yellow Pages for Vauxhall parts.

Waste Oil Disposal
There are 1,300 listed waste oil disposal sites in the UK alone. PLEASE don't foul the environment by tipping waste oil into the drains or the ground. Find your nearest oil disposal point by ringing the National Rivers Authority on **FREEFONE 0800 663366.**

APPENDIX 3
SERVICE HISTORY

This Chapter helps you keep track of all the servicing carried out on your vehicle and can even save you money! A vehicle with a Service History is always worth more than one without, and you can make full use of this section, even if you have a garage or mechanic carry out the work for you. It enables you to specify the jobs you want to have carried out to your vehicle and, of course, it enables you to keep that all-important Service History. And even if your vehicle doesn't have a 'history' going back to when it was new, keeping this Chapter complete will add to your vehicle's value when you come to sell it. Mind you, it obviously won't be enough to just to tick the boxes: keep all your receipts when you buy oil, filters and other consumables or parts. That way, you'll also be able to return any faulty parts if needs be.

Buying Parts

Before carrying out a service on your car, you will need to purchase the right parts. Please refer to **Chapter 2, Buying Guide** for information on how to buy the right parts at the right prices and for information on how to find your car's 'identity numbers'; information that you will need in order to buy the right parts, first time!

Month, whichever comes first, is repeated at each one of the following Service Intervals. The same applies to the **6,000 Miles or Six Months** interval: much of it is repeated at **12,000 Miles or Twelve Months.** Every time a Job or set of Jobs is 'repeated' from an earlier Interval, we show it in a tinted area on the page. You can then see more clearly which jobs are unique to the level of Service Interval that you are on.

The Job Lists

Wherever possible, the Jobs listed in this section have been placed in a logical order or placed into groups that will help you make progress on the car. We have tried to save you too much in the way of unnecessary movement by grouping jobs around areas of the car. Therefore, at each Service Interval, you will see the work grouped into Jobs that need carrying out in The Engine Bay, Around The Car or Under The Car.

You'll also see space at each Service Interval for you to write down the date, price and seller's name every time you buy consumables or accessories. And once again, do remember to keep your receipts! There's also space for you to date and sign the Service Record or for a garage's stamp to be applied.

As you move through the Service Intervals. you will notice that the work carried out at say, **1,500 Miles or Every**

You will also find that all the major Intervals, right up to the 'longest', contain Jobs that are unique to that Service Interval. That's why we have continued this Service History right up to the **36,000 Miles or every Three Years** interval. So now, you will be able to service your car and keep a full record of the work, in the knowledge that your car has been looked after as well as anyone could wish for!

Important Note!

The Service Jobs listed here are intended as a check list and a means of keeping a record of your vehicle's service history, *not* as a set of instructions for working on your car. It is most important that you refer to **Chapter 3, Servicing Your Car** for full details of how to carry out each Job listed here and for essential SAFETY information and, see also, **Chapter 1, Safety First!**.

EVERY 500 MILES, WEEKLY OR BEFORE A LONG JOURNEY

This list is shown, complete, only once. It would have been a bit much to have provided the list 52 times over for use once a week throughout the year! Each job is, however, included with every longer Service list from 3,000 miles/Three Months-on so that each of the 'weekly' Jobs is carried out as part of every service.

Every 500 Miles - The Engine Bay

- [ ] Job 1. Engine oil level.
- [ ] Job 2. Check coolant level.
- [ ] Job 3. Brake fluid level.
- [ ] Job 4. Battery electrolyte.
- [ ] Job 5. Screenwash level.

Every 500 Miles - Around the Car

- [ ] Job 6. Check tyre pressures.
- [ ] Job 7. Check headlights, sidelights and front indicators.
- [ ] Job 8. Rear lights and indicators.
- [ ] Job 9. Interior lights.
- [ ] Job 10. Number plate lights.
- [ ] Job 11. Side repeater light bulbs.
- [ ] Job 12. Check horn.
- [ ] Job 13. Check windscreen wipers.
- [ ] Job 14. Windscreen washers.

EVERY 1,500 MILES - OR EVERY MONTH, WHICHEVER COMES FIRST

These Jobs are similar to the 500 Mile Jobs but don't need carrying out quite so regularly. Once again, these Jobs are not shown with a separate listing for each 1,500 miles/1 Month interval but they are included as part of every 3,000 miles/Three Months Service list and for every longer Service interval.

Every 1,500 Miles - Around the Car

- [ ] Job 15. Check tyres.
- [ ] Job 16. Check spare tyre.
- [ ] Job 17. Wash bodywork.
- [ ] Job 18. Touch-up paintwork.
- [ ] Job 19. Aerial/Antenna.
- [ ] Job 20. Valet interior.
- [ ] Job 21. Improve visibility.

Every 1,500 miles - Under the Car

- [ ] Job 22. Clean mud traps.

EVERY 3,000 MILES - OR THREE MONTHS, WHICHEVER COMES FIRST

All the Service Jobs in the tinted area have been carried forward from earlier service intervals and are to be repeated at this service.

Every 3,000 miles - The Engine Bay

First carry out all Jobs listed under earlier Service Intervals as applicable.
- [ ] Job 2. Check coolant level.
- [ ] Job 3. Brake fluid level.
- [ ] Job 4. Battery electrolyte.
- [ ] Job 5. Screenwash level.

- [ ] Job 23. Generator drive belt.
- [ ] Job 24. Check brake/fuel lines.
- [ ] Job 25. **DIESEL ENGINES ONLY** Drain fuel filter.
- [ ] Job 26. **DIESEL ENGINES UP TO 1987 ONLY** Renew engine oil.
- [ ] Job 27. **DIESEL ENGINES UP TO 1987 ONLY** Replace oil filter.

Every 3,000 miles - Around The Car

First carry out all Jobs listed under earlier Service Intervals as applicable.
- [ ] Job 6. Check tyre pressures.
- [ ] Job 7. Check headlights, sidelights and front indicators.
- [ ] Job 8. Rear lights and indicators.
- [ ] Job 9. Interior lights.
- [ ] Job 10. Number plate lights.
- [ ] Job 11. Side repeater light bulbs.
- [ ] Job 12. Check horn.
- [ ] Job 13. Check windscreen wipers.
- [ ] Job 14. Windscreen washers.
- [ ] Job 15. Check tyres.
- [ ] Job 16. Check spare tyre.
- [ ] Job 17. Wash bodywork.
- [ ] Job 18. Touch-up paintwork.

Job 19. Aerial/Antenna.

Job 20. Valet interior.

Job 21. Improve visibility.

Job 28. Check wheel bolts.

Job 29. Check brake/fuel lines.

Job 30. Check handbrake adjustment.

Job 31. Door and tailgate seals.

Job 32. Check windscreen.

Job 33. Rear view mirrors.

Every 3,000 miles - Under the Car

First carry out all Jobs listed under earlier Service Intervals as applicable.

Job 22. Clean mud traps.

Job 34. Check exhaust system.

Job 35. Check exhaust mountings.

Job 36. Check steering rack gaiters.

Job 37. Check drive-shaft gaiters.

Job 38. Steering joints.

Job 39. Check suspension ball-joints.

Job 40. Inspect for leaks.

Every 3,000 miles - Road Test

Job 41. Clean controls.

Job 42. Check instruments.

Job 43. Throttle pedal.

Job 44. Brakes and steering road test.

Date serviced:..

Carried out by: ....
Garage Stamp or signature:

Parts/Accessories purchased (date, parts,

source) ....

....

....

....

....

EVERY 4,500 MILES - OR EVERY SIX MONTHS, WHICHEVER COMES FIRST

Job 45. DIESEL ENGINES FROM 1987-1992 ONLY Change engine oil and filter.

EVERY 6,000 MILES - OR EVERY SIX MONTHS, WHICHEVER COMES FIRST

All the Service Jobs in the tinted area have been carried forward from earlier service intervals and are to be repeated at this service.

Every 6,000 miles - The Engine Bay

First carry out all Jobs listed under earlier Service Intervals as applicable.

Job 3. Brake fluid level.

Job 4. Battery electrolyte.

Job 5. Screenwash level.

Job 23. Generator drive belt.

Job 24. Check brake/fuel lines.

Job 25. DIESEL ENGINES ONLY Drain fuel filter.

Job 26. DIESEL ENGINES UP TO 1987 ONLY Renew engine oil.

Job 27. DIESEL ENGINES UP TO 1987 ONLY Replace oil filter.

Job 46. Change engine oil/oil filter.

Job 47. Replace oil filter.

Job 48. PETROL ENGINES ONLY Spark plugs.

Job 49. 1300cc MODELS UP TO 1986 ONLY Distributor.

Job 50. NOT DIESEL OR V6, OR 1.6, 1.8 AND 2.0 LITRE MODELS AFTER 1987 Ignition timing.

Job 51. Accelerator controls.

Job 52. Check clutch adjustment.

Job 53. Radiator matrix.

Job 54. Coolant check.

Job 55. Check water pump.

Job 56. Check manual gearbox oil.

Job 57. Automatic transmission fluid.

Job 58. Four wheel drive transmission.

Job 59. Power steering.

Job 60. Lubricate carburettor linkage.

Job 61. Lubricate throttle cable.

Job 62. Check exhaust emission.

Job 63. Adjust carburettor.

Job 64. FUEL INJECTION PETROL ENGINES ONLY Idle speed and mixture.

Job 65. DIESEL ENGINES ONLY Replace fuel filter.

Every 6,000 miles - Around the Car

First carry out all Jobs listed under earlier Service Intervals as applicable.

Job 6. Check tyre pressures.

Job 7. Check headlights, sidelights and front indicators.

Job 8. Rear lights and indicators.

Job 9. Interior lights.

Job 10. Number plate lights.

Job 11. Side repeater light bulbs.

Job 12. Check horn.

Job 13. Check windscreen wipers.

Job 14. Windscreen washers.

Job 15. Check tyres.

Job 16. Check spare tyre.

Job 17. Wash bodywork.

Job 18. Touch-up paintwork.

Job 19. Aerial/Antenna.

Job 20. Valet interior.

Job 21. Improve visibility.

Job 28. Check wheel bolts.

Job 29. Check brake/fuel lines.

Job 30. Check handbrake adjustment.

Job 31. Door and tailgate seals.

Job 32. Check windscreen.

Job 33. Rear view mirrors.

Job 66. Check seat belts.

Job 67. Locks and hinges.

Job 68. Bonnet release mechanism.

Job 69. Check seats.

☐ Job 70. Test shock absorbers.

☐ Job 71. Check/renew front disc brake pads.

☐ Job 72. **2.0 LITRE ENGINED MODELS ONLY** Check/replace rear disc pads.

☐ Job 73. **ALL MODELS EXCEPT 2.0 LITRE** Check/adjust/renew rear drum brakes.

☐ Job 74. Check brake proportioning valve.

Every 6,000 miles - Under the Car

First carry out all Jobs listed under earlier Service Intervals as applicable.

☐ Job 22. Clean mud traps.

☐ Job 34. Check exhaust system.

☐ Job 35. Check exhaust mountings.

☐ Job 36. Check steering rack gaiters.

☐ Job 37. Check drive-shaft gaiters.

☐ Job 38. Steering joints.

☐ Job 39. Check suspension ball-joints.

☐ Job 40. Inspect for leaks.

Every 6,000 miles - Road Test

First carry out all Jobs listed under earlier Service Intervals as applicable.

☐ Job 41. Clean controls.

☐ Job 42. Check instruments.

☐ Job 43. Throttle pedal.

☐ Job 44. Brakes and steering road test.

Date serviced:..

Carried out by:..
Garage Stamp or signature:

Parts/Accessories purchased (date, parts,

source) ....

....

....

....

....

EVERY 9,000 MILES - OR EVERY NINE MONTHS, WHICHEVER COMES FIRST

All the Jobs at this Service Interval have been carried forward from earlier Service Intervals and are to be repeated at this service.

Every 9,000 miles - The Engine Bay

☐ Job 2. Check coolant level.

☐ Job 3. Brake fluid level.

☐ Job 4. Battery electrolyte.

☐ Job 5. Screenwash level.

☐ Job 23. Generator drive belt.

☐ Job 24. Check brake/fuel lines.

☐ Job 25. **DIESEL ENGINES ONLY** Drain fuel filter.

☐ Job 26. **DIESEL ENGINES UP TO 1987 ONLY** Renew engine oil.

☐ Job 27. **DIESEL ENGINES UP TO 1987 ONLY** Replace oil filter.

☐ Job 45. **DIESEL ENGINES FROM 1987-1992 ONLY** Change engine oil and filter.

Every 9,000 miles - Around The Car

First carry out all Jobs listed under earlier Service Intervals as applicable.

☐ Job 6. Check tyre pressures.

☐ Job 7. Check headlights, sidelights and front indicators.

☐ Job 8. Rear lights and indicators.

☐ Job 9. Interior lights.

☐ Job 10. Number plate lights.

☐ Job 11. Side repeater light bulbs.

☐ Job 12. Check horn.

☐ Job 13. Check windscreen wipers.

☐ Job 14. Windscreen washers.

☐ Job 15. Check tyres.

☐ Job 16. Check spare tyre.

☐ Job 17. Wash bodywork.

☐ Job 18. Touch-up paintwork.

☐ Job 19. Aerial/Antenna.

☐ Job 20. Valet interior.

☐ Job 21. Improve visibility.

☐ Job 28. Check wheel bolts.

☐ Job 29. Check brake/fuel lines.

☐ Job 30. Check handbrake adjustment.

☐ Job 31. Door and tailgate seals.

☐ Job 32. Check windscreen.

☐ Job 33. Rear view mirrors.

Every 9,000 miles - Under the Car

First carry out all Jobs listed under earlier Service Intervals as applicable.

☐ Job 22. Clean mud traps.

☐ Job 34. Check exhaust system.

☐ Job 35. Check exhaust mountings.

☐ Job 36. Check steering rack gaiters.

☐ Job 37. Check drive-shaft gaiters.

☐ Job 38. Steering joints.

☐ Job 39. Check suspension ball-joints.

☐ Job 40. Inspect for leaks.

Every 9,000 miles - Road Test

First carry out all Jobs listed under earlier Service Intervals as applicable.

- [ ] Job 41. Clean controls.
- [ ] Job 42. Check instruments.
- [ ] Job 43. Throttle pedal.
- [ ] Job 44. Brakes and steering road test.

Date serviced:... .

Carried out by: ....
Garage Stamp or signature:

Parts/Accessories purchased (date, parts,

source) ....

....

....

....

....

EVERY 12,000 MILES - OR EVERY TWELVE MONTHS, WHICHEVER COMES FIRST

All the Service Jobs in the tinted area have been carried forward from earlier service intervals and are to be repeated at this service.

Every 12,000 miles - The Engine Bay

First carry out all Jobs listed under earlier Service Intervals as applicable.

- [ ] Job 4. Battery electrolyte.
- [ ] Job 5. Screenwash level.
- [ ] Job 23. Generator drive belt.
- [ ] Job 24. Check brake/fuel lines.
- [ ] Job 25. **DIESEL ENGINES ONLY** Drain fuel filter.
- [ ] Job 26. **DIESEL ENGINES UP TO 1987 ONLY** Renew engine oil.
- [ ] Job 27. **DIESEL ENGINES UP TO 1987 ONLY** Replace oil filter.
- [ ] Job 46. Change engine oil/oil filter.
- [ ] Job 47. Replace oil filter.
- [ ] Job 48. **PETROL ENGINES ONLY** Spark plugs.
- [ ] Job 49. **1300cc MODELS UP TO 1986 ONLY** Distributor.
- [ ] Job 50. **NOT DIESEL OR V6, OR 1.6, 1.8 AND 2.0 LITRE MODELS AFTER 1987** Ignition timing.
- [ ] Job 51. Accelerator controls.
- [ ] Job 52. Check clutch adjustment.
- [ ] Job 53. Radiator matrix.
- [ ] Job 54. Coolant check.
- [ ] Job 55. Check water pump.
- [ ] Job 56. Check manual gearbox oil.
- [ ] Job 57. Automatic transmission fluid.
- [ ] Job 58. Four wheel drive transmission.
- [ ] Job 59. Power steering.
- [ ] Job 60. Lubricate carburettor linkage.
- [ ] Job 61. Lubricate throttle cable.
- [ ] Job 62. Check exhaust emission.
- [ ] Job 63. Adjust carburettor.
- [ ] Job 64. FUEL INJECTION **PETROL ENGINES ONLY** Idle speed and mixture.
- [ ] Job 65. **DIESEL ENGINES ONLY** Replace fuel filter.

- [ ] Job 75. Read stored engine codes.
- [ ] Job 76. UP TO 1987 ONLY Check camshaft belt.
- [ ] Job 77. CAVALIERS FROM 1991 ONLY Emission control equipment.
- [ ] Job 78. Air cleaner element.
- [ ] Job 79. Air cleaner intake.
- [ ] Job 80. Check/renew fuel filter.
- [ ] Job 81. FUEL INJECTION ENGINES ONLY Renew fuel microfilter.
- [ ] Job 82. Check coolant hoses.
- [ ] Job 83. Replace coolant.
- [ ] Job 84. Check power steering hoses and belt.
- [ ] Job 85. Check air conditioning.
- [ ] Job 86. Battery terminals.
- [ ] Job 87. Glow plug maintenance.

Every 12,000 miles - Around the Car

First carry out all Jobs listed under earlier Service Intervals as applicable.

- [ ] Job 6. Check tyre pressures.
- [ ] Job 7. Check headlights, sidelights and front indicators.
- [ ] Job 8. Rear lights and indicators.
- [ ] Job 9. Interior lights.
- [ ] Job 10. Number plate lights.
- [ ] Job 11. Side repeater light bulbs.
- [ ] Job 12. Check horn.
- [ ] Job 13. Check windscreen wipers.
- [ ] Job 14. Windscreen washers.
- [ ] Job 15. Check tyres.
- [ ] Job 16. Check spare tyre.
- [ ] Job 17. Wash bodywork.
- [ ] Job 18. Touch-up paintwork.
- [ ] Job 19. Aerial/Antenna.
- [ ] Job 20. Valet interior.
- [ ] Job 21. Improve visibility.
- [ ] Job 28. Check wheel bolts.
- [ ] Job 29. Check brake/fuel lines.
- [ ] Job 30. Check handbrake adjustment.
- [ ] Job 31. Door and tailgate seals.
- [ ] Job 32. Check windscreen.
- [ ] Job 33. Rear view mirrors.

SERVICE HISTORY

☐ Job 66. Check seat belts.

☐ Job 67. Locks and hinges.

☐ Job 68. Bonnet release mechanism.

☐ Job 69. Check seats.

☐ Job 70. Test shock absorbers.

☐ Job 71. Check/renew front disc brake pads.

☐ Job 72. **2.0 LITRE ENGINED MODELS ONLY** Check/replace rear disc pads.

☐ Job 73. **ALL MODELS EXCEPT 2.0 LITRE** Check/adjust/renew rear drum brakes.

☐ Job 74. Check brake proportioning valve.

☐ Job 88. Toolkit and jack.

☐ Job 89. Lamp seals.

☐ Job 90. Alarm sender unit.

☐ Job 91. Adjust headlights.

☐ Job 92. Renew wiper blades.

☐ Job 93. Check hub bearings.

☐ Job 94. Check steering and suspension.

☐ Job 95. **CONVERTIBLE CARS ONLY** Check soft-top frame.

Every 12,000 miles - Under the Car

First carry out all Jobs listed under earlier Service Intervals as applicable.

☐ Job 22. Clean mud traps.

☐ Job 34. Check exhaust system.

☐ Job 35. Check exhaust mountings.

☐ Job 36. Check steering rack gaiters.

☐ Job 37. Check drive-shaft gaiters.

☐ Job 38. Steering joints.

☐ Job 39. Check suspension ball-joints.

☐ Job 40. Inspect for leaks.

☐ Job 96. Engine/gearbox mounts.

☐ Job 97. Inspect underside.

☐ Job 98. Clear drain holes.

☐ Job 99. **FOUR WHEEL DRIVE ONLY** Check prop shaft U.J.'s.

☐ Job 100. Renew brake fluid.

Every 12,000 miles - Road Test

First carry out all Jobs listed under earlier Service Intervals as applicable.

☐ Job 41. Clean controls.

☐ Job 42. Check instruments.

☐ Job 43. Throttle pedal.

☐ Job 44. Brakes and steering road test.

EVERY 13,500 MILES

☐ Job 45. **DIESEL ENGINES FROM 1987-1992 ONLY** Change engine oil and filter.

Date serviced:....................................

Carried out by:....................................
Garage Stamp or signature:

Parts/Accessories purchased (date, parts, source) ....
....
....
....
....

EVERY 15,000 MILES - OR EVERY FIFTEEN MONTHS, WHICHEVER COMES FIRST

All the Jobs at this Service Interval have been carried forward from earlier Service Intervals and are to be repeated at this service.

Every 15,000 miles - The Engine Bay

☐ Job 2. Check coolant level.

☐ Job 3. Brake fluid level.

☐ Job 4. Battery electrolyte.

☐ Job 5. Screenwash level.

☐ Job 23. Generator drive belt.

☐ Job 24. Check brake/fuel lines.

☐ Job 25. **DIESEL ENGINES ONLY** Drain fuel filter.

☐ Job 26. **DIESEL ENGINES UP TO 1987 ONLY** Renew engine oil.

☐ Job 27. **DIESEL ENGINES UP TO 1987 ONLY** Replace oil filter.

Every 15,000 miles - Around The Car

First carry out all Jobs listed under earlier Service Intervals as applicable.

- [ ] Job 6. Check tyre pressures.
- [ ] Job 7. Check headlights, sidelights and front indicators.
- [ ] Job 8. Rear lights and indicators.
- [ ] Job 9. Interior lights.
- [ ] Job 10. Number plate lights.
- [ ] Job 11. Side repeater light bulbs.
- [ ] Job 12. Check horn.
- [ ] Job 13. Check windscreen wipers.
- [ ] Job 14. Windscreen washers.
- [ ] Job 15. Check tyres.
- [ ] Job 16. Check spare tyre.
- [ ] Job 17. Wash bodywork.
- [ ] Job 18. Touch-up paintwork.
- [ ] Job 19. Aerial/Antenna.
- [ ] Job 20. Valet interior.
- [ ] Job 21. Improve visibility.
- [ ] Job 28. Check wheel bolts.
- [ ] Job 29. Check brake/fuel lines.
- [ ] Job 30. Check handbrake adjustment.
- [ ] Job 31. Door and tailgate seals.
- [ ] Job 32. Check windscreen.
- [ ] Job 33. Rear view mirrors.

Every 15,000 miles - Under the Car

First carry out all Jobs listed under earlier Service Intervals as applicable.

- [ ] Job 22. Clean mud traps.
- [ ] Job 34. Check exhaust system.
- [ ] Job 35. Check exhaust mountings.
- [ ] Job 36. Check steering rack gaiters.
- [ ] Job 37. Check drive-shaft gaiters.
- [ ] Job 38. Steering joints.
- [ ] Job 39. Check suspension ball-joints.
- [ ] Job 40. Inspect for leaks.

Every 15,000 miles - Road Test

First carry out all Jobs listed under earlier Service Intervals as applicable.

- [ ] Job 41. Clean controls.
- [ ] Job 42. Check instruments.
- [ ] Job 43. Throttle pedal.
- [ ] Job 44. Brakes and steering road test.

Date serviced:...

Carried out by: ....
Garage Stamp or signature:

Parts/Accessories purchased (date, parts, source) ....

....

....

....

....

EVERY 18,000 MILES - OR EVERY EIGHTEEN MONTHS, WHICHEVER COMES FIRST

All the Jobs at this Service Interval have been carried forward from earlier Service Intervals and are to be repeated at this service.

Every 18,000 miles - The Engine Bay

First carry out all Jobs listed under earlier Service Intervals as applicable.

- [ ] Job 3. Brake fluid level.
- [ ] Job 4. Battery electrolyte.
- [ ] Job 5. Screenwash level.
- [ ] Job 23. Generator drive belt.
- [ ] Job 24. Check brake/fuel lines.
- [ ] Job 25. **DIESEL ENGINES ONLY** Drain fuel filter.
- [ ] Job 26. **DIESEL ENGINES UP TO 1987 ONLY** Renew engine oil.
- [ ] Job 27. **DIESEL ENGINES UP TO 1987 ONLY** Replace oil filter.
- [ ] Job 45. **DIESEL ENGINES FROM 1987-1992 ONLY** Change engine oil and filter.
- [ ] Job 46. Change engine oil/oil filter.
- [ ] Job 47. Replace oil filter.
- [ ] Job 48. **PETROL ENGINES ONLY** Spark plugs.
- [ ] Job 49. **1300cc MODELS UP TO 1986 ONLY** Distributor.
- [ ] Job 50. **NOT DIESEL OR V6, OR 1.6, 1.8 AND 2.0 LITRE MODELS AFTER 1987** Ignition timing.
- [ ] Job 51. Accelerator controls.
- [ ] Job 52. Check clutch adjustment.
- [ ] Job 53. Radiator matrix.
- [ ] Job 54. Coolant check.
- [ ] Job 55. Check water pump.
- [ ] Job 56. Check manual gearbox oil.
- [ ] Job 57. Automatic transmission fluid.
- [ ] Job 58. Four wheel drive transmission.
- [ ] Job 59. Power steering.
- [ ] Job 60. Lubricate carburettor linkage.
- [ ] Job 61. Lubricate throttle cable.
- [ ] Job 62. Check exhaust emission.

SERVICE HISTORY

☐ Job 63. Adjust carburettor.

☐ Job 64. FUEL INJECTION **PETROL ENGINES ONLY** Idle speed and mixture.

☐ Job 65. **DIESEL ENGINES ONLY** Replace fuel filter.Job 64. FUEL INJECTION **PETROL ENGINES ONLY** Idle speed and mixture.

Every 18,000 miles - Around the Car

First carry out all Jobs listed under earlier Service Intervals as applicable.

☐ Job 6. Check tyre pressures.

☐ Job 7. Check headlights, sidelights and front indicators.

☐ Job 8. Rear lights and indicators.

☐ Job 9. Interior lights.

☐ Job 10. Number plate lights.

☐ Job 11. Side repeater light bulbs.

☐ Job 12. Check horn.

☐ Job 13. Check windscreen wipers.

☐ Job 14. Windscreen washers.

☐ Job 15. Check tyres.

☐ Job 16. Check spare tyre.

☐ Job 17. Wash bodywork.

☐ Job 18. Touch-up paintwork.

☐ Job 19. Aerial/Antenna.

☐ Job 20. Valet interior.

☐ Job 21. Improve visibility.

☐ Job 28. Check wheel bolts.

☐ Job 29. Check brake/fuel lines.

☐ Job 30. Check handbrake adjustment.

☐ Job 31. Door and tailgate seals.

☐ Job 32. Check windscreen.

☐ Job 33. Rear view mirrors.

☐ Job 66. Check seat belts.

☐ Job 67. Locks and hinges.

☐ Job 68. Bonnet release mechanism.

☐ Job 69. Check seats.

☐ Job 70. Test shock absorbers.

☐ Job 71. Check/renew front disc brake pads.

☐ Job 72. **2.0 LITRE ENGINED MODELS ONLY** Check/replace rear disc pads.

☐ Job 73. **ALL MODELS EXCEPT 2.0 LITRE** Check/adjust/renew rear drum brakes.

☐ Job 74. Check brake proportioning valve.

Every 18,000 miles - Under the Car

First carry out all Jobs listed under earlier Service Intervals as applicable.

☐ Job 22. Clean mud traps.

☐ Job 34. Check exhaust system.

☐ Job 35. Check exhaust mountings.

☐ Job 36. Check steering rack gaiters.

☐ Job 37. Check drive-shaft gaiters.

☐ Job 38. Steering joints.

☐ Job 39. Check suspension ball-joints.

☐ Job 40. Inspect for leaks.

Every 18,000 miles - Road Test

First carry out all Jobs listed under earlier Service Intervals as applicable.

☐ Job 41. Clean controls.

☐ Job 42. Check instruments.

☐ Job 43. Throttle pedal.

☐ Job 44. Brakes and steering road test.

Date serviced:...

Carried out by:..
Garage Stamp or signature:

Parts/Accessories purchased (date, parts, source)..

....

....

....

....

EVERY 21,000 MILES - OR EVERY TWENTY ONE MONTHS, WHICHEVER COMES FIRST

All the Jobs at this Service Interval have been carried forward from earlier Service Intervals and are to be repeated at this service.

Every 21,000 miles - The Engine Bay

☐ Job 2. Check coolant level.

☐ Job 3. Brake fluid level.

☐ Job 4. Battery electrolyte.

☐ Job 5. Screenwash level.

☐ Job 23. Generator drive belt.

☐ Job 24. Check brake/fuel lines.

☐ Job 25. **DIESEL ENGINES ONLY** Drain fuel filter.

☐ Job 26. **DIESEL ENGINES UP TO 1987 ONLY** Renew engine oil.

☐ Job 27. **DIESEL ENGINES UP TO 1987 ONLY** Replace oil filter.

Every 21,000 miles - Around The Car

First carry out all Jobs listed under earlier Service Intervals as applicable.

- [ ] Job 6. Check tyre pressures.
- [ ] Job 7. Check headlights, sidelights and front indicators.
- [ ] Job 8. Rear lights and indicators.
- [ ] Job 9. Interior lights.
- [ ] Job 10. Number plate lights.
- [ ] Job 11. Side repeater light bulbs.
- [ ] Job 12. Check horn.
- [ ] Job 13. Check windscreen wipers.
- [ ] Job 14. Windscreen washers.
- [ ] Job 15. Check tyres.
- [ ] Job 16. Check spare tyre.
- [ ] Job 17. Wash bodywork.
- [ ] Job 18. Touch-up paintwork.
- [ ] Job 19. Aerial/Antenna.
- [ ] Job 20. Valet interior.
- [ ] Job 21. Improve visibility.
- [ ] Job 28. Check wheel bolts.
- [ ] Job 29. Check brake/fuel lines.
- [ ] Job 30. Check handbrake adjustment.
- [ ] Job 31. Door and tailgate seals.
- [ ] Job 32. Check windscreen.
- [ ] Job 33. Rear view mirrors.

Every 21,000 miles - Under the Car

First carry out all Jobs listed under earlier Service Intervals as applicable.

- [ ] Job 22. Clean mud traps.
- [ ] Job 34. Check exhaust system.
- [ ] Job 35. Check exhaust mountings.
- [ ] Job 36. Check steering rack gaiters.
- [ ] Job 37. Check drive-shaft gaiters.
- [ ] Job 38. Steering joints.
- [ ] Job 39. Check suspension ball-joints.
- [ ] Job 40. Inspect for leaks.

Every 21,000 miles - Road Test

First carry out all Jobs listed under earlier Service Intervals as applicable.

- [ ] Job 41. Clean controls.
- [ ] Job 42. Check instruments.
- [ ] Job 43. Throttle pedal.
- [ ] Job 44. Brakes and steering road test.

EVERY 22,500 MILES

- [ ] Job 45. DIESEL ENGINES FROM 1987-1992 ONLY Change engine oil and filter.

Date serviced:..

Carried out by: ....
Garage Stamp or signature:

Parts/Accessories purchased (date, parts, source) ....

....

....

....

....

EVERY 24,000 MILES - OR EVERY TWO YEARS, WHICHEVER COMES FIRST

All the Service Jobs in the tinted area have been carried forward from earlier service intervals and are to be repeated at this service.

Every 24,000 miles - The Engine Bay

First carry out all Jobs listed under earlier Service Intervals as applicable.

- [ ] Job 4. Battery electrolyte.
- [ ] Job 5. Screenwash level.
- [ ] Job 23. Generator drive belt.
- [ ] Job 24. Check brake/fuel lines.
- [ ] Job 25. DIESEL ENGINES ONLY Drain fuel filter.
- [ ] Job 26. DIESEL ENGINES UP TO 1987 ONLY Renew engine oil.
- [ ] Job 27. DIESEL ENGINES UP TO 1987 ONLY Replace oil filter.
- [ ] Job 46. Change engine oil/oil filter.
- [ ] Job 47. Replace oil filter.
- [ ] Job 48. PETROL ENGINES ONLY Spark plugs.
- [ ] Job 49. 1300cc MODELS UP TO 1986 ONLY Distributor.
- [ ] Job 50. NOT DIESEL OR V6, OR 1.6, 1.8 AND 2.0 LITRE MODELS AFTER 1987 Ignition timing.
- [ ] Job 51. Accelerator controls.
- [ ] Job 52. Check clutch adjustment.
- [ ] Job 53. Radiator matrix.
- [ ] Job 54. Coolant check.
- [ ] Job 55. Check water pump.
- [ ] Job 56. Check manual gearbox oil.
- [ ] Job 57. Automatic transmission fluid.
- [ ] Job 58. Four wheel drive transmission.
- [ ] Job 59. Power steering.
- [ ] Job 60. Lubricate carburettor linkage.
- [ ] Job 61. Lubricate throttle cable.
- [ ] Job 62. Check exhaust emission.
- [ ] Job 63. Adjust carburettor.
- [ ] Job 64. FUEL INJECTION PETROL ENGINES ONLY Idle speed and mixture.
- [ ] Job 65. DIESEL ENGINES ONLY Replace fuel filter.

☐ Job 75. Read stored engine codes.

☐ Job 76. **UP TO 1987 ONLY** Check camshaft belt.

☐ Job 77. **CAVALIERS FROM 1991 ONLY** Emission control equipment.

☐ Job 78. Air cleaner element.

☐ Job 79. Air cleaner intake.

☐ Job 80. Check/renew fuel filter.

☐ Job 81. **FUEL INJECTION ENGINES ONLY** Renew fuel microfilter.

☐ Job 82. Check coolant hoses.

☐ Job 83. Replace coolant.

☐ Job 84. Check power steering hose and belt.

☐ Job 85. Check air conditioning.

☐ Job 86. Battery terminals.

☐ Job 87. Glow plug maintenance.

☐ Job 101. Radiator pressure cap.

Every 24,000 miles - Around the Car

First carry out all Jobs listed under earlier Service Intervals as applicable.

☐ Job 6. Check tyre pressures.

☐ Job 7. Check headlights, sidelights and front indicators.

☐ Job 8. Rear lights and indicators.

☐ Job 9. Interior lights.

☐ Job 10. Number plate lights.

☐ Job 11. Side repeater light bulbs.

☐ Job 12. Check horn.

☐ Job 13. Check windscreen wipers.

☐ Job 14. Windscreen washers.

☐ Job 15. Check tyres.

☐ Job 16. Check spare tyre.

☐ Job 17. Wash bodywork.

☐ Job 18. Touch-up paintwork.

☐ Job 19. Aerial/Antenna.

☐ Job 20. Valet interior.

☐ Job 21. Improve visibility.

☐ Job 28. Check wheel bolts.

☐ Job 29. Check brake/fuel lines.

☐ Job 30. Check handbrake adjustment.

☐ Job 31. Door and tailgate seals.

☐ Job 32. Check windscreen.

☐ Job 33. Rear view mirrors.

☐ Job 66. Check seat belts.

☐ Job 67. Locks and hinges.

☐ Job 68. Bonnet release mechanism.

☐ Job 69. Check seats.

☐ Job 70. Test shock absorbers.

☐ Job 71. Check/renew front disc brake pads.

☐ Job 72. **2.0 LITRE ENGINED MODELS ONLY** Check/replace rear disc pads.

☐ Job 73. **ALL MODELS EXCEPT 2.0 LITRE** Check/adjust/renew rear drum brakes.

☐ Job 74. Check brake proportioning valve.

☐ Job 88. Toolkit and jack.

☐ Job 89. Lamp seals.

☐ Job 90. Alarm sender unit.

☐ Job 91. Adjust headlights.

☐ Job 92. Renew wiper blades.

☐ Job 93. Check hub bearings.

☐ Job 94. Check steering and suspension.

☐ Job 95. **CONVERTIBLE CARS ONLY** Check soft-top frame.

☐ Job 102. Check brake discs/drums and calipers.

Every 24,000 miles - Under the Car

First carry out all Jobs listed under earlier Service Intervals as applicable.

☐ Job 22. Clean mud traps.

☐ Job 34. Check exhaust system.

☐ Job 35. Check exhaust mountings.

☐ Job 36. Check steering rack gaiters.

☐ Job 37. Check drive-shaft gaiters.

☐ Job 38. Steering joints.

☐ Job 39. Check suspension ball-joints.

☐ Job 40. Inspect for leaks.

☐ Job 96. Engine/gearbox mounts.

☐ Job 97. Inspect underside.

☐ Job 98. Clear drain holes.

☐ Job 99. **FOUR WHEEL DRIVE ONLY** Check prop shaft U.J.'s.

☐ Job100. Renew brake fluid.

Every 24,000 miles - Road Test

First carry out all Jobs listed under earlier Service Intervals as applicable.

- [ ] Job 41. Clean controls.
- [ ] Job 42. Check instruments.
- [ ] Job 43. Throttle pedal.
- [ ] Job 44. Brakes and steering road test.

EVERY 27,000 MILES - OR EVERY TWENTY SEVEN MONTHS, WHICHEVER COMES FIRST

All the Jobs at this Service Interval have been carried forward from earlier Service Intervals and are to be repeated at this service.

Every 27,000 miles - The Engine Bay

- [ ] Job 2. Check coolant level.
- [ ] Job 3. Brake fluid level.
- [ ] Job 4. Battery electrolyte.
- [ ] Job 5. Screenwash level.
- [ ] Job 23. Generator drive belt.
- [ ] Job 24. Check brake/fuel lines.
- [ ] Job 25. **DIESEL ENGINES ONLY** Drain fuel filter.
- [ ] Job 26. **DIESEL ENGINES UP TO 1987 ONLY** Renew engine oil.
- [ ] Job 27. **DIESEL ENGINES UP TO 1987 ONLY** Replace oil filter.
- [ ] Job 45. **DIESEL ENGINES FROM 1987-1992 ONLY** Change engine oil and filter.

Every 27,000 miles - Around The Car

First carry out all Jobs listed under earlier Service Intervals as applicable.

- [ ] Job 6. Check tyre pressures.
- [ ] Job 7. Check headlights, sidelights and front indicators.
- [ ] Job 8. Rear lights and indicators.
- [ ] Job 9. Interior lights.
- [ ] Job 10. Number plate lights.
- [ ] Job 11. Side repeater light bulbs.
- [ ] Job 12. Check horn.
- [ ] Job 13. Check windscreen wipers.
- [ ] Job 14. Windscreen washers.
- [ ] Job 15. Check tyres.
- [ ] Job 16. Check spare tyre.
- [ ] Job 17. Wash bodywork.
- [ ] Job 18. Touch-up paintwork.
- [ ] Job 19. Aerial/Antenna.
- [ ] Job 20. Valet interior.
- [ ] Job 21. Improve visibility.
- [ ] Job 28. Check wheel bolts.
- [ ] Job 29. Check brake/fuel lines.
- [ ] Job 30. Check handbrake adjustment.
- [ ] Job 31. Door and tailgate seals.
- [ ] Job 32. Check windscreen.
- [ ] Job 33. Rear view mirrors.

Every 27,000 miles - Under the Car

First carry out all Jobs listed under earlier Service Intervals as applicable.

- [ ] Job 22. Clean mud traps.
- [ ] Job 34. Check exhaust system.
- [ ] Job 35. Check exhaust mountings.
- [ ] Job 36. Check steering rack gaiters.
- [ ] Job 37. Check drive-shaft gaiters.
- [ ] Job 38. Steering joints.
- [ ] Job 39. Check suspension ball-joints.
- [ ] Job 40. Inspect for leaks.

Date serviced: ....

Carried out by: ....
Garage Stamp or signature:

Parts/Accessories purchased (date, parts, source) ....
....
....
....
....

Every 27,000 miles - Road Test

First carry out all Jobs listed under earlier Service Intervals as applicable.

- ☐ Job 41. Clean controls.
- ☐ Job 42. Check instruments.
- ☐ Job 43. Throttle pedal.
- ☐ Job 44. Brakes and steering road test.

Date serviced:..

Carried out by: ....
Garage Stamp or signature:

Parts/Accessories purchased (date, parts, source) ....
....
....
....
....

EVERY 30,000 MILES - OR EVERY THIRTY MONTHS, WHICHEVER COMES FIRST

All the Jobs at this Service Interval have been carried forward from earlier Service Intervals and are to be repeated at this service.

Every 30,000 miles - The Engine Bay

First carry out all Jobs listed under earlier Service Intervals as applicable.

- ☐ Job 3. Brake fluid level.
- ☐ Job 4. Battery electrolyte.
- ☐ Job 5. Screenwash level.
- ☐ Job 23. Generator drive belt.
- ☐ Job 24. Check brake/fuel lines.
- ☐ Job 25. **DIESEL ENGINES ONLY** Drain fuel filter.
- ☐ Job 26. **DIESEL ENGINES UP TO 1987 ONLY** Renew engine oil.
- ☐ Job 27. **DIESEL ENGINES UP TO 1987 ONLY** Replace oil filter.
- ☐ Job 45. **DIESEL ENGINES FROM 1987-1992 ONLY** Change engine oil and filter.
- ☐ Job 46. Change engine oil/oil filter.
- ☐ Job 47. Replace oil filter.
- ☐ Job 48. **PETROL ENGINES ONLY** Spark plugs.
- ☐ Job 49. **1300cc MODELS UP TO 1986 ONLY** Distributor.
- ☐ Job 50. **NOT DIESEL OR V6, OR 1.6, 1.8 AND 2.0 LITRE MODELS AFTER 1987** Ignition timing.
- ☐ Job 51. Accelerator controls.
- ☐ Job 52. Check clutch adjustment.
- ☐ Job 53. Radiator matrix.
- ☐ Job 54. Coolant check.
- ☐ Job 55. Check water pump.
- ☐ Job 56. Check manual gearbox oil.
- ☐ Job 57. Automatic transmission fluid.
- ☐ Job 58. Four wheel drive transmission.
- ☐ Job 59. Power steering.
- ☐ Job 60. Lubricate carburettor linkage.
- ☐ Job 61. Lubricate throttle cable.
- ☐ Job 62. Check exhaust emission.

- ☐ Job 63. Adjust carburettor.
- ☐ Job 64. **FUEL INJECTION PETROL ENGINES ONLY** Idle speed and mixture.
- ☐ Job 65. **DIESEL ENGINES ONLY** Replace fuel filter.

Every 30,000 miles - Around the Car

First carry out all Jobs listed under earlier Service Intervals as applicable.

- ☐ Job 6. Check tyre pressures.
- ☐ Job 7. Check headlights, sidelights and front indicators.
- ☐ Job 8. Rear lights and indicators.
- ☐ Job 9. Interior lights.
- ☐ Job 10. Number plate lights.
- ☐ Job 11. Side repeater light bulbs.
- ☐ Job 12. Check horn.
- ☐ Job 13. Check windscreen wipers.
- ☐ Job 14. Windscreen washers.
- ☐ Job 15. Check tyres.
- ☐ Job 16. Check spare tyre.
- ☐ Job 17. Wash bodywork.
- ☐ Job 18. Touch-up paintwork.
- ☐ Job 19. Aerial/Antenna.
- ☐ Job 20. Valet interior.
- ☐ Job 21. Improve visibility.
- ☐ Job 28. Check wheel bolts.
- ☐ Job 29. Check brake/fuel lines.
- ☐ Job 30. Check handbrake adjustment.
- ☐ Job 31. Door and tailgate seals.
- ☐ Job 32. Check windscreen.
- ☐ Job 33. Rear view mirrors.
- ☐ Job 66. Check seat belts.
- ☐ Job 67. Locks and hinges.
- ☐ Job 68. Bonnet release mechanism.
- ☐ Job 69. Check seats.
- ☐ Job 70. Test shock absorbers.
- ☐ Job 71. Check/renew front disc brake pads.
- ☐ Job 72. **2.0 LITRE ENGINED MODELS ONLY** Check/replace rear disc pads.
- ☐ Job 73. **ALL MODELS EXCEPT 2.0 LITRE** Check/adjust/renew rear drum brakes.
- ☐ Job 74. Check brake proportioning valve.

Every 30,000 miles - Under the Car

First carry out all Jobs listed under earlier Service Intervals as applicable.

- [ ] Job 22. Clean mud traps.
- [ ] Job 34. Check exhaust system.
- [ ] Job 35. Check exhaust mountings.
- [ ] Job 36. Check steering rack gaiters.
- [ ] Job 37. Check drive-shaft gaiters.
- [ ] Job 38. Steering joints.
- [ ] Job 39. Check suspension ball-joints.
- [ ] Job 40. Inspect for leaks.

Every 30,000 miles - Road Test

First carry out all Jobs listed under earlier Service Intervals as applicable.

- [ ] Job 41. Clean controls.
- [ ] Job 42. Check instruments.
- [ ] Job 43. Throttle pedal.
- [ ] Job 44. Brakes and steering road test.

EVERY 31,500 MILES

- [ ] Job 45. **DIESEL ENGINES FROM 1987-1992 ONLY** Change engine oil and filter.

Date serviced:..

Carried out by: ....
Garage Stamp or signature:

Parts/Accessories purchased (date, parts,

source) ....

....

....

....

....

EVERY 33,000 MILES - OR EVERY THIRTY THREE MONTHS, WHICHEVER COMES FIRST

All the Jobs at this Service Interval have been carried forward from earlier Service Intervals and are to be repeated at this service.

Every 33,000 miles - The Engine Bay

- [ ] Job 2. Check coolant level.
- [ ] Job 3. Brake fluid level.
- [ ] Job 4. Battery electrolyte.
- [ ] Job 5. Screenwash level.
- [ ] Job 23. Generator drive belt.
- [ ] Job 24. Check brake/fuel lines.
- [ ] Job 25. **DIESEL ENGINES ONLY** Drain fuel filter.
- [ ] Job 26. **DIESEL ENGINES UP TO 1987 ONLY** Renew engine oil.
- [ ] Job 27. **DIESEL ENGINES UP TO 1987 ONLY** Replace oil filter.

Every 33,000 miles - Around The Car

First carry out all Jobs listed under earlier Service Intervals as applicable.

- [ ] Job 6. Check tyre pressures.
- [ ] Job 7. Check headlights, sidelights and front indicators.
- [ ] Job 8. Rear lights and indicators.
- [ ] Job 9. Interior lights.
- [ ] Job 10. Number plate lights.
- [ ] Job 11. Side repeater light bulbs.
- [ ] Job 12. Check horn.
- [ ] Job 13. Check windscreen wipers.
- [ ] Job 14. Windscreen washers.
- [ ] Job 15. Check tyres.
- [ ] Job 16. Check spare tyre.
- [ ] Job 17. Wash bodywork.
- [ ] Job 18. Touch-up paintwork.
- [ ] Job 19. Aerial/Antenna.
- [ ] Job 20. Valet interior.
- [ ] Job 21. Improve visibility.
- [ ] Job 28. Check wheel bolts.
- [ ] Job 29. Check brake/fuel lines.
- [ ] Job 30. Check handbrake adjustment.
- [ ] Job 31. Door and tailgate seals.
- [ ] Job 32. Check windscreen.
- [ ] Job 33. Rear view mirrors.

Every 33,000 miles - Under the Car

First carry out all Jobs listed under earlier Service Intervals as applicable.

- [ ] Job 22. Clean mud traps.
- [ ] Job 34. Check exhaust system.
- [ ] Job 35. Check exhaust mountings.
- [ ] Job 36. Check steering rack gaiters.
- [ ] Job 37. Check drive-shaft gaiters.
- [ ] Job 38. Steering joints.
- [ ] Job 39. Check suspension ball-joints.
- [ ] Job 40. Inspect for leaks.

Every 33,000 miles - Road Test

First carry out all Jobs listed under earlier Service Intervals as applicable.

- [ ] Job 41. Clean controls.
- [ ] Job 42. Check instruments.
- [ ] Job 43. Throttle pedal.
- [ ] Job 44. Brakes and steering road test.

Date serviced:....................................

Carried out by: ....
Garage Stamp or signature:

Parts/Accessories purchased (date, parts, source) ....
....
....
....
....

EVERY 36,000 MILES - OR EVERY THREE YEARS, WHICHEVER COMES FIRST

All the Service Jobs in the tinted area have been carried forward from earlier service intervals and are to be repeated at this service.

Every 36,000 miles - The Engine Bay

First carry out all Jobs listed under earlier Service Intervals as applicable.

- [ ] Job 4. Battery electrolyte.
- [ ] Job 5. Screenwash level.
- [ ] Job 23. Generator drive belt.
- [ ] Job 24. Check brake/fuel lines.
- [ ] Job 25. **DIESEL ENGINES ONLY** Drain fuel filter.
- [ ] Job 26. **DIESEL ENGINES UP TO 1987 ONLY** Renew engine oil.
- [ ] Job 27. **DIESEL ENGINES UP TO 1987 ONLY** Replace oil filter.
- [ ] Job 45. **DIESEL ENGINES FROM 1987-1992 ONLY** Change engine oil and filter.
- [ ] Job 46. Change engine oil/oil filter.
- [ ] Job 47. Replace oil filter.
- [ ] Job 48. **PETROL ENGINES ONLY** Spark plugs.
- [ ] Job 49. **1300cc MODELS UP TO 1986 ONLY** Distributor.
- [ ] Job 50. **NOT DIESEL OR V6, OR 1.6, 1.8 AND 2.0 LITRE MODELS AFTER 1987** Ignition timing.
- [ ] Job 51. Accelerator controls.
- [ ] Job 52. Check clutch adjustment.
- [ ] Job 53. Radiator matrix.
- [ ] Job 54. Coolant check.
- [ ] Job 55. Check water pump.
- [ ] Job 56. Check manual gearbox oil.
- [ ] Job 57. Automatic transmission fluid.
- [ ] Job 58. Four wheel drive transmission.
- [ ] Job 59. Power steering.
- [ ] Job 60. Lubricate carburettor linkage.
- [ ] Job 61. Lubricate throttle cable.
- [ ] Job 62. Check exhaust emission.
- [ ] Job 63. Adjust carburettor.
- [ ] Job 64. **FUEL INJECTION PETROL ENGINES ONLY** Idle speed and mixture.
- [ ] Job 65. **DIESEL ENGINES ONLY** Replace fuel filter.
- [ ] Job 75. Read stored engine codes.
- [ ] Job 76. **UP TO 1987 ONLY** Check camshaft belt.
- [ ] Job 77. **CAVALIERS FROM 1991 ONLY** Emission control equipment.
- [ ] Job 78. Air cleaner element.
- [ ] Job 79. Air cleaner intake.
- [ ] Job 80. Check/renew fuel filter.
- [ ] Job 81. **FUEL INJECTION ENGINES ONLY** Renew fuel microfilter.
- [ ] Job 82. Check coolant hoses.
- [ ] Job 83. Replace coolant.
- [ ] Job 84. Check power steering hose and belt.
- [ ] Job 85. Check air conditioning.
- [ ] Job 86. Battery terminals.
- [ ] Job 87. Glow plug maintenance.
- [ ] Job 101. Radiator pressure cap.

- [ ] Job 103. Renew camshaft belt.

Every 36,000 miles - Around the Car

First carry out all Jobs listed under earlier Service Intervals as applicable.

- [ ] Job 6. Check tyre pressures.
- [ ] Job 7. Check headlights, sidelights and front indicators.
- [ ] Job 8. Rear lights and indicators.
- [ ] Job 9. Interior lights.
- [ ] Job 10. Number plate lights.
- [ ] Job 11. Side repeater light bulbs.
- [ ] Job 12. Check horn.
- [ ] Job 13. Check windscreen wipers.
- [ ] Job 14. Windscreen washers.
- [ ] Job 15. Check tyres.
- [ ] Job 16. Check spare tyre.
- [ ] Job 17. Wash bodywork.
- [ ] Job 18. Touch-up paintwork.
- [ ] Job 19. Aerial/Antenna.
- [ ] Job 20. Valet interior.
- [ ] Job 21. Improve visibility.
- [ ] Job 28. Check wheel bolts.
- [ ] Job 29. Check brake/fuel lines.
- [ ] Job 30. Check handbrake adjustment.
- [ ] Job 31. Door and tailgate seals.
- [ ] Job 32. Check windscreen.
- [ ] Job 33. Rear view mirrors.
- [ ] Job 66. Check seat belts.
- [ ] Job 67. Locks and hinges.
- [ ] Job 68. Bonnet release mechanism.
- [ ] Job 69. Check seats.
- [ ] Job 70. Test shock absorbers.
- [ ] Job 71. Check/renew front disc brake pads.
- [ ] Job 72. **2.0 LITRE ENGINED MODELS ONLY** Check/replace rear disc pads.
- [ ] Job 73. **ALL MODELS EXCEPT 2.0 LITRE** Check/adjust/renew rear drum brakes.
- [ ] Job 74. Check brake proportioning valve.
- [ ] Job 88. Toolkit and jack.
- [ ] Job 89. Lamp seals.
- [ ] Job 90. Alarm sender unit.
- [ ] Job 91. Adjust headlights.

- [ ] Job 92. Renew wiper blades.
- [ ] Job 93. Check hub bearings.
- [ ] Job 94. Check steering and suspension.
- [ ] Job 95. **CONVERTIBLE CARS ONLY** Check soft-top frame.
- [ ] Job 102. Check brake discs/drums and calipers.

Every 36,000 miles - Under the Car

First carry out all Jobs listed under earlier Service Intervals as applicable.

- [ ] Job 22. Clean mud traps.
- [ ] Job 34. Check exhaust system.
- [ ] Job 35. Check exhaust mountings.
- [ ] Job 36. Check steering rack gaiters.
- [ ] Job 37. Check drive-shaft gaiters.
- [ ] Job 38. Steering joints.
- [ ] Job 39. Check suspension ball-joints.
- [ ] Job 40. Inspect for leaks.
- [ ] Job 96. Engine/gearbox mounts.
- [ ] Job 97. Inspect underside.
- [ ] Job 98. Clear drain holes.
- [ ] Job 99. **FOUR WHEEL DRIVE ONLY** Check prop shaft U.J.'s.
- [ ] Job 100. Renew brake fluid.

- [ ] Job 104. Change gearbox oil/transmission fluid.
- [ ] Job 105. Rustproofing.
- [ ] Job 106. Renew HT leads.

Every 36,000 miles - Road Test

First carry out all Jobs listed under earlier Service Intervals as applicable.

- [ ] Job 41. Clean controls.
- [ ] Job 42. Check instruments.
- [ ] Job 43. Throttle pedal.
- [ ] Job 44. Brakes and steering road test.

Date serviced:..

Carried out by: ....
Garage Stamp or signature:

Parts/Accessories purchased (date, parts, source) ....
....
....
....
....

SERVICE HISTORY

LONGER TERM SERVICING

Every 63,000 miles

☐ Job 107. Replace glow plugs.

Date serviced:...

Carried out by: ....
Garage Stamp or signature:

Parts/Accessories purchased (date, parts,

source) ....

....

....

....

LONGER TERM SERVICING

NOTES